RETURN
TO SENDER

RETURN
TO SENDER

UNANSWERED LETTERS TO
THE PRESIDENT 2001–2015

Ralph Nader

Seven Stories Press

New York • Oakland

Seven Stories Press
140 Watts Street
New York, NY 10013
www.sevenstories.com

College professors and high school and middle school teachers may order free examination copies of Seven Stories Press titles. To order, visit www.sevenstories.com/contact or send a fax on school letterhead to (212) 226-1411.

Book design by Jon Gilbert

Library of Congress Cataloging-in-Publication Data

Nader, Ralph.
  Return to sender : unanswered letters to Presidents Bush & Obama, 2001-2015 / Ralph Nader. -- Seven Stories Press first edition.
    pages cm
  ISBN 978-1-60980-626-2 (hardcover)
  1. United States--Politics and government--2001-2009--Sources. 2. United States--Politics and government--2009---Sources. 3. United States--Social policy--1993---Sources. 4. United States--Politics and government--Decision making--Sources. 5. Bush, George W. (George Walker), 1946---Correspondence. 6. Obama, Barack--Correspondence. 7. Presidents--United States--Correspondence. 8. American letters. I. Title.
  E902.N34 2015
  973.932092--dc23
                                        2014038291

Printed in the United States of America

9 8 7 6 5 4 3 2 1

Contents

Letters to President Barack Obama

Introduction

As a teenager, I was enthralled by the letters between Thomas Jefferson and John Adams into their last years, and Justice Oliver Wendell Holmes's correspondence with scholar Harold Laski. Many of the letters had a continuity of exchanged thoughts that added up to much more than the sum of their parts.

I have always preferred the ink-and-paper, written letter method of communicating with elected officials. This method proved fruitful in the heyday of consumer and environmental activism during the sixties and seventies when many such letters received media attention and subsequently sparked action. This book contains my letters to Presidents George W. Bush and Barack Obama, presented in reverse chronological order for each presidency.

The letters in this volume recount missed opportunities by presidents who increasingly are being preoccupied with fundraising trips, avoidable foreign wars and hostilities, and ceremonial photo opportunities interspersed with White House gatherings with sports stars and other celebrities of the moment. Since taking office in 2009, President Obama has attended over 425 fundraisers with the rich all over the country. Sadly, besides draining time away from substantive presidential engagements, these events are antithetical to serious civic and political discourse, and destructive to what Abraham Lincoln called "the public sentiment." They are just fancy auctions between candidates and friendly affluent bidders, whose presence cues the former about what is expected in return. Given how presidents spend their time, it is fair to say that they *misspend* much of their time with such pursuits.

Imagine the benefits to us all of a president who empowers the people by mobilizing them to form better, self-reliant communities, or who pays close attention to the neglected federal civil service and the improved running of executive departments and agencies.

I harbor the hope that sparing some attention for thoughtful letters would provide presidents with periods of reflection and help them escape from their tightly programmed schedules. Reading serious letters sent by citizens might induce presidents to send out thoughtful responses in the form of public feelers for fresh approaches, recommendations, or timely alerts about important matters. Additionally, reading and responding to these letters would set an example that would encourage others to share their valued thoughts and break down the barrier of communication between the White House and the citizenry. How else can citizens ever hope to communicate with their president on anything other than a symbolic level? Inaugurating a new tradition of presidential replies can enrich deliberative democracy by bringing forth otherwise inhibited feedback from people of experience, wisdom and imagination whose voices otherwise aren't heard from.

I hope readers will find a concrete example by one citizen in what follows and be encouraged to follow suit.

Rhetoric by both Presidents George W. Bush and Barack Obama would have you think that these presidents encourage and support citizens sharing their opinions with their commander in chief. However, once delivered to the White House, my letters to Presidents George W. Bush and Barack Obama could not penetrate the multi-layered White House bubble. What happens to them upon arriving at 1600 Pennsylvania Avenue is a mystery. I have no idea if anyone reads them, refers them to other departments and agencies in the executive branch, or puts them in circular files or warehouses for the archives or presidential libraries. With very few exceptions, I received no response from anyone on staff, nor even an acknowledgement of receipt. Many others have had similar experiences, including, at a critical time for our country, the leaders of more than thirteen diverse national organizations with millions of members such as the National Council of Churches and national labor, veteran, women, student and business groups. Each organization independently requested an urgent meeting with the single-minded President Bush shortly before his invasion of Iraq in 2003. Not one received even the courtesy of an acknowledgement (see: https://nader.org/iraq-letters).

Occasionally, letters from average citizens surface when a president wants to use them for political spin. Or presidents will mention their interest in citizens' pleas, as President Obama does when he mentions that he reads ten letters from "the people" before sleeping every night, to take him out of his self-imposed bubble.

As I am involved in many issues and citizen groups, I frequently wrote to these presidents and hoped for some reaction from them or even from an assistant. In order to avoid redundancy, I restricted those epistles to viewpoints not often made and to taboos not often discussed. For example, I sent letters discussing Israel's devastation of Lebanon and Gaza while receiving, with knee-jerk predictability, military, economic and diplomatic support from Washington contrary to federal law and international treaties.

Breaking through this communication bubble using other portals is nearly impossible. The bubble controls the quality and quantity of presidential news conferences as well as who is called on among the White House Press Corps, and therefore shapes the resulting headlines.

This disturbing trend of nonresponse and discourtesy to citizens extends to many cabinet secretaries and agency heads. It is in the self-interest of these federal officials to give the perception of listening to their constituents by, at the very least, acknowledging receipt of their letters and e-mails. Yet, it seems that like presidents, cabinet secretaries and agency heads largely treat paper letters with indifference, as the Securities and Exchange Commission (SEC) did to knowledgeable writers who for several years repeatedly conveyed in letters to the SEC the essence of the Madoff scandal. All this spells the degradation of an elementary relationship between the citizens and their elected officials and those agency heads appointed by elected officials.

The lack of any response at all is astonishing, so I sought to find out if this uniformity of indifference was policy. I wrote letters asking Presidents Bush and Obama just about their general policy or guidelines regarding answering letters. No response.

The right to petition your government implies some possibility of learning whether the petition arrived and whether it will receive notice. Our Founding Fathers would not accept the use of the First Amendment that only is "crying in the wilderness."

We are in the Information Age. Never before has there been a greater disparity between sending messages and receiving replies. Such a failure to respond will diminish the number of people who try to correspond, which was never a sizable percentage of the citizenry to begin with, and reduce what would have been well-crafted letters into brief e-mails.

Consider the matter from the viewpoint of the president. He receives hundreds of thousands of letters a year. Staff and volunteers do not do much more than open, sort and pass along those designated to receive responses from the president and/or staff. Some letters to presidents are similar, stemming from a letter-writing campaign through grassroots organizing or AstroTurf campaigns, in the case of commercial interests. These letter-writing campaigns sometimes simply generate form letters signed by different people. They do not require substantive responses because these letters were not crafted with any sort of individual, personal thought; they can simply be tabulated as public opinion on a certain issue. Then there are the single, individual letters supporting or opposing some major, high-profile White House decision, such as the auto industry bailout. These might receive a pro forma specific acknowledgement, as do letters inviting the president to some specific ceremony or function.

Letters on matters of public significance that are collectively signed by notable scientists, physicians, attorneys, professors or other groups with specific expertise may reach the president's personal attention. For example, back in the mid-twentieth century, scientists signing letters urging proposed nuclear arms controls received wide media coverage and subsequently did affect White House decisions.

A response by the president usually means a letter signed by a White House staffer. It is rare for the president to sign letters personally, as he is reported to do for the letters to families of soldiers who have lost their lives in Iraq or Afghanistan. There is, however, robo-signing of Christmas holiday cards or robo-signatures on political letters or "first family" photographs to the Party faithful or potential campaign donors. Amusingly, I have received some such letters addressed to me asking for political contributions.

Sound judgment is needed to determine which letters volunteers and staff should answer. After all, issue letters vary in their gravity, novelty, accuracy or timely significance. Nevertheless, a blanket no-response policy is unwise. The White House should not abandon its role in respecting people who speak their minds in a democratic society woefully characterized by mass withdrawal and cynicism regarding politics.

My motivation to test this bubble had two goals. First, I sought a substantive response that would result in action, such as greater presidential attention to global infectious diseases and workplace safety. Second, failing in that objective, I wanted to document this lack of two-way, substantive communication with anyone either in the White House or with appointees from executive departments and agencies.

During the Bush years there were two responses from his office. The first response was to a letter I wrote in May of 2001. I had suggested President Bush's proposed tax cuts would make it impossible for the necessary programs to be funded if the budget surpluses were to be absorbed by tax reductions heavily weighted for the wealthiest citizens and corporations. A form letter arrived in October of 2001 from the President's Assistant for Economic Policy. The assistant replied: "President Bush is committed to defeating international terrorism and providing the American people with the security they want and deserve. Second, the president is committed to providing the economic leadership necessary to keep the economy thriving in the months and years ahead."

I did not expect substantive responses to more than a third of these letters, including any replies from departments and agencies in lieu of a response from the Executive Office of the President, but I saw no reason why all of them could not be acknowledged, as apparently does the Office of the Prime Minister of Canada—a practice that I pointed out to President Obama in yet another letter that went unanswered. Other than two letters from First Lady Michelle Obama's staff—one explaining why President Obama could not meet with a *proposed* large assembly near the White House of national civic, charitable and labor groups and another thanking me for my support of the first lady's nutrition campaigns—and a one-page form letter from President Obama in 2010 in response to my letter about the GM bailout, there were no substantive replies to any of my letters.

The second response was to a letter I wrote on May 8, 2006, to the president asking him to meet with people knowledgeable about the auto industry apart from the heads of the failing major auto companies. In June of 2006, the Deputy Director of Appointments and Scheduling wrote to tell me the White House would contact me if President Bush wanted to discuss automotive industry issues. President Bush's staff never got back to me about a meeting.

As for my letters, some signed with colleagues, they covered important ground urging action, inaction or the adoption of new priorities, such as giving a "seat at the table" to labor, consumer, environmental, peace and other civic groups, instead of just the business and war lobbies. I sent letters on pending legislation, aggressive wars and military actions without a basis in law, the violation of civil liberties and due process of law, and convenient facilities enabling consumers to band together. My recurrent missives dealt with the proliferating privileges and immunities of giant corporations engaged in corporate crime waves and escaping because of anemic regulatory enforcement budgets. I chided President Obama when he forgot about specific campaign assurances in 2008 regarding raising the minimum wage, congressional voting rights for the District of Columbia, addressing structural problems of poverty, revising NAFTA, corporate tax reform, and importantly, his repeatedly declared assurance of compliance with our Constitution.

My letters expressed a desire to lift up presidential standards and performances in the general interest of all Americans and their constitutional sovereignty over artificial entities called corporations. Most of my entreaties and criticism probably would have been well received by a majority of the citizenry. Public discussion and media coverage of these letters, which were publically distributed, could have encouraged more people to engage or at least voice their substantive commentary and suggestions. But, sadly, the White House reporters, or their colleagues, rarely cover such letters, no matter how relevant or unique. Once, I wrote to President Obama from the perspective of "a captured" E. coli, seeking redemption, in a petri dish that made a poignant case that the real global "terrorists" are deadly bacteria and viruses. The expiring E. coli urged him to push for greater resources to protect our citizens from possible epidemics. No response. But, I was told some scientists at the Centers for Disease Control—who could use a larger budget—enjoyed the approach.

I have one final note on the importance of collecting letters written to presidents to prevent them from disappearing into history. The more leisurely days when exchanges of letters between writers, illustrious or not, were collected in book form are likely over. Here the Internet can step in and partially fill this gap. Web sites for unrequited letters could store these letters, along with pertinent unpublished letters to media outlets such as the *New York Times* and the *Wall Street Journal*. These are, after all, the voices of the people and part of our history.

—Ralph Nader, Washington, DC, January 2015

Publisher's Note: The letters have been edited for stylistic consistency, grammar, and accuracy, but the content has not been changed. This collection contains letters written to President Bush while he was still governor of Texas (October 5, 2000: The Auto Safety Wake-up Call; September 21, 2000: Your Views on Personal Privacy?; September 11, 2000: Legalize Hemp!). They were included to give further context of the communication, or lack thereof, by George W. Bush, regardless of his title/position.

Letters to President George W. Bush

The George W. Bush Presidential Center

Dear President Bush,

A few days ago I received *a personalized letter* from your Presidential Center that included a solicitation card for donations that actually provided words for my reply. They included "I'm honored to help tell the story of the Bush Presidency" and "I'm thrilled that the Bush Institute is advancing timeless principles and practical solutions to the challenges facing our world." (Below were categories of "tax deductible contributions" starting with $25 and going upward.)

Did you mean the "timeless principles" that drove you and Mr. Cheney to invade the country of Iraq which, contrary to your fabrications, deceptions and cover-ups, never threatened the United States? Nor could Iraq, under its dictator and his dilapidated military, threaten its far more powerful neighbors, even if the Iraqi regime wanted to do so.

Today, Iraq remains a country (roughly the size and population of Texas) you destroyed, a country where over a million Iraqis, including many children and infants (remember Fallujah?) lost their lives, millions more were sickened or injured, and millions more were forced to become refugees, including most of the Iraqi Christians. Iraq is a country rife with sectarian strife that your prolonged invasion provoked into what is now open warfare. Iraq is a country where al-Qaeda is spreading with explosions taking 20, 30, 40, 50 or 60 lives per day. Just this week, it was reported that the U.S. has sent Hellfire air-to-ground missiles to Iraq's air force to be used against encampments of "the country's branch of al-Qaeda." There was no al-Qaeda in Iraq before your invasion. Al-Qaeda and Saddam Hussein were mortal enemies.

The Bush/Cheney sociocide of Iraq, together with the loss of tens of thousands of U.S. soldiers' lives, injuries, and illnesses, registers, with the passage of time, no recognition by you that you did anything wrong nor have you accepted responsibility for the illegality of your military actions without a congressional declaration of war. You even turned your back on Iraqis who worked with U.S. military occupation forces as drivers, translators, etc. at great risk to themselves and their families and were desperately requesting visas to the U.S., often with the backing of U.S. military personnel. Your administration allowed fewer Iraqis into the U.S. than did Sweden in that same period and far, far fewer than Vietnamese refugees coming to the U.S. during the nineteen-seventies.

When you were a candidate, I called you a corporation running for the presidency masquerading as a human being. In time you turned a metaphor into a reality. As a corporation, you express no remorse, no shame, no compassion and resistance admitting anything other than that you have done nothing wrong.

Day after day, Iraqis, including children, continue to die or suffer terribly. When the paraplegic U.S. army veteran Tomas Young* wrote you last year seeking some kind of recognition of the many things that went horribly criminal for many American soldiers and Iraqis, you did not deign to reply, as you did not deign to reply to Cindy Sheehan, who lost her son, Casey, in Iraq. As you said, "the interesting thing about being the president" is that you "don't feel like [you] owe anybody an explanation." As a former president, nothing has changed as you make very lucrative speeches before business groups and, remarkably, ask Americans for money to support your "continued work in public service."

Pollsters have said that they believe a majority of Iraqis would say that life today is worse for them than under the brutal

---

* See http://www.truthdig.com/dig/item/the_last_letter_20130318 for more information.

dictatorship of Saddam Hussein. They also say George W. Bush left Iraq worse off than when he entered it, despite the U.S.-led sanctions prior to 2003 that took so many lives of Iraqi children and damaged the health of so many civilian families.

Your national security advisor, Condoleezza Rice, said publicly in 2012 that while "the arc of history" may well turn out better for postinvasion Iraq than the present-day violent chaos, she did "take personal responsibility" for the casualties and the wreckage. Do you?

Can you, at the very least, publicly urge the federal government to admit more civilian Iraqis, who served in the U.S. military occupation, to this country to escape the retaliation that has been visited on their similarly situated colleagues? Isn't that the *minimum* you can do to very slightly lessen the multiple, massive blowbacks that your reckless military policies have caused? It was your own antiterrorism White House advisor, Richard Clarke, who wrote in his book, *Against All Enemies: Inside America's War on Terror*, soon after leaving his post, that the U.S. played right into Osama bin Laden's hands by invading Iraq.

Are you privately pondering what your invasion of Iraq did to the Iraqis and American military families, the economy, and to the spread of al-Qaeda attacks in numerous countries?

Sincerely,

P.S. I am enclosing as a contribution in kind to your Presidential Center Library the book *Rogue Nation: American Unilateralism and the Failure of Good Intentions* by Clyde Prestowitz (2003), whom I'm sure you know. Note the positive remark on the back cover by General Wesley Clark.

Silent Bush

Dear President Bush,

In your public statement after the Supreme Court of the United States (5 to 4) selected you for the White House and stopped the Florida Supreme Court from completing its work in reviewing a seriously flawed election process, you said you were determined to bring "common courtesy" to your new residence.

Apparently, "common courtesy" does not include you or your extensive staff responding to substantive letters. Many others have experienced similar stonewalling.

During your eight years in office, I have written you dozens of letters which have received no reply. This correspondence has encompassed many domestic and foreign policy issues and practices pertinent to your actions, inactions, and policy positions. The only response ever received was from a staff member of the Office of Special Counsel regarding inquiries as to whether Karl Rove filed the required accounting reports on his political campaign expenses, and his public servant duties in the White House.*

The question here is generic and simple:

Why have you and your far-flung subordinates in the White House and executive branch never responded to any of my letters, save one, between the years 2001 and 2009?

Sincerely,

---

* There were two pro forma responses from White House Staff on other issues (see: October 9, 2001 and June 26, 2006).

Post-presidency Questions

Dear President Bush,

You may have had your last softball news conference at the White House, but judging by the many people in our country who have serious criticisms of your eight-year tenure, there are numerous unanswered questions that should be addressed to you for the record and for your possible contemplation during retirement.

1. How could you have presided daily over the invasion and war in Iraq and allowed over 900 American soldiers to die and more injured due to the lack of body armor or vehicle armor? With billions of dollars going to Halliburton and other companies and much money available for such soldier protection, why have you never explained such a serious widely reported dereliction of duty?

2. Why did you and Secretary of Defense Donald Rumsfeld define injuries by U.S. soldiers in Iraq so as to exclude two-thirds of them? Your definition of official injuries is ones incurred in the midst of battle, even though most of that country became a theater of war, with much unilateral, unopposed action by the armed forces. CBS's *60 Minutes* on October 2004 demonstrated the feelings of seriously injured U.S. soldiers, who were not officially counted, in order not to arouse further the opposition to the war by the American people. One quadriplegic solider used the words "a disgrace." What is your response?

3. You have made one last lap speaking to military audiences, but you did not speak to one peace audience or group. This is not surprising, given the observation that your role as commander in chief was your most pleasurable task. However, for the historians, if not for your own sense of

balance and example, you could have spoken to a gathering at the United States Institute of Peace (USIP) in Washington, D.C. USIP is a national institution established and funded by Congress to help prevent, manage, and resolve international conflicts. You could have broken new mental ground for yourself in preparing for such an address. Why did you not do something like this in the interest of focusing on waging peace, not just waging war?

4. Why have you prohibited, at all times, the families of their fallen sons and daughters from going to Dover, Delaware, to pay their respects to their loved ones? Mothers and fathers have been deeply hurt by your desire to avoid any public focus or associations with this destination for political reasons. You have not explained this inhumane exclusion. Why not?

5. Tens of thousands of Iraqis, who worked with the U.S. Armed Forces in Iraq and therefore are jeopardized, have tried to emigrate. Some became refugees in nearby countries. For their reasons, whether economic need or support, they provided critical civilian services for the U.S. occupying facilities. Yet you have allowed very few to enter the United States as immigrants. Sweden has received more Iraqi refugees by far than has been permitted under your administration. Recall how over 150,000 Vietnamese refugees were admitted in the mid-seventies. Less than 10 percent of those numbers of Iraqis have been given immigrant visas. Those Iraqis have been widely praised by U.S. soldiers for what was essentially civil service work. Why have you turned your back on these people when you describe yourself as a person of personal loyalty?

6. In the last few days, you finally admitted some mistakes but in a backhanded way. You have made many very destructive mistakes here in the United States that have harmed American workers and consumers.

There is far too much to recount here regarding your antagonism to vigorous enforcement of regulations for consumer and worker health, safety and economic justice. Their neglect and subversion in favor of corporate demands have cost many lives, injuries and illnesses among innocent American people, children and families. Your oft-repeated statement that your highest priority is to "keep America safe" obviously did not include the 58,000 American workers who lost their lives to occupational diseases and injuries annually (OSHA estimate) or the 65,000 Americans whose lives are taken yearly due to air pollution (EPA estimate) or the nearly 100,000 people who die from medical malpractice just in hospitals (Harvard School of Public Health study) every year. You have devoted massively more rhetoric and capital in your chosen role as the ruler of Iraq than to the plight of these three categories of preventable violence to innocent Americans. You have regulatory duties here that you swore to uphold. Why did you not do so?

Instead you kept harping about taking the federal cops off the corporate damage beat (deregulation) and even made a speech in Louisiana about medical malpractice tort litigation that may set a record for the insensitivity of a monetized presidential mind.

7. During your continuing blanket support of anything and everything militarily that the Israeli government does to the helpless and defenseless Palestinian Arabs and Lebanese civilians (including cluster bombs), did it ever occur to you (most recently in devastated civilian Gaza) that such actions, funded by the U.S. taxpayers, could accurately be called "anti-Semitism against Arabs?" Did you ever consult with your father's advisors, James Baker or Brent Scowcroft, on this continuing conflict?

8. Hardly a week goes by without reports of food contamination or food poisoning affecting innocent Americans. The most recent tragedy involves salmonella sickness affecting hundreds due to contaminated peanut butter. Both the FDA and the USDA suffer from lack of funds, authority and will-power. You did very little to change this situation—which would have been heralded by 99 percent of the people and opposed by a handful of companies and China. Chinese imports have been shown to be contaminated (e.g., farm-raised fish and medical ingredients) and lethal. Yet, you spent your time as an American Caesar focusing on Iraq and neighboring lands without attending to the necessities of the American people. Why?

9. It remained for the final weeks of your regime to inform our country just how deep your ruinous "corporations *uber alles*" character is. Lou Dubose, editor of the *Washington Spectator* (January 15, 2009 issue), issued a partial recounting of what he called your "final run at environmental safeguards and what remains of protections for American workers."

In an utterly shameless and cowardly obeisance to your corporate masters, you have overturned worker protections, allowed the coal mining barons to dump, more easily, rock and dirt from the gouging of sacred mountains into valleys, streams and rivers in Appalachia.

You have weakened the Endangered Species Act for the mining, drilling, logging, and damming interests. Promoting further water pollution, you issued a rule allowing corporate factory farms to bypass the Clean Water Act and dump hundreds of thousands of tons of fecal waste into waterways without obtaining EPA permits.

In recent weeks you have issued rules allowing the burning of hazardous wastes as fuel, emitting more toxic benzene and toluene into people's lungs, opening a million acres of federal land near the Grand Canyon for uranium mining and two million acres of federal land in Wyoming, Utah and Colorado to oil shale mining and refining with future devastation to the region. In addition, you issued a rule that will obstruct the Mine Safety and Health Administration and OSHA from their duty to collect information pertinent to dealing with workplace hazards.

You must know that these rules may be challenged and probably repealed by a Democratic Congress because they are so extreme and cruel. Why did you further defile your exit with such cruel and inhumane decisions?

10. How would you characterize the political fortitude of the congressional Democrats, most of whom believe you have committed many repeated impeachable offenses but never did uphold their constitutional oaths to do anything about their documented evaluation of your "unitary" presidency?

11. The nontreatment and mistreatment under your administration of returning veterans are filling books written or about to be published. The problem of "recognition of injury" remains a serious one. Follow-up rehabilitation is too often missing in action. Long waits leading to impoverishment are not infrequent. Also, as reported in the award-winning series by the *Hartford Courant*, soldiers with serious mental stress and damage were redeployed back to Iraq due to the shortage of manpower. One hundred and fifty thousand of our veterans are homeless.

Why haven't you given them the kind of attention you rhetorically give to these soldiers when they are on their way to Iraq or Afghanistan?

Should you wish to catch up on your correspondence, kindly consider responding to these questions that are on

the minds of millions of people here and abroad. You are
not known for exchanging letters—to put it mildly—but
sometimes the postpresidential period affords opportunities for
modest measures of redemption.

Sincerely,

JANUARY 12, 2009
I Beg Your Non-pardon

Dear President Bush,

We strongly urge you to refrain from presidential pardons
for any current or former White House, cabinet or agency
official in your administration for torture, illegal surveillance,
unconstitutional imprisonments, obstruction of justice, perjury,
violation of the Intelligence Identities Protection Act of 1982,
or otherwise. The pardons would be tantamount to shredding
the rule of law which all presidents are constitutionally
obligated to honor.

Supreme Court Justice Louis D. Brandeis declared in
Olmstead v. United States:

"Decency, security, and liberty alike demand that
government officials shall be subjected to the same rules of
conduct that are commands to the citizen. In a government
of laws, existence of the government will be imperiled if it
fails to observe the law scrupulously. Our Government is the
potent, the omnipresent teacher. For good or for ill, it teaches
the whole people by its example. Crime is contagious. If the
Government becomes a lawbreaker, it breeds contempt for law;

it invites every man to become a law unto himself; it invites anarchy."

The list of officials you should exclude from pardons under this standard includes, but is not limited to: Vice President Richard Cheney, former Secretary of Defense Donald Rumsfeld, Defense Department General Counsel William Haynes, former National Security Advisor and Secretary of State Condoleezza Rice, former Attorney General John Ashcroft, former Deputy Secretary of Defense Paul Wolfowitz, former Deputy Secretary of State Richard Armitage, former Under Secretary of Defense Douglas Feith, former White House Counsel and Attorney General Alberto Gonzales, former White House political director Karl Rove, former White House Counsel Harriet Miers, former Deputy Assistant Attorney General for the Office of Legal Counsel John Yoo, Chief of Staff to the Vice President David Addington, Director of Central Intelligence General Michael Hayden, and former Director of Central Intelligence George Tenet. It goes without saying that you should not pardon yourself in light of the time-honored constitutional principle that no man should be a judge in his own case. This principle stems back to *Dr. Bonham's Case* in 1610. Further, the resignation of President Richard M. Nixon under an impeachment cloud rejected the contention that if the president does it, it's legal.

That you and the enumerated officials were involved in fighting the so-called War on Terror or that your and their crimes may have been committed in connection with the Iraq War is not exculpatory. To the contrary, Congress and the courts have extended to the executive branch in general, and your administration in particular, extraordinary latitude in purportedly defending the United States. Any criminal acts committed in this context are thus particularly egregious because they exceeded even lawful authority to impinge on cherished freedoms. The crimes also set troublesome precedents for maltreatment of the United States military or civilians if captured or detained by our adversaries.

Nor does the excuse of "emergency" obtain. It remains for future juries to determine definitively whether official actions were criminal, but the range of actions potentially transgressing the law is long, varied, and persistent. Criminality that continues day after day for years cannot be rationalized as inescapable emergency irregularities. The suspected crimes reflected deliberate policies, not "heat of battle" errors of judgment.

During the Constitutional Convention, George Mason worried that a president might use the pardon power to evade rather than achieve justice by "pardon[ing] crimes which were advised by himself," or before formal accusation "to stop inquiry and prevent detection." But James Madison, father of the Constitution, answered that the constitutional deterrent or remedy would be impeachment by the House and conviction by the Senate: "If the President be connected, in any suspicious manner, with any person, and there be grounds [to] believe he will shelter him, the House of Representatives can impeach him; they can remove him if found guilty."

Later as a member of Congress, Madison underscored that a conspicuous difference between the president and the British monarch was that the former would be subject to impeachment for pardon abuses. In other words, the pardon was never intended to be an instrument of the president to conceal his own wrongdoing.

In 2000, you trumpeted to the American people: "I'm running for president because I want to help usher in the responsibility era, where people understand they are responsible for the choices they make and are held accountable for their actions." To pardon yourself or your inner circle to circumvent criminal responsibility would make a mockery of that high-minded pledge.

Such pardons would be condemned by the rule of law teaching and practices of President Abraham Lincoln:

"As the patriots of seventy-six did to the support of the Declaration of Independence, so to the support of the Constitution and Laws, let every American pledge his life, his property, and his sacred honor—let every man remember that to violate the law, is to trample on the blood of his father, and to tear the character of his own, and his children's liberty. Let reverence for the laws . . . be preached from the pulpit, proclaimed in legislative halls, and enforced in courts of justice."

As president during the Civil War, Lincoln's actions at Fort Sumter and unilateral suspension of the Great Writ of habeas corpus were presented to Congress for repudiation or endorsement according to law.

To frustrate justice and the rule of law with pardons for the powerful would also disrespect the Bible, which you celebrate. It preaches in Amos 5:18-24: "Let justice roll down like waters, and righteousness like an ever-flowing stream."

Sincerely,
Bruce Fein
Ralph Nader

Protect Gaza

Dear President Bush,

Congressman Barney Frank said recently that Barack Obama's declaration that "there is only one president at a time" overestimated the number. He was referring to the economic crisis. But where are you on the Gaza crisis where the civilian population of Gaza, its civil servants and public facilities are being massacred and destroyed respectively by U.S.-built F-16s and U.S.-built helicopter gunships?

The deliberate suspension of your power to stop this terrorizing of 1.5 million people, mostly refugees, blockaded for months by air, sea and land in their tiny slice of land, is in cowardly contrast to the position taken by President Dwight Eisenhower in 1956. That year he single-handedly stopped the British, French, and Israeli aircraft attack against Egypt during the Suez Canal dispute.

Fatalities in Gaza are already over 400 and injuries close to 2,000 so far as is known. Total Palestinian civilian casualties are 400 times greater than the casualties incurred by Israelis. But why should anyone be surprised at your blanket support for Israel's attacks given what you have done to a far greater number of civilians in Iraq and now in Afghanistan?

Confirmed visual reports show that Israeli warplanes and warships have destroyed or severely damaged police stations, homes, hospitals, pharmacies, mosques, fishing boats, and a range of public facilities providing electricity and other necessities.

Why should this trouble you at all? It violates international law, including the Geneva Conventions and the U.N. Charter. You too have repeatedly violated international law and committed serious constitutional transgressions.

Then there is the matter of the Israeli government blocking imports of critical medicines, equipment such as dialysis machines, fuel, food, water, spare parts, and electricity at varying intensities for almost two years. The depleted U.N. aid mission there has called this illegal blockade a humanitarian crisis especially devastating to children, the aged and the infirm. Chronic malnutrition among children is rising rapidly. U.N. rations support 80 percent of this impoverished population.

How do these incontrovertible facts affect you? Do you have any empathy or what you have called Christian charity?

What would a vastly shrunken Texas turned in an encircled Gulag do up against the 4th most powerful military in the world? Would these embattled Texans be spending their time chopping wood?

Gideon Levy, the veteran Israeli columnist for *Haaretz*, called the Israeli attack a "brutal and violent operation" far beyond what was needed for protecting the people in its south. He added:

"The diplomatic efforts were just in the beginning, and I believe we could have got to a new truce without this bloodshed—to send dozens of jets to bomb a total helpless civilian society with hundreds of bombs—just today, they were burying five sisters. I mean, this is unheard of. This cannot go on like this. And this has nothing to do with self-defense or with retaliation even. It went out of proportion, exactly like two-and-a-half years ago in Lebanon."

Apparently, thousands of Israelis, including some army reservists, who have demonstrated against this destruction of Gaza agree with Mr. Levy. However, their courageous stands have not reached the mass media in the U.S., whose own reporters cannot even get into Gaza due to Israeli prohibitions on the international press.

Your spokespeople are making much ado about the breaking of the six-month truce. Who is the occupier? Who is the most powerful military force? Who controls and blocks the necessities of life? Who has sent raiding missions across the border most often? Who has sent artillery shells and missiles at close range into populated areas? Who has refused the repeated comprehensive peace offerings of the Arab countries issued in 2002 if Israel would agree to return to the 1967 borders and agree to the creation of a small independent Palestinian state possessing just 22 percent of the original Palestine?

The "wildly inaccurate rockets," as reporters describe them, coming from Hamas and other groups cannot compare with the modern precision armaments and human damage generated from the Israeli side.

There are no rockets coming from the West Bank into Israel. Yet, the Israeli government is still sending raiders into that essentially occupied territory, further entrenching its colonial outposts that are still taking water and land and increasing the checkpoints. This is going on despite a most amenable West Bank leader, Mahmoud Abbas, whom you have met with at the White House and praised repeatedly. Is it all vague words and no real initiatives with you and your emissary Condoleezza Rice?

Peace was possible, but you provided no leadership, preferring instead to comply with all wishes and demands by the Israeli government—even resupplying it with the still-active cluster bombs in south Lebanon during the invasion of that country in 2006.

The arguments about who started the latest hostilities go on and on with Israel always blaming the Palestinians to justify all kinds of violence and harsh treatment against innocent civilians.

From the Palestinian standpoint, you would do well to remember the origins of this conflict, which was the dispossession of their lands. To afford you some empathy, recall the oft-quoted comment by the founder of Israel, David Ben-Gurion, who told the Zionist leader, Nahum Goldmann: "There has been anti-Semitism—the Nazis, Hitler, Auschwitz—but was that their [the Palestinians] fault? They only see one thing: We have come here and stolen their country. Why should they accept that?"

Alfred North Whitehead once said: "Duty arises out of the power to alter the course of events." By that standard, you have shirked mightily your duty over the past eight years to bring peace to both Palestinians and Israelis and more security to a good part of the world.

The least you can do in your remaining days at the White House is adopt a modest profile in courage, and vigorously demand and secure a ceasefire and a solidly based truce. Then your successor, President-elect Obama, can inherit something more than the usual self-censoring Washington puppet show that eschews a proper focus on the national interests of the United States.

Sincerely,

MAY 12, 2008
Revive the National Highway Traffic Safety Administration

Dear President Bush,

You and your White House have been sitting on the National Highway Traffic Safety Administration (NHTSA) since your arrival in January 2001, thus assuring the giant auto companies that NHTSA—toothless under President Bill Clinton and previous administrations—continues to morph even further away from the technology-forcing, life-saving regulatory agency it is supposed to be and to an industry consulting firm.

The result has been tens of thousands of American fatalities and serious injuries that could have been prevented had you and President Clinton simply urged NHTSA to follow its statutory obligations, lately under congressionally mandated deadlines, with readily feasible, practical safety technologies.

Instead, you stacked the deck with your Chief of Staff, Andrew Card, former president and CEO of the American Automobile Manufacturers Association (AAMA). The rest, as they say, "is commentary."

NHTSA is now set to replace an obsolete motor vehicle roof crush resistance standard that became effective in 1973. You can continue to condemn thousands of Americans to preventable deaths by permitting NHTSA to issue a new, deficient standard, or you can take command and smoke out the corporate lobbyists from Detroit and allow NHTSA to issue FMVSS 216—Roof Crush Resistance at a strength-to-weight (SWR) ratio of at least 4 from the present inadequate standard of 1.5.

Eight models from such companies as Volvo, Saab, Toyota, VW and Honda already meet or exceed the SWR of 4. Note the countries of origin. Note the absence of U.S. manufacturers. The Dodge Ram pickup truck and the Ford F-250 pickup truck have a SWR down at 1.7.

You may wish to brief yourself about the horrible toll on our country's highways during the past 35 years due to marshmallow-structured roofs. The American fatalities and serious injuries alone total more than the entire number of soldiers you have driven to Iraq, many of whom were deployed without adequate body and Humvee armor.

Then there are the quadriplegics and the paraplegics and the thousands of other human beings left defenseless by an auto safety agency under your command that has been at a standstill for years instead of functioning as a law enforcement branch in the Department of Transportation.

You need to see the visuals. You need to see the pictures of the crushed, the pictures of the vehicles whose roofs displaced the "survival space" of the drivers and passengers. You need to speak to the families of the victims who were on the receiving end of such obstinate, criminal negligence by the auto manufacturer executives who will not let their own engineers put in the simple technical fixes year after year.

Remove the corporatists from your White House schedule for a day and invite some of these suffering citizens, their families, and champions. Include Senators Mark Pryor and Tom Coburn who will preside over a Senate hearing on this subject in early June.

Keep in mind that even NHTSA, in its industry-indentured cautious fashion, managed to declare the obvious in 2005: "In sum, the agency believes that there is a relationship between the amount of roof intrusion and the risk of injury to belted occupants in rollover events." But the agency still mimics the resistance of GM, Ford, and Chrysler to any dynamic rollover test that safety advocates favor to assure effective compliance.

A president is not selected or elected to close the doors of state courts to wrongfully injured people who want and need to hold their corporate perpetrators accountable. You must recall your oft-repeated phrase about holding people responsible for their behavior and actions, with the exception of yourself, and drop your attack on our civil justice system. Therefore, delete the federal preemption clause expected in the forthcoming standards that prevent the state judiciaries from hearing product liability suits in this area of vehicle design and construction.

Your legal advisors should point out that in the National Traffic and Motor Vehicle Safety Act of 1966, there is a specific provision that reads: "Compliance with a motor vehicle safety standard prescribed under this chapter does not exempt a person from liability at common law."

Those words were put in the law to prevent just such a federal preemption as NHTSA now prepares to facilitate. Twenty-six state attorneys general opposed preemption in a letter to NHTSA back in 2005. With your invited guests, suggested above, hold a White House news conference. Point to the CEOs in Detroit, and exclaim "Bring 'em on!" Remember, you're either with the American people or you're with the big auto bosses.

Sincerely,

[signature]

APRIL 11, 2008

Save Darfur, Part 2*

Dear President Bush,

Much of the world has condemned the violence and called on the Sudanese government to end the slaughter. You and your administration have, properly, called the mass killing "genocide," and urged a peace process.

But the horror in Darfur continues. Tens of thousands more

---

* See page 43 for original letter from September 15, 2006.

have been displaced in the last month. Violence has intensified in western Darfur. Meanwhile, millions of displaced people are giving up hope of returning to their homes.

The noble words of your administration and the outside world have not been enough to change the course of the Sudanese government.

The United States knows how to deploy its political power and influence. It is now time to put more political muscle behind the effort to end the genocide, and achieve a peaceful solution to this conflict.

One leverage point is normalization of relations with the Sudanese government. You and your administration should announce that the United States will not normalize its relationship with Sudan until the Sudanese government removes all obstacles to the full deployment of the multilateral United Nations–African Union peacekeeping operation (UNAMID), fully implements the Comprehensive Peace Agreement (CPA) and engages in good faith in a comprehensive, open and inclusive peace process in Darfur.

It is vital that the Sudanese government not be permitted to delay and derail UNAMID. A report in the *International Herald Tribune* succinctly captures the urgency of the situation:

"As Darfur smolders in the aftermath of a new government offensive, a long-sought peacekeeping force, expected to be the world's largest, is in danger of failing even before it begins its mission because of bureaucratic delays, stonewalling by the Sudanese government, and reluctance from troop-contributing countries to send peacekeeping forces into an active conflict."

Rather than blaming the U.N. for delays, the United States should exercise leverage to accelerate the deployment of the personnel and resources that would make UNAMID into an effective force, and to overcome the Chinese government's objections to deployment.

The United States has a complicated and interconnected relationship with China, but much more could be done to dissuade China from its ongoing support of the Sudanese government. The United States is willing to file claims against China at the World Trade Organization to protest failures to enforce patents, copyright, and trademarks. Is it too much to ask for an equally robust effort to stop the slaughter of innocent human beings?

The U.S. Special Envoy for Sudan is the direct means for the United States to press Sudan to get peace negotiations jump-started and to remove obstacles to the full deployment of UNAMID. The Special Envoy's office should be fully and adequately staffed, commensurate with the seriousness of his mission.

We look forward to your reply.

Sincerely,

Ralph Nader

Robert Weissman

OSHA and the "Culture of Life"

Dear President Bush,

I was listening to your address before the self-described Conservative Political Action Committee gathering in Washington, D.C. last week, while reviewing materials on occupational hazards in the workplace. The contrast between your declarations and the ongoing annual tragedy of 58,000 Americans losing their lives due to workplace diseases and traumas (OSHA figures) was astonishing and deplorable.

Your remarks included such phrases as "You and I believe in accountability"; "People should be held responsible for their actions"; "Maintaining a culture of life"; "My number one priority is to protect you"; and "All human life is precious and deserves to be protected."

These are words and phrases that you have been using year after year in your capacity as a judicially-selected president who has sworn to uphold the Constitution and the laws of the land.

Therefore, let us apply your verbal sensitivities about accountability, responsibility and the safety of working Americans to your sworn duty to uphold the job safety laws of your administration.

Having been deeply involved in the creation of the Occupational Safety and Health Administration (OSHA) in 1970—during the Nixon administration—I know that its principal mission was regulatory: to establish federal workplace safety standards, enforce them, and upgrade them to avoid obsolescence.

Although in its 38-year history, OSHA regulations and inspections saved many lives, the latter two-thirds of its history has witnessed a serious deterioration in its performance. It is now a captive of industry, underbudgeted, understaffed, and with a consulting attitude rather than a law-and-order, life-saving determination.

Under the Clinton administration, not one chemical control regulation was initiated and issued in eight years. Under your regime, OSHA is dormant. Your secretary of labor ignores it where she does not actually operate to keep it asleep. Yet, on average, over 1,000 Americans die every week from workplace exposures.

Under the Reagan administration, the White House rejected an urgent request by the physicians at the Centers for Disease

Control for a $3 million budget to send certified letters to 250,000 workers found in a lengthy field study to be exposed to significant hazards—chemical and particulate—in their factories, foundries, and mines. The letters were to urge the workers to have their doctors check them out for actual or incipient diseases. Instead, the workers were left defenseless.

Last week, an explosive fireball imploded the century-old Dixie Crystal sugar refinery in Port Wentworth, Georgia, taking, at latest count, seven lives and causing many serious injuries. This is only the latest of a steady series of explosions, mine collapses, cave-ins at construction sites, and other fatally traumatic occurrences.

And who can forget the gripping, prize-winning series in the *New York Times* in January 2003 that began with these words:

"Tyler, Texas—It is said that only the desperate seek work at Tyler Pipe, a sprawling, rusting pipe foundry out on Route 69, just past the flea market. Behind a high metal fence lies a workplace that is part Dickens and part Darwin, a dim, dirty, hellishly hot place where men are regularly disfigured by amputations and burns, where turnover is so high that convicts are recruited from local prisons."

Tyler Pipe is owned by McWane, Inc. of Birmingham, Alabama, which is a very large manufacturer of cast-iron sewer and water pipe. Since 1995, according to a nine-month investigation by the *Times*, PBS and the Canadian Broadcasting Corporation, "at least 4,600 injuries have been recorded in McWane foundries, many hundreds of them serious ones." They included fatalities.

Numerous coal companies were finally caught a few years ago faking their coal dust samples to avoid federal regulations designed to diminish coal miners' pneumoconiosis. Fines for these deliberate violations were, as usual, slaps on the companies' wrists. Since 1900, more coal miners have lost their lives from coal dust and mine collapses than all the Americans lost in World War II. And that is just one industry!

So, where is George W. Bush? The man who says his number one job is to protect the safety of Americans. Has he visited any of their disasters caused by corporate wrongdoing, not by natural disasters? Has he ever made a major speech or proposed a decent budget and stronger enforcement and authority for the federal worker safety and health agencies?

Has he been maintaining "a culture of life" under an "accountability" framework? Does he believe that he and his top appointees have "been responsible for their actions"? Not at all.

Perhaps you are not worried about this lonely epidemic of death, disease, and injury day after day, since it is not caused by terrorists. Even if every three weeks, workplace conditions lead to a fatality toll greater than 9/11. Imagine, every three weeks, on average.

Remember Mr. Bush, you said "all human life is precious and deserves to be protected."

This is especially so when the perils are so preventable by timely regulatory inspections and enforcement of up-to-date life-saving standards.

It comes back, in the final analysis, to that oath of office you took, doesn't it, to enforce the laws under our Constitution whose preamble starts with "We the People." Not "We the Corporations."

Sincerely,

The Shameful Reign of Alberto Gonzales

Dear President Bush,

As you evaluate candidates to replace Alberto R. Gonzales as attorney general it would be appropriate for you to consider all the things Mr. Gonzales has done that have tarnished the reputation of the Justice Department and undermined the rule of law in our country. Mr. Gonzales will be spared from impeachment because of his resignation, but repairing the damage he has done to the integrity of the Justice Department can only begin if you rise above partisan and personal considerations in selecting his replacement. First and foremost, the next attorney general must truly embrace the importance of the Constitution and the rights it establishes for the citizenry and the responsibilities it imposes on government employees.

The oath of office taken by Attorney General Gonzales and previous attorneys general reads:

"I, (Name), do solemnly swear (or affirm) that I will support and defend the Constitution of the United States against all enemies, foreign and domestic; that I will bear true faith and allegiance to the same; that I take this obligation freely, without any mental reservation or purpose of evasion; and that I will well and faithfully discharge the duties of the office on which I am about to enter. So help me God" (5 U.S.C. §3331).

When Mr. Gonzales was installed as the eightieth Attorney General of the United States on February 14, 2005, he said, "So, I rise today to reassure you that I understand the special role of this office, and to commit to do my best on behalf of the American people to fulfill the confidence and trust reflected in my appointment." Unfortunately, Mr. Gonzales has shattered the trust and confidence that the citizens of the United States have in the Justice Department.

Mr. Gonzales repeatedly misled Congress—and the American people—and likely perjured himself in seeking to cover up an astonishing array of policies and practices that contravened the Justice Department's historic independence, violated core constitutional protections, and authorized violations of fundamental international proscriptions against torture and abuse. And, in his role as attorney general and previously as White House counsel, he played an instrumental role in advancing policies that shredded longstanding American civil liberties and human rights protections.

After reviewing the following questions and comments, even you might be willing to concede that Mr. Gonzales has shamed the Justice Department and darkened our country's reputation.

Did Mr. Gonzales mislead Congress about his role in the firing of federal prosecutors?

Mr. Gonzales insisted that each of the attorneys had been fired for "performance" reasons and stated that, "I would never, ever make a change in a United States attorney for political reasons, or if it would in any way jeopardize an ongoing serious investigation. I just would not do it."

The *New York Times* reported six of the eight prosecutors had, however, recently received good performance reviews between 2003 and 2006.

Mr. Gonzales testified that "this focus has been on the eight United States attorneys that were asked to resign last December 7th and June 14th."

Published reports, however, show that D. Kyle Sampson, then–Attorney General Gonzales's chief of staff, considered more than two dozen U.S. attorneys for termination, according to lists compiled by him and his colleagues.

Did Mr. Gonzales mislead Congress about whether the president could authorize warrantless wiretapping?

Mr. Gonzales said that "It is not the policy or the agenda of this president to authorize actions that would be in contravention of our criminal statutes."

The *Washington Post* reported, "In fact, the president did secretly authorize the National Security Agency to begin warrantless monitoring of calls and e-mails between the United States . . ."

Did Mr. Gonzales mislead Congress on April 27, 2005, when he testified before the Senate Select Committee on Intelligence that "the track record established over the past three years has demonstrated the effectiveness of the safeguards of civil liberties put in place when the Act was passed? There has not been one verified case of civil liberties abuse."

The *Washington Post* reported Mr. Gonzales was in possession of at least six FBI reports detailing unlawful surveillance, searches, and improper use of national security letters.

Later, again under oath, Mr. Gonzales testified that his statement had been truthful because they were not "intentional" abuses of the Patriot Act.

Did Mr. Gonzales mislead Congress when on July 24, 2007, he testified before the Senate Judiciary Committee that the subject of an emergency meeting with the hospitalized then–Attorney General John Ashcroft on March 10, 2004, was not the surveillance program, which allowed the National Security Agency (NSA) to eavesdrop on suspects in the United States without receiving court approval?

Mr. Gonzales said: "The disagreement that occurred and the reason for the visit to the hospital, Senator, was about other intelligence activities. It was not about the terrorist surveillance program that the president announced to the American people."

"A four-page memorandum [dated May 17, 2006] from the national intelligence director's office, obtained by The Associated Press, shows that the briefing was about the surveillance program."

Did Mr. Gonzales mislead Congress when he testified before the Senate Judiciary Committee on January 18, 2007, about the appointment of "interim" U.S. Attorneys?

A provision quietly added to the Patriot Act in 2005 allowed the president to appoint "interim" U.S. attorneys for an indefinite period of time, without Senate confirmation. Mr. Gonzales testified under oath that "I am fully committed, as the administration's fully committed, to ensure that, with respect to every United States attorney position in this country, we will have a presidentially appointed, Senate-confirmed United States attorney."

The *Washington Post* reported:

"Justice officials discussed bypassing the two Democratic senators in Arkansas, who normally would have had input into the appointment, as early as last August. By mid-December, [D. Kyle] Sampson [former chief of staff to Attorney Gonzales] was suggesting that Gonzales exercise his newfound appointment authority to put [Tim] Griffin in place until the end of Bush's term."

President Bush, the next attorney general must respect the Constitution and the rule of law.

Our country cannot afford and does not deserve an attorney general who puts political loyalty above his sworn obligation to respect and defend civil liberties and civil rights.

Sincerely,

Second Verse, Same as the First

Dear President Bush,

I have read your address to the nation on "The New Way Forward in Iraq" and wish to share some observations.

You say, "Where mistakes have been made, the responsibility rests with me." You then quickly change the subject. Whoa now, what does it mean when you say the responsibility for mistakes rests with you?

Responsibility for "mistakes" that led to the invasion—an invasion which other prominent officials and former officials say was based on inaccurate information, deceptions, and cover-ups?

Responsibility for the condoning of torture, even after the notorious events at Abu Ghraib prison were disclosed?

Responsibility for months and months of inability to equip our soldiers with body armor and vehicle armor that resulted in over 1,000 lost American lives and many disabilities?

Responsibility for the gross mismanagement over outsourcing both service and military tasks to corporations, such as Halliburton, that have wasted tens of billions of dollars, including billions that simply disappeared without account?

Responsibility for serious undercounting of official U.S. injuries in Iraq—because the injuries were not incurred in direct combat—so as to keep down political opposition to the war in this country?

Over and over again, during your political campaigns you called for consequences to attach to bad or failing behavior. Responsibility means consequences, you said.

Well just how does that belief apply to you, as a failed and disastrous commander in chief and caretaker of American soldiers, American tax dollars and, under international law, the safety of Iraqi civilians?

You said, "I've made it clear to the prime minister . . . that America's commitment is not open-ended. If the Iraqi government does not follow through on its promises, it will lose the support of the American people. . . ." But you have stated on many prior occasions that a U.S. retreat from Iraq would be catastrophic. Now you imply that if the Iraqi government does not deliver, the U.S. commitment will end. Which is it?

And the Iraq War has lost the support of the American people some time ago.

What are the people to believe "not open-ended" means? Especially since your new secretary of defense told the Congress that within two months it will be known whether your troop escalation strategy is working or not.

You said that your administration will "partner a Coalition brigade with every Iraqi Army division." Why do you continue to use misleading euphemisms? They are not "Coalition brigades"—they are U.S. soldier brigades. Even the British want to draw down their small number of troops.

You said that a discovered al-Qaeda document describes "the terrorists' plan to infiltrate and seize control of [Anbar Province]." "This would bring al Qaeda," you asserted, "closer to its goals of taking down Iraq's democracy, building a radical Islamic empire, and launching new attacks on the United States at home and abroad." Since your field "commanders" estimate a total of 1,300 al-Qaeda, mostly foreign, fighters, widely disliked and increasingly opposed by the local people and their tribal leaders, why are you continuing to engage in this preposterous sequence of doom, this politics of mega-fear à la your neoconservative advisors? Why indeed, do you do this when your own intelligence officials, including the former

Director of the CIA Porter J. Goss, and military leaders in Iraq, have said publicly that the U.S. military occupation has been a magnet for the attraction and training of more and more terrorists, including those from other countries who will acquire demolition and other skills before leaving Iraq.

Your comment that victory in Iraq will bring a "functioning democracy that . . . upholds the rule of law, respects fundamental human liberties and answers to its people," invites the response, "Have you done this in our country?"

Given your serial civil liberties violations, frequent mockery of the rule of law and our Constitution, and your ignoring the judgment of last November's election (not to mention the desire by 70 percent of U.S. soldiers polled last January in Iraq wanting you to leave within 6 to 12 months), there is a pronounced lack of consistency here.

Finally, you conclude that "we mourn the loss of every fallen American, and we owe it to them to build a future worthy of their sacrifice. Fellow citizens: The year ahead will demand more patience, sacrifice, and resolve."

Why not some exemplary sacrifice from the Bush family? What is keeping those bright, capable daughters—Jenna and Barbara—from showing that the family is not expecting everybody but the Bush family to sacrifice? Why are they not demonstrating their sacrifice and resolve for your Iraq democracy war by enlisting into the armed forces?

Could it be that they disagree with your policies? Or could it be that they do not consider your war-quagmire "worthy of their sacrifice?"

Sincerely,

Save Darfur, Part 1

Dear President Bush,

We join with the thousands of Americans who are calling on you to intensify your efforts to end the slaughter in Darfur.

This genocide unfolding before our eyes stands in danger of worsening drastically in coming weeks, if African Union peacekeepers are forced out of the area. But the current situation itself is unconscionable.

As you know, the U.N. Security Council has authorized a plan to send a U.N. force to Darfur to supplement the African Union presence and transition to a U.N. operation. U.S. leadership is needed to turn this plan into reality, especially by persuading other nations to back and immediately implement the plan.

When you address the United Nations this coming Tuesday we urge you to set aside your likely agenda to defend the disastrous war and occupation in Iraq, or prepare for perilous military actions against Iran.

Instead, use the opportunity for a nobler purpose—to exert leadership on the Darfur issue and challenge the international community to act now, before the situation descends into an even worse humanitarian nightmare.

Sincerely,
Ralph Nader
John Richard
Robert Weissman

Lebanon: A Nation Under Attack

Dear President Bush,

The widespread destruction of a defenseless Lebanon—its civilians, its life-sustaining public services, its environment—is a grim and indelible testament to your consummate cruelty and ignorance. Nearly two weeks ago when your tardy secretary of state met with the Israeli Prime Minister, the message she carried was summarized in a large headline across page one of an Israeli newspaper: "TAKE YOUR TIME."

Yes, take your time, says George W. Bush, while there are pulverized fleeing refugees in cars full of families and bombings of apartment buildings, hospitals and the poor huddled in large south Beirut slums.

Take your time, says George W. Bush, while bridges, roads, gasoline stations, airports, seaports, wheat silos, vehicles with medical supplies, clearly marked ambulances taking the wounded to clinics, even a milk factory are destroyed.

Take your time, says George W. Bush, while shelters are demolished with bodies of little children together with their mothers and fathers buried in the rubble.

Take your time, says George W. Bush, while the number of fleeing refugees nears one million Lebanese, many exposed to hunger, disease, lack of potable water and medicines. All this in a country friendly to the United States, which played by your rules, protested the Syrian army back into Syria and was trying democratically to put itself together.

Take your time, says George W. Bush, while he speeds up the supply of precision missiles containing deadly anti-personnel cluster bombs, which will claim the lives of innocent children for years into the future. The phosphorus bombs are laying waste to fields growing crops and horribly burning innocents come from the U.S.A., under your direction.

Do you think the taxpayers of America would approve of such shipped weapons, were they ever asked?

Are there words in the English language suitable for the impeachable serial war crimes you are intimately involved in committing not only in Iraq, but also now through your encouragement and supplying of the once again invading Israeli government?

Are there words to describe your strategic stupidity, which will further increase opposition and peril to the United States, around the world and especially in the Middle East? Your own generals and former CIA Director Porter Goss, among others in your administration, have declared that your occupation of Iraq is a magnet attracting the recruiting and training of more and more "terrorists" from Iraq and other countries. And so now this will be the case in Lebanon. All this is a growing "blowback" to use the CIA word for a boomeranging foreign policy that is endangering the security of the United States.

The calibrated Israeli terror bombing of Lebanon came in three stages. With its electronic pinpoint precision bombing and artillery, the Israeli government went after civilians, their homes, cities, towns, and villages. Then after telling some to abandon their neighborhoods, it cut population centers off from each other by destroying transportation facilities into and inside Lebanon, making both refugee flight and delivery of emergency relief efforts either impossible or very difficult. Then its planes, tanks, and artillery endangered or destroyed what food, water and relief efforts managed to get through to the injured and dying. Warehouse food supplies were incinerated. About four hundred small fishing boats north of Beirut on the oil-polluted coastline were demolished as well.

All the above mayhem and much more have been reported in the U.S., European, Lebanese and Israeli media. The bulk of the fatalities in Lebanon have been civilians. The bulk of the fatalities on the Israeli side have been soldiers. Very fortunately for the Israelis, the Hezbollah rockets are very inaccurate, the vast majority falling harmlessly. Unfortunately for the Lebanese, the precision American armaments of the Israelis are very accurate, which serves to account for why the total casualties and physical destruction are 100 times greater in Lebanon than in Israel.

Most of these accurate munitions come from your decision to send them. Knowing they will be used for offensive purposes, including the lethal demolition of a long-established U.N. compound in violation of the Arms Export Control Act which you have sworn to uphold, places the responsibility of being a domestic lawbreaker squarely on your shoulders.

There is another law that is not being enforced—the Humanitarian Aid Corridor Act of 1996 sponsored by then-Senator (and Republican) Robert Dole. Foreign aid is supposed to be cut off to any nation that obstructs the provision of humanitarian aid to another country. As one example, press reports that two tankers, each with 30,000 tons of diesel fuel critical for operating Lebanese hospitals and water pumping stations, are idling in Cyprus from fear of the totally dominant Israeli navy and air force.

There are only a few days left of fuel in Lebanon, which is heading for a larger wave of secondary casualties. They and other critical suppliers need safe passage, which the U.S. Navy in the area can readily provide, should it receive orders from the commander in chief.

You heard high Israeli officials accurately say on the day the massive bombing of Lebanon began, which was not preceded by

Hezbollah rockets, that "nothing is safe" in Lebanon. That huge overreaction to the recent Hezbollah border raid, in addition to many more previous air, sea and land border violations by the Israeli government, certainly put you on public notice.

Since you view yourself as a reborn Christian, and since you have the power to stop the Israeli state terror assaults on Lebanon, you may wish to reflect on Leviticus 19:16: "Neither shalt thou stand idly by the blood of thy neighbor." Lebanon was a friendly country to you and you have stood by not just idly, but are willfully aiding and abetting its devastation.

Sincerely,

JULY 17, 2006
Lebanon

Dear President Bush,

You have been a weak president, despite your strutting and barking, when it comes to doing the right things for the American people within the Constitution and its rule of law. This trait is now in bold relief over the Israeli government's escalating war crimes pulverizing the defenseless people and country of Lebanon.

With systematic efficiency, the Israeli government has already destroyed innocent homes and basic public facilities—ports, airports, highways, bridges, power stations—which are critical to delivery of food, medicines, health care, ambulances, water, and other essentials for a civilian population. This bombardment, by U.S.-made bombers, military vehicles, ships, and missiles with American taxpayer subsidies, places an inescapable responsibility upon your shoulders, which does not mix with your usual vacuous messianic rigidity.

As the leading player in official Washington's puppet show, it is time for you to assert the interests of the American people and those of the broad Israeli and Palestinian peace movements by standing up to the puppeteers. For without this conflict, Hezbollah would not be in today's news.

The time has come for you to return to Texas for a private meeting with your father, his former national security advisor, Brent Scowcroft, and his former secretary of state, James Baker. You need to say to them "I can't trust my advisors anymore; there have been so many tragic blunders. What do you advise me to do about the destruction of a friendly nation by the world's fifth most powerful military?"

Here is what I think they should say to you:

1. Take personal command of an immediate rescue effort for the tens of thousands of Americans trapped in Lebanon by Israel's calculated blocking of air, land, and sea escape routes. You've said the safety of Americans is your top priority. Prove it by using the U.S. Air Force and the U.S. Navy facilities to immediately evacuate all our people desperate to escape the terrorization of Lebanon.

2. You have been so docile and permissive to Israeli demands that any modest deviation from this posture will make your next move credible. Announce that you are sending two prominent negotiators—perhaps James Baker (Republican) and former Senate Majority Leader George Mitchell (Democrat) to Israel and Lebanon to arrange for a cease fire between the combatants.

Announced at a televised White House news conference with your two envoys, you can punctuate your seriousness by raising the questions of violations of the Arms Export Control

Act and the Foreign Assistance Act. Using U.S.-supplied weapons systems to commit civilian atrocities on homes and fleeing vehicles with children and to inflict collective punishment on mass civilian populations is not using these weapons for legitimate self-defense and internal policing, as our federal law requires. Israeli planes have even fire bombed wheat silos and gasoline stations in Lebanon. More mayhem is on the way.

3. Stop acting like an impulsive, out-of-control West Texas sheriff and start reading, thinking, and listening for a change. When Israel, Britain, and France violated international treaties against aggression in 1956 by invading the Suez Canal, President Dwight Eisenhower used his influence to make them withdraw from Egypt.

In 1982, following a year without any PLO skirmishes over the Lebanese-Israeli border, Israeli armed forces invaded Lebanon anyway. They created a path of destruction all the way to Beirut and militarily occupied south Lebanon for 18 years before they withdrew, except for retaining Shebaa Farms. In 1982 the *New York Times* reported "indiscriminate bombing" of Beirut by Israeli planes. At least 20,000 Lebanese civilians lost their lives in that invasion and many more were injured. From that conflict Hezbollah was born, composed of many people whose relatives were casualties in that illegal invasion.

History, George, does not start two weeks or two months ago. You must read about past U.S. presidents who, at least, sent high-level emissaries to quell similar border fighting. It worked and prisoners were often exchanged.

You are doing and saying nothing about what the rest of the world believes is a hugely disproportionate attack against innocent adults and children in violation of the Geneva Conventions, the U.N. Charter and other treaties and federal statutes. You've sworn to uphold these laws. Do so. Because of the Israeli government's overwhelming military power, the imbalance of terror against civilians and their property has always been to its advantage. As has its occupation of Palestine and confiscation of land and water sources.

4. You can't take sides and be an honest broker. Just about all our knowledgeable retired military, diplomatic, and intelligence officials believe resolving the Israeli-Palestinian conflict is the key to deflating other agitations in the region. Freedom and justice for the Palestinian state and security and stability for the Israeli state must both be achieved.

You have turned your back on the courageous and prominent Israeli peace movement which normally reflects the positions of half of the Israeli population. You've never met with any of its leaders—even those in the Knesset or former officials in the military, intelligence, and justice ministries. Hundreds of reserve combat officers and soldiers of the IDF have refused, in their words, "to fight beyond the 1967 borders to dominate, expel, starve, and humiliate an entire people." They pledged only to fight for Israel's legitimate defense.*

5. Once in a while, ask your aides for a sample of Israeli opinion that rejects the notion that there can be a military solution to this conflict, despite the military imbalance. For example, reports and editorials in *Haaretz*, arguably the most respected newspaper in Israel, would educate your judgment. In a recent editorial, *Haaretz* argued that the present Israeli government has "lost its reason" through the brutal incarceration, devastation, and deprivation of innocent people in Gaza.

In another *Haaretz* commentary dated July 16th, Gideon Levy writes:

"In Gaza, a soldier is abducted from the army of a state that frequently abducts civilians from their homes and locks

---

* See www.seruv.org.il/defaulteng.asp for more information.

them up for years without a trial—but only we're allowed to do that. And only we're allowed to bomb civilian population centers."

6. One final bit of advice could come from Papa Bush's circle. If the Israeli army decides to invade Lebanon with troops, your support of the aggression can possibly unleash a domino of warring actions and reactions over there. As it is, Americans are increasingly fed up with the Iraq quagmire.

Moreover, we know they don't like many of your domestic policies favoring the wealthy, the post-Katrina debacle, exporting jobs, and among our conservative base, your enormous deficits. So, your Republican Party's control of government is at stake in November. Don't you have your hands full with Iraq, whose invasion we all urged you to avoid in 2003?

Sincerely,

[signature]

MAY 8, 2006
GM, Ford, and Chrysler . . .
What About Consumer Groups?

Dear President Bush,

Your scheduled meeting with the leaders of the American auto industry is unhelpfully lopsided.

Numerous news sources report that you have agreed to meet later this month with the leaders of the domestic auto industry, but the accounts indicate that the invitation list only includes the heads of General Motors Corporation, Ford Motor Company, and DaimlerChrysler's Chrysler Group, and not the auto suppliers whose many practical innovations are repeatedly turned down by the Big Three.

Reports of the meeting indicate that the talks will cover energy and the environment, pension and health care costs, and currency issues affecting Japanese automakers.

A broad agenda should have you seeking a broad variety of opinions reflecting all auto industry stakeholders, including consumers.

My learned associates and I request a personal meeting with you to discuss these matters, including auto safety and emissions subjects.

THE WHITE HOUSE
WASHINGTON

June 26, 2006

Dear Mr. Nader:

Thank you for your letter inviting President Bush to discuss automotive industry issues in Washington, DC.

We appreciate your invitation and the valuable opportunity it presents. As the President's schedule continues to develop, your request will be given every consideration. We will contact you once a final decision has been made. If you have any questions regarding your request, you may contact the Office of Appointments and Presidential Scheduling at 202-456-5324.

Sincerely,

La Rhonda M. Houston
Deputy Director
Office of Appointments and Scheduling

Today the most effective treatment for the domestic industry's decline is an injection of innovative technology and orientation of design priorities. Unfortunately, the giants of the domestic auto industry—the same manufacturers you are meeting with—have demonstrated a congenital disinterest in applying the creative ability of their engineering corps to advance efficient, clean, and safe vehicle designs.

Our recent report, *Innovation and Stagnation in Automotive Safety and Fuel Efficiency*, details numerous examples of life-saving and fuel-saving technologies that have been ignored by the Detroit automakers. Moreover, the institutions we have entrusted to prod and regulate the industry on fuel economy and safety—Congress and the National Highway Traffic Safety Administration—have been derelict in their duties. I have enclosed a copy of our report by Rob Cirincione for your perusal.

A revitalized attention to efficient, clean, and safe motor vehicle design can simultaneously square motorists' interests with domestic labor's and shareholders' interests—improving automobile safety performance, energy consumption, the environment, *and* the competitive position of the domestic industry. As several industry observers have said, the solution to the domestic auto companies' stagnation problems is product, product, product.

We look forward to a productive exchange geared toward action.
Sincerely,

Clinton to Bush: Help Move the Trailers

Dear President Bush,

The enclosed exchange of letters between the undersigned and former President William J. Clinton are self-explanatory. I asked him to "raise the roof" on the bureaucratic nightmare that comprises 10,000 trailers or mobile homes parked unused in his hometown of Hope, Arkansas, at a cost to the taxpayers of over $400 million.

Mr. Clinton wrote back to express his frustration with the situation and his attempt to "expedite the process" to as of now no avail. He urged me to write you directly to see if you can "expedite the process" in getting the trailers out of Hope, Arkansas, to where they are needed. Therefore, this letter.

I look forward to hearing from you. Please send a copy of your response to Mr. Clinton with whom you have appeared in public from time to time and reportedly are on good terms.

Sincerely,

Enclosed: two letters.

ENCLOSURE I: MARCH 15, 2006:
LETTER TO PRESIDENT CLINTON

Dear President Clinton,

When I heard that 10,000 (yes, ten thousand) FEMA-purchased new trailers for the displaced victims of Katrina have been languishing for weeks in a little-used airfield in Hope, Arkansas, without being shipped to the families in desperate need for shelter, my first reaction was:

"Why that's Bill Clinton's hometown! Why isn't he raising the roof on this bureaucratic nightmare?"

So I ask you, why aren't you trying to expedite delivery of these mobile homes (valued at $400 million) out of your hometown? It is not because you are unfamiliar with the back and forth between federal, state, and local jurisdictions over Katrina-induced needs. You are identified with the Bush-Clinton Katrina Fund and have visited the devastated area. You can cut through the perceived overcome-able obstacles, like the floodplain policy that has been described as a snag between the state of Louisiana and Washington, D.C.

Hope, Arkansas, as you well know, is a town with a population around 10,000. Often you used the name of your hometown as the metaphor for your 1992 presidential campaign: "the man from Hope." Well, I am sure that many families displaced by Katrina who are now homeless or huddling with friends or relatives or in shacks wish that you would give them some hope. They were certainly encouraged in that regard by your many expressions of hope and support post-Katrina.

Let's say that the situation in your hometown, where some say the trailers in the mud are deteriorating, is a special responsibility of yours.

Along with many other Americans, I look forward to hearing from you.

Sincerely,

WILLIAM JEFFERSON CLINTON

April 5, 2006

Dear Ralph:

Thank you for your letter about the FEMA trailers in Hope, Arkansas. Like many Americans, I share your concerns about Hurricane Katrina survivors who lack sufficient housing and your frustration that these trailers have so far gone unused.

I have worked to right this wrong since I first heard reports of the trailers' existence. My staff and I have contacted Don Powell and others involved in the reconstruction effort to see if there was anything we could do to expedite the process.

I explored the possibility of providing Bush Clinton Katrina Fund financial assistance to move the trailers, but my understanding is that the issue is not financing. Many communities have been unwilling to host the trailers because they don't want them in their neighborhoods, lack the capacity to house them, or face utility problems.

I will continue to monitor the situation and have asked Don Powell to keep me informed. I appreciate your concern about this important issue, and I assure you that I will continue to do everything I can to help the people and communities affected by Hurricane Katrina.

All the best to you.

Sincerely,

Bill Clinton

Do You Have Time for the Casualties?

Dear President Bush,

As the tragic number of fallen U.S. soldiers nears the 2,500 mark in Iraq, many due to the lack of adequate body and vehicle armor, skepticism is being expressed over whether you are, in fact, personally signing the condolence letters which you are reported to be sending their next of kin.

You will note that this skepticism is based, in part, on the previous admission by Secretary of Defense Donald Rumsfeld that he was allowing these letters to be machine signed—a delegation that was presumably reversed back to his own fingers after the press wrote about his handwriting fatigue.

The question is: Are you personally signing in your own handwriting the letters of condolences which go out to bereaved parents, spouses or relatives under your signature?

There is a need to inform accurately those who are wondering.

Sincerely,

MARCH 3, 2006
Debunking "Situational Information"

Dear President Bush,

I saw you on the CBS evening news the other day using a new phrase: "situational information." You were referring to the conditions just before and during the Katrina hurricane levee disaster in New Orleans. The "situational information" was not what it should have been, you declared. This was your way of saying that you did not receive prompt information about the risk the giant hurricane posed for the breaching of the city's levees.

Now it appears that you were given advance warning. This was the thrust of the CBS television news report by Bob Orr. Anchor Russ Mitchell introduced the segment with these words: "In the days following Hurricane Katrina, President Bush insisted that no one in his administration anticipated the failure of the levees protecting New Orleans. But newly released videotape shows that as the huge storm approached the Gulf Coast, the president and his top advisors WERE warned it posed just such a threat to the low-lying city" (emphasis in the original).

These advisors included National Hurricane Center Director Max Mayfield and FEMA Director Michael Brown, who told top administration officials, including Homeland Security Secretary Michael Chertoff, of the "looming danger . . . a day before landfall."

These tapes caused the *Wall Street Journal*'s article on March 2 to have this headline: "Tape of Pre-Katrina Briefing Shows Bush Was Warned of Dangers." Sounds like you received quite explicit "situational intelligence" which you still decline to acknowledge getting. Maybe the White House has a problem with "situational credibility."

Since that day when Hurricane Katrina struck the city of New Orleans and surrounding coastal areas, tens of thousands of displaced people—the survivors—have felt abandoned by the federal government. Scores of newspaper, television and radio eyewitness reports record this abandonment in places like Ward 9 in New Orleans and Pearlington, Mississippi. The level of failure under your presidential watch is massive, ringed with private corporate contracting graft, corruption, and waste. Prime ministers in parliamentary nations would have fallen by now.

Recall your dramatic, nationally televised choreographed assurance, standing near the French Quarter, that the federal government would take the lead in rebuilding New Orleans for its desperate residents and the return of those who fled. Get that videotape out and watch it, over six months of little action later. Maybe it will teach you something about the price that a destroyed area of America and its people are paying because you are expensively preoccupied being the mayor of Baghdad.

Your regime's debacle after Katrina continues to leave tens of thousands of people without their homes. They are either in some motels temporarily, with some friends or relatives or simply just homeless.

Yet next to the little-used municipal airport in Hope, Arkansas—Bill Clinton's hometown—ten thousand or more FEMA mobile homes/trailers are sitting immobile week after week. The trailers were delivered to that staging area by the manufacturer, and await shipment to the needy, displaced families down south around New Orleans and the Gulf Coast communities. These families wait day after day, week after week.

You always tell reporters that the federal government's response could have been better. What about your response from late August to now? You are supposed to lead the federal government, so start leading directly by example.

Why not call up your friend Bill Clinton, with whom you and your father often have been seen together at social, ceremonial, and charitable occasions? The telephone conversation can go like this:

GWB: "Hey Bill, how about you and me hopping on Air Force One pronto and heading down to your old stomping grounds around Hope. Let's show we can break up that bureaucratic logjam and leave Hope with 10,000 fewer trailers. I'm the president, you were the president. You were the Governor of Arkansas. Hometown boy comes home to do good. What a great photo opportunity for bipartisanship?"

WJC: "Not a bad idea, George. But the bureaucracy starts in Washington, D.C., so there will have to be some bureaucracy-busting advance work done to make the visit a success. Then there is the matter of getting floodplain rules waived and all the other state and local rules which Washington has not confronted for months."

GWB: "Hmmm, Bill, you've been doing your homework."

WJC: "Not really, George, just reading the newspapers."

GWB: "OK, OK, I get the snide remark. But I've been running a war for freedom."

WJC: "Didn't mean it that way, George. Sure, let's go down and get those trailers on the road. Where do you want to meet up . . . in Hope?"

GWB: "Very funny, Bill, like you are summoning me. We meet at the White House, get on the presidential helicopter and head for Andrews Air Force base. You know the protocols."

WJC: "What do you think our chances of success will be?"

GWB: "Well, heh, heh, Bill, what's that phrase—'Hope Springs Eternal.'"

Sincerely,

On the Himalayan Earthquake

Dear President Bush,

A humanitarian catastrophe of almost unimaginable proportions is unfolding in the Himalayas, yet your administration seems remarkably unorganized in applying more resources. Has anyone shown you the wire service photos of frightened children standing in the rubble with nothing between them and the impending winter but a blanket? Reports tell of two to three million people who are without homes, hundreds of thousands who have received no aid whatsoever, and helicopter flights facing cutbacks because they have no aid to deliver. Is the global community prepared to turn its back on these people? Are you, the self-proclaimed leader of the compassionate forces in the world, looking askance?

While hundreds of millions of dollars in aid have been promised by the international community, only a fraction of it has been received. What is urgently needed are tents for shelter and equipment for removing rubble, reconstruction, and other materials in advance of the approaching winter. Lack of medical care is causing relatively minor infections to fester to the point where doctors are forced to resort to amputation. Reports from the scene tell us that the 80,000 dead from the earthquake may be matched by a second wave of preventable deaths, deaths attributable to disinterest and neglect among those who have the capacity to preserve these lives.

Our nation has large and well-organized communities of both Indians and Pakistanis. If the reports and the images of this tidal wave of human disaster do not move you, perhaps you and your Party should prepare to explain to these communities why their brothers and sisters were not worth saving. The aid pledged by your administration so far amounts to a few hours worth of what you are spending on the boomerang Iraq War opposed by a growing majority of the American people. Please spare us from the suggestion that you, our history's largest tax-cutter for the wealthy, including yourself, cannot afford to do more.

You have often loudly and publicly proclaimed your Christian beliefs, most recently in your support for Ms. Miers's nomination to the United States Supreme Court. Perhaps your religious beliefs could offer you some guidance in determining what is the decent course of action for the president to do in this moment of grave crisis for so many helpless families.

Sincerely,

OCTOBER 24, 2005
The Avian Flu: A Wake-up Call for Our Pharmaceutical System

Dear President Bush,

As you know, the world faces the possibility in the near future of an avian flu outbreak that many experts say could take millions of lives worldwide. The United States may not be spared from this devastation, according to the Centers for Disease Control, in the absence of any control measures (vaccination or drugs), it has been estimated that in the United States a "medium-level" pandemic could cause 89,000 to 207,000 deaths, 314,000 to 734,000 hospitalizations, 18 to 42 million outpatient visits, and another 20 to 47 million people being sick. Between 15 percent and 35 percent of the U.S. population could be affected by an influenza pandemic, and the economic impact could range between $71.3 and $166.5 billion.*

There are a number of steps that need to be taken to address this threat. We are writing about just one component of a public health response to the prospect of an avian flu outbreak: that is the stockpiling of antiviral medications.

As you also know, the World Health Organization and other public health experts have recommended that countries which can afford to do so should stockpile appropriate antivirals sufficient for 25 percent of their population or more. But the United States is far below this level. The U.S. stockpile is sufficient to provide medications to less than 1 percent of Americans. U.S. government officials state that they believe stockpiling is important; therefore their failure to obtain stockpiles is simply a failure of organization and prioritization. Secretary Leavitt has indicated the United States will work to increase its stockpile, but the single manufacturer of a key antiviral, oseltamivir (sold by Roche under license from Gilead under the brand name Tamiflu), says it cannot meet demand.

With pressure escalating on Roche, last week it indicated it will issue licenses to other manufacturers. It remains to be seen what the terms of these licenses will be. If they are collusive and continue to restrain supply or keep prices artificially inflated, and assuming a public health finding that stockpiling is important, then the government should invoke 28 U.S.C. §1498, authorizing the government and its contractors to use the patents on oseltamivir. §1498 permits the government to use any patent it deems necessary, conditioned only on payment of appropriate compensation to the patent holder.

For the longer term, there must be a serious assessment of

---

* See http://www.cdc.gov/flu/avian/gen-info/pandemics.htm for more information.

how the United States finds itself hostage to pharmaceutical manufacturers who cannot manufacture sufficient quantities of drugs or vaccines to deal with priority public health concerns, or who charge too much for what they do sell.

The federal government has long offered major subsidies to the pharmaceutical industry, including through federally funded research at the National Institutes of Health and technology transfer and licensing giveaways, as well as through extensive tax credits. The public may reasonably ask what kind of treatment it receives in return, especially in emergency situations.

With some exceptions, shortfalls in pharmaceutical and vaccine supplies and high prices do not relate to manufacturing challenges. Rather, they are due to the policy choice of relying on patent monopolists who for one reason or another fail to adequately supply the market or choose to use their monopoly power to price gouge.

There are at least two appropriate remedies to prevent a recurrence of these problems. We urge you to pursue both.

First, the provision of a marketing monopoly to drug innovators invites abuse. Innovators—to the extent they actually innovate with their own monies—must be compensated, including for the risk they take that their investments might fail. But there is no reason they should be rewarded with a marketing monopoly. The marketing monopoly gives them the ability to restrict supply dangerously—whether by inattention to public health needs or otherwise. It enables them to price gouge. It gives them an incentive to pour resources into marketing and advertising, which hurts public health by leading to overuse and inappropriate use of pharmaceuticals. And it gives them an incentive to conduct research in areas where a marketing monopoly will give them the biggest dollar payouts (frequently copycat drugs, and less important treatment areas) at the expense of higher public health priorities (such as vaccines, or products to treat diseases of high prevalence in developing countries with little buying power).

There are many ways that innovators could be compensated other than with a marketing monopoly. One such proposal is for a Medical Innovation Prize Fund,* which would have an independently administered government fund pay innovators, but not grant innovators a marketing monopoly. Under this proposal, generic versions of any pharmaceutical or related product would be available from multiple suppliers immediately or shortly after a product received FDA approval.

Second, there should be an expanded role for government in the development and manufacture of pharmaceuticals and vaccines. The federal government is already a major funder of basic drug research through the National Institutes of Health and other agencies, and contributes as well a large amount of funding to drug and vaccine development. But at some point along the line, the government turns over the fruits of its investment to private corporations, frequently for little or no compensation. They complete the development process and then typically gain monopoly rights to manufacture the resultant product, with the familiar attendant abuses. Rather than turn over the fruits of its investment, the government should consider carrying forward the development process to conclusion and

---

* For an iteration of this proposal, see H.R. 417, The Medical Innovation Prize Fund Act, introduced by Representative Bernie Sanders. In the Sanders proposal, the fund would come from general tax revenues. The amount expended would be equal to 0.5 percent of gross domestic product (roughly $60 billion currently). This is more than the industry now spends on research and development. However, the expenditure would enable a huge net savings for the United States as a whole, which currently spends more than $200 billion a year on pharmaceuticals. Under the Medicare prescription drug benefit, the U.S. is on course to spend $849 billion over the next 10 years, according to the Congressional Budget Office. The Medicare savings alone from H.R. 417 would go a long way to funding the prize fund.

licensing the final products on a nonexclusive basis to generic makers. Or, it might manufacture the products itself, especially during a fast-developing emergency.

In light of the oseltamivir shortfall, as well as ongoing problems in securing adequate flu vaccines, it would seem not imprudent for the government to develop and maintain some significant manufacturing capacity for drugs and vaccines. It seems clear that the United States, and the world, will be faced with an ongoing series of evolving and relatively sudden public health demands; and the corporate sector has demonstrated that it will frequently fail to provide sufficient supply of essential medicines and vaccines at appropriate prices. It was such recognition of the pharmaceutical industry's resistance that led the Pentagon to expand the Walter Reed Army Institute of Research, with naval research participation, during the Vietnam War, to do successful, efficient malaria and other drug and vaccine development at costs far below those of the private drug companies.

The first responsibility of a government must be to provide for the safety of the citizenry. We must take measures to ensure we are not held hostage to the whims of profit-before-people drug corporations. That means ending the marketing monopoly for pharmaceutical and vaccine innovators and expanding the government role in pharmaceutical and vaccine development and manufacture, especially for emergency conditions.

Sincerely,
Ralph Nader
Robert Weissman

Harriet Miers: Questionable Integrity

Dear President Bush,

Your position regarding the nomination of Harriet Miers to become an Associate Justice of the Supreme Court of the United States is increasingly untenable, even within your own Party, for reasons well known to you.

Moreover, before the general public, the nomination has a distinct aroma of cronyism deeply marinated in a sauce of secrecy. You have chosen your chief legal counsel and loyal political supporter. Nominating your confidante and insisting that her White House record be confidential is a difficult sell to the American people. They may believe that you can't have it both ways. If you wish to maintain internal White House confidentiality, then do not nominate a confidante to the highest court in the land.

A major responsibility of the White House counsel is to advise the president on the legality of various courses of action. This, undoubtedly, has kept her very busy. The Senate and the people deserve to learn how she has performed in this regard.

Our experience with this responsibility has not been encouraging. In a letter dated July 18, I, along with Kevin Zeese, wrote to Ms. Miers in her role as Counsel to the resident concerning a matter of integrity in your administration. Under 5 U.S.C. 7321, Karl Rove was required to allocate his expenditures separating time and resources spent on political activity from his time spent as a staff member in the White House. It was a simple request by fax and hard copy regarding the allocation of Mr. Rove's expenditures during the 2004 presidential campaign. Mr. Rove was the central figure in your reelection campaign. Indeed, you described Mr. Rove as "the architect" of your reelection. At the same time he was working on your reelection campaign, he was also serving as your senior advisor overseeing planning, political affairs, public liaison, and intergovernmental affairs. He took no leave of absence from his taxpayer-funded position during the campaign. Three months later we still have not received a response of any kind. Why? The failure to respond now also raises questions about Ms. Miers, whom you described today as "a leader of unquestioned integrity."

The Miers nomination has more and more signs of being unsustainable. Any defection by already outspoken Republicans on the Senate Judiciary Committee, together with the Democrats' votes, could block her nomination in committee.

You would be well advised to withdraw the nomination and cease searching for ideologically-driven judicial nominees who are essentially "prejudgers" of cases.

Sincerely,

JULY 28, 2005

Iraq: Poor Families Sacrifice,
War Corporations Profit

Dear President Bush,

On June 28, 2005 you addressed the nation in prime time about the situation in Iraq. You called the casualties, destruction and suffering in that country "horrifying" and "real." Then you declared: "I know Americans ask the question: Is the sacrifice worth it? It is worth it," you asserted and went on to explain your position.

My question to you is this: "Who is doing the sacrificing on the U.S. side besides our troops and their families and other Americans whose dire necessities and protections cannot be met due to the diversion of huge spending for the Iraq War and occupation?"

Let's start with the wealthy. In the midst of the ravages of war, you gave them a double tax cut, pushing these enormous windfalls through Congress at the same time as concentrations of wealth among the top one percent richest were accelerating.

You also cut taxes for the large corporations that benefit most from arcane, detailed tax legislation. Many of these corporations have profited greatly from the tens of billions of dollars in contracts which you have handed them.

Companies like Halliburton, from which Vice President Dick Cheney receives handsome retirement benefits, keep getting multibillion contracts even though the Pentagon auditors and investigations by Rep. Henry Waxman have shown vast waste, nonperformances, and not a little corruption. Not much corporate sacrifice there.

You and Mr. Cheney need to be reminded that your predecessors pressed, during wartime, for surcharges on corporate profits of the largest corporations. As Rep. Major R. Owens pointed out recently in introducing such legislation (H.R. 1804), the precedents for such an equitable policy, at a time of growing federal deficits, occurred during World War I, World War II, and the Korean and Vietnam Wars. Ponder the difference. Past presidents increased taxes on the large companies as a way of spreading out the economic sacrifice a little. Instead, during a time of record—even staggering— corporate profits, you reduce their contributions to the U.S. Treasury and military expenditures.

Where is the presence of the sons and daughters of the

top political and economic rulers in the Iraq theater, where they can see the suffering of millions of innocent Iraqi people? You can count on the fingers of one hand the number of family members serving over there among the 535 members of Congress and the White House. No specific data is available for the families of the CEOs of the Fortune 500. But we can guess that very few are stationed in and around the Sunni Triangle these days. Can't get much tennis, golf or sailing in if that were the case. How often have you extolled the patriotic sacrifice of members of the armed forces, the Reserves and the National Guard? How often have you praised their work as the highest form of service to their nation, its security and future? Well, what about your daughters having this sublime opportunity to be on the receiving end of their father's encomiums? Remember Major John Eisenhower, among others.

In an earlier unanswered letter, I urged you and Mr. Cheney to announce that you would reject the tens of thousands of dollars in personal tax cuts that passage of your tax cut legislation for the wealthy would have accorded both of your fortunes. Recusing yourselves would have conveyed the message that it is unseemly to sign your own personal tax reduction. It would also have furthered the principle of the moral authority to govern.

Well, you did sign your own tax cut, while tens of thousands of Americans had to leave their employment and small businesses and go to Iraq, often at a reduced pay and worrying about inadequate protective equipment and insufficient training.

I refer you to the *New York Times* of July 4, 2005, which published a featured story on Phil Sorenson and Cody Wentz, from Williston, North Dakota, who after graduation from high school joined the National Guard and were shipped out to Iraq as part of the 141st Engineer Combat Battalion. In the article the *Times* reporter wrote:

"Sorenson said his unit was initially told it would conduct searches for insurgents. But for the next year, the 141st's mission was to travel 15 to 20 miles an hour in search of roadside bombs, a task for which Sorenson said they had trained for about one day" (emphasis added).

"Infuriated by poor equipment and the lack of preparation, Wentz wrote a four-page letter to Lloyd Omdahl, a former lieutenant governor of North Dakota who writes a newspaper column."

Soon thereafter a roadside bomb took the life of Cody Wentz and the leg of Phil Sorenson, who has returned to North Dakota to try to rebuild his life.

President Harry Truman used to say, "The buck stops here." At what point does the buck stop at your desk in the Oval Office?

Those rulers who send young men and women into undeclared wars on platforms of fabrications, deceptions, and cover-ups do not have proper incentives for responsible, effective behavior and politics. Some degrees of shared sacrifice provide prudent restraint against the manipulations and recklessness of politicians and the supporting avarice of their fellow oligarchs.

Without some measure of sacrifice, programs are mis-designed to pursue stateless terrorists in ways and areas that actually produce recruitment opportunities for more such terrorists. Note your own CIA Director Porter Goss's testimony before the Senate earlier this year. But the resulting warmongering, where the "intelligence and the facts" are fixed to the policy, became unsavory reelection strategies in 2004.

You have often told us that you want to nominate federal judges who believe in a strict construction of the Constitution. How about a president who believes in the strict constitutional authority of article one, section eight, which gives Congress and Congress alone the power to declare war? Requiring a declaration of war, together with legislation requiring, upon such a declaration, the conscription of all eligible members of congressional and White House families, would assure that only "unavoidable and necessary wars" are declared and fought.

Sincerely,

[signature]

Why Meet with Foreign Dissidents but Not Domestic Ones?

Dear President Bush,

On June 15, 2005, the *Washington Post* had a page-one story reporting that you have begun meeting in the White House with foreign dissidents challenging their political leaders. Hmm. You probably sense the obvious question. Why don't you ever meet with dissident groups of Americans who question your policies? On the hustings, in town after town, you screen out people peaceably critical of your war or social insecurity positions or have them escorted out of your audiences. Apparently you and your associates prefer an audience of 100 percent ditto-heads. This is unbecoming a president of a country that is "the land of the free and the home of the brave."

Let one example do for many. During the weeks before

your March 2003 invasion of Iraq, civic organizations, representing millions of Americans each requested in writing a meeting with you regarding the Iraq situation. Some had firsthand information and much experience.

Asking to see you were organizations of veterans, retired intelligence officials, churches, business persons, labor, minorities, women of peace, and students. Quite a cross section of America. You not only refused to see them, but also you did not even accord them the propriety of sending them a letter of declination. You just turned your back on these decent Americans.

You once told your circle of advisors in the White House that you don't have to explain yourself, because, unlike them, you are the president. What do you think your grandfather, my former courteous, responsive Senator Prescott Bush from Connecticut would have said about such boorish and imperious behavior by his grandson?

Clearly you needed more of his tutelage years ago.

Again, please respond to the above question about meeting with domestic critics.

Sincerely,

MAY 30, 2005
Mothers and Grandparents Against Iraq

Dear President Bush,

As the United States moves toward the third year of the war and occupation of Iraq, U.S. soldiers are still dying because of lack of armor. This war has already lasted longer than the U.S.

participation in World War I—and our soldiers are still not properly equipped. There is no satisfactory rationale for this reality. There is no explanation as to why you are not publicly taking to task those personnel more directly entrusted with procuring this equipment over the past 26 months.

It is bad enough that based on fabrications, deceptions, and distortions, you plunged our nation into war. It is duplicitous enough that you wrap yourself around the soldiers and their families for photo opportunities while underreporting their casualties, cutting their benefits, and putting them in harm's way. But to send them into battle ill equipped—for a war of choice, not of necessity—this is not something that any patriotic American should accept or tolerate.

Here is a sample of what Americans are saying about the dangers our troops are facing as a result of you not supporting those soldiers in combat:

"I wish that the same leaders who are so eager to proclaim that every life is sacred were half as eager to act on behalf of our military men and women, who are dying needlessly. The Bush Administration and Congress are negligent for allowing this . . ." —Mother from Devon, PA

"Who is holding President Bush, Vice President Dick Cheney and Defense Secretary Donald H. Rumsfeld accountable for the heavy human toll from this questionable war fought for nonexistent weapons of mass destruction; for soldiers being killed while driving in poorly armored vehicles; and for the innocent people—Americans, Iraqis, and others— who have died or been maimed?" —Grandmother from Houston, TX

"My son, an infantry officer in the Marine Corps, is home from Iraq and is safe, but I can't help mourning the loss of those brave, selfless, fallen boys of Company E. I feel so angry about the lack of relatively simple protection that they deserved." —Mother from San Clemente, CA

"Two years into the Iraq War, and the Humvee armor program is still incomplete. Two and a half years into World War II, and we were a few months away from D-Day. I guess that tax cuts must be more important to the White House. Sad, sad." —Grandfather from West Hartford, CT

The anger Americans feel for this dereliction is understandable. When they read reports about the deaths and serious injuries of thousands of soldiers because of lack of body armor and protection for their vehicles, they have to wonder. And, when those same reports describe how our allies were able to order body armor from a Michigan manufacturer in 12 days—while U.S. soldiers still waited months and years—it is amazing their frustration can be ignored by you.

The *Wall Street Journal* reported on how the Pentagon is slow to react with protective equipment (Greg Jaffe, "Pentagon Procurement Slows Supply Flow," May 24, 2005). They review the example of a jammer to block the detonation of roadside bombs. Their story demonstrates how General Abizaid called the roadside bombs his "number one threat in Iraq" in June 2004 but today, nearly one year later, the Pentagon continues to manufacture jammers that don't jam frequencies used by the resistance. But the source of the problem runs deeper; as the *New York Times* pointed out, procurement is a problem but the real problem is your leadership of the war/occupation:

"The roots of this problem lie in the Bush Administration's stubborn self-delusion about the reception American troops were likely to face in Iraq. Then it took the Pentagon many months to acknowledge that it was facing a determined long-term insurgency, not just a clutch of desperate holdouts from Saddam Hussein's inner circle. By the time reality started sinking in during the early months of 2004, the insurgents were on a fast learning curve that Washington has been trying to catch up with ever since. Insurgents' tactics keep growing more sophisticated and their firepower more intense. As a result, American units in the field have discovered that even their armored Humvees must now be refitted with stronger armor to protect against the increasingly lethal improvised explosive devices that have become this war's signature weapon ("Support Our Troops," *New York Times* editorial, May 1, 2005).

We are requesting that you answer with your best estimates:

—How many of the more than 1,600 U.S. soldiers died because of inadequate protective gear?
—How many have been injured because of inadequate protective gear?
—How many vehicles in Iraq are currently ill equipped with inadequate protective armor?
—How many soldiers still do not have sufficient body armor?

We are writing to request that you meet with some of the American military families and Veterans for Peace, who have spoken out about the failure of your administration to protect U.S. soldiers. Don't you think it would be useful for you, as the commander in chief, to explain to them and the American people directly why you sent U.S. soldiers into battle ill-equipped and now, two and a half years later, have still failed to fully remedy the problem when you clearly had the funds to procure this equipment on the double? Under the U.S. tort law, which you are targeting to destroy in increments, this behavior would be considered gross negligence. Under the penal codes, it would meet the criteria for criminal negligence.

Isn't it way past time for you to level with the people of this country?

Sincerely,

[signature]

FEBRUARY 6, 2005
Bush's Twisted Priorities

Dear President Bush,

With the transmission of your federal budget tomorrow, you will extend your record of massive deficits, privileges, and tax cuts for the wealthy and corporations, and sharp reductions in the budgets for health care and protection of the poor, children and all Americans from hazards to their health and safety under the purview of weakened regulatory agencies.

From public health to education to home energy assistance to environmental programs to Amtrak, budget cuts reflect the twisted priorities of your administration. The bloated, wasteful, redundant military expenditures, including the boondoggle unworkable missile defense program at over $9 billion last year, come at the expense of programs that save the lives and health of the American people here at home. Your own agencies estimate that 58,000 Americans die each year due to worker-related diseases and trauma, that about 65,000 Americans die from air pollution annually, and the School of Public Health study at Harvard puts the fatality toll from hospital malpractice at over 100,000 a year. These are just lethal samples of the conditions you ignore, reduce responses toward, or make worse by pushing to restrict the victims from having their full day in court for compensatory justice.

You have finally awoken, slightly, to the threat of a global flu epidemic which received prominent treatment in the *Washington Post* and *New York Times* this weekend. But increasing that budget to $120 million, an increase of 21 percent over the prior year, is not enough to post infectious disease specialists in the Far East, conduct the surveillance of its incipient spread, and prepare our country for the possibly catastrophic onslaught. Recall, after U.N. inspectors and our troops could not find any WMDs in Iraq, you spent well over half a billion dollars with 1,500 inspectors, under David Kay, and found nothing. Is there a priority problem here for a president in need of redefining national security to include virulent epidemics? Then, to make matters worse, you propose cutting the budget of the Centers for Disease Control and Prevention by 9 percent.

Your arguments reveal false scenarios. You speak of being "wise with the people's money," while your trillions of dollars in deficits will inflict the most gigantic tax on our children and grandchildren in all of American history, while your Homeland Security and Defense budgets are full of waste, fraud and abuse by contractors. Do you ever read the GAO reports, the internal audits of your own administration?

You wish to further tighten the restrictions on mothers on welfare, but, with few exceptions, your budget does not cut huge corporate welfare expenditures, subsidies, giveaways, handouts, bailouts, and guarantees—all which could recover important revenues for your budget. Don't you read the criticisms of corporate welfare by the Cato Institute and the Heritage Foundation in order to see many ways to reduce your federal deficit? You decry "lawsuit abuse" and move to usurp the state courtrooms by federal power without looking at the data showing too little—not too much—access to the courts, and untold fatalities, injuries, and diseases wrongfully inflicted on innocent Americans, including veterans, that are endured without compensation or deterrence.

You travel about the county declaring that Social Security is heading for bankruptcy (when the most obvious simple changes, such as increasing the wealthy's income subject to Social Security taxes, can pay benefits until the next century). Yet, you preside over a federal government that by your definition of "bankruptcy" is deep into that condition since you became president, adding nearly three trillion dollars to the national debt. You are indeed the commander in chief of deficit spending, false scenarios, waste in government, corporate rip-offs of Uncle Sam, welfare for the rich, penury for the increasing poor, and tax-shifting on to the shrinking middle class.

I recommend that you end your isolation and insulation from the American people on these matters and open up your mind to nonrigged town meetings around the country that are not dominated by your orchestrated fawning partisans. The people have a right to access their president with their concerns, complaints, and broader inquiries regarding the future of our country and its place in the world. Enough of your mass-media-transmitted soliloquies to the American people.

Sincerely,

DECEMBER 9, 2004
The Destruction of Mosques in Iraq

Dear President Bush,

Reading the news accounts of the recurring destruction of many mosques in Iraq, I recall the words of your own former counterterrorism chief, Richard Clarke, who wrote earlier this year: "Far from addressing the popular appeal of the enemy that attacked us, Bush handed that enemy precisely what it wanted and needed, proof that America was at war with Islam, that we were the new Crusaders to come to occupy Muslim land." Clarke was referring to your "unprovoked invasion of an oil-rich Arab country," namely Iraq.

Together with your reference to "crusade" during the drumbeats of pending war, and your invoking religious inspiration for your mission to overthrow the dictator, it is not surprising that many Muslims in these countries hold the impressions alluded to by Mr. Clarke.

The city of mosques—Fallujah—now lies mostly in ruins. So do many of its mosques. You believe this was unavoidable because mosques are being used as locations of arms caches or resistance to the advancing U.S. troops. It is their fault if these insurgents bring down their mosques on themselves, not that of the policies initiated by you as commander in chief, you would say.

This is too facile because you have often said the U.S. has to win the "hearts and minds of the Iraqi people." This is your declared objective. If Iraqi Muslims believe that the U.S. is attacking Islam, then to them it may well be that, in the words of Annemarie Brown, "Islamist respect for insurgency brings mosques into a supportive role." Another way of putting it: fighting against what they perceive as an attack on their religion means they will defend their religion even, or especially, from their holy places of worship. How many of these mosques have been destroyed or rendered unusable for prayers?

Your justification for responding to mosques as battlegrounds knows neither any public policy boundaries, nor any program of if, when, and how you plan to rebuild these beautiful structures. All over the Islamic world, great numbers of Muslims see pictures and believe the United States is destroying their most sacred buildings. Memory is long in the Middle East.

Recently retired intelligence and counterterrorist specialists in your government view the Iraq invasion as enhancing recruitment of al-Qaeda or al-Qaeda clones. What must they think of this latest escalation?

Within the framework of an unconstitutional war based on a platform of fabrications and deceptions driving an invasion that is clearly illegal under international law, why do you think that demolishing Iraqi cities and towns, which generate mosque-based resistance, does anything to reach the "hearts and minds" of Iraqi Muslims? Many of these people say they find their lives more disrupted and insecure after the overthrow than under Saddam Hussein.

There are too many ambiguities in your instructions to military forces with regard to their invasive or destructive moves against mosques. The recent raid on the Abu Hanifa Mosque in Baghdad for suspected insurgents pushes the threshold and expands the arenas of unbridled discretion. Even an official dispatch by the American Forces Information Services quoted a senior defense official in Baghdad regarding the raid that was staged after Friday prayers as saying it "could have been timed better," adding "We still have after-action critiquing to do."

There is the additional provocation to many Muslims of U.S. forces or directed forces using the seized mosques as military occupation public address systems replacing the historic daily call to prayer by muezzins. Do you have any idea how this affects Muslims?

Envision for an empathetic instant, a gigantically more powerful Islamic country invading a weak U.S. after toppling a dictator in Washington (who was once supported by this Islamic superpower), going after the U.S. resistance forces, and blowing apart Baptist and Catholic churches, for example, that the resistance used for arms caches or defense maneuvers against the invaders. For just a hypothetical moment, put the shoe on the other foot, if that is the only way to sensitize yourself to what is going on in Iraq—i.e., assaulting the religious sensibilities of Iraqis, causing them to turn even more forcefully against the U.S. occupation.

Destruction of cities by the world's most powerful military machine is relatively easy. How are you going to reconstruct these cities? Congress appropriated some $18 billion months ago for this purpose and less than $2 billion has been used and not entirely for reconstruction.

Tell the American people what you are going to do about rebuilding these mosques, about possibly pursuing military tactics and technologies that can avoid the occasion for destroying these holy buildings.

Will you meet with and answer questions on this subject by representatives of millions of Muslim Americans in this country who have to be seeking some assurances, some way out of this inflammatory expansion of the battlefield that can only boomerang against U.S. security and safety interests in the coming months and years?

Americans who have either been against this illegal war

from the outset or have turned against the war in the interim months (now around half of those polled) deserve some more sobering thoughts than they have been receiving from messianic militarists in political positions repeating unfounded and long-rebutted pretexts for this war.

Sincerely,

[signature]

DECEMBER 8, 2004

Stand Up and Face the Casualty Count

Dear President Bush,

On June 30, 2004, I wrote you an open letter urging that your administration include in the U.S. casualty toll in Iraq: (1) injuries in noncombat situations; (2) personnel who have come down with disabling diseases; and (3) cases of mental trauma requiring evacuation from Iraq. You did not respond, nor did Senator John Kerry, who received a copy of the letter.

I should have added three additional categories which are also not part of the official casualty count: (4) fatalities that occur after U.S. military personnel are brought stateside; (5) soldiers committing suicide in Iraq; and (6) injuries and fatalities incurred by corporate contractors operating in the Iraqi war theater.

On November 21, 2004, CBS's *60 Minutes* led its program with a segment on the subject of uncounted "non-combat" casualties. They interviewed badly injured soldiers who were upset by their being excluded from the official count, even though they were, in one soldier's words, "in hostile territory." The Pentagon declined to be interviewed, instead sending a letter that contained information not included in published casualty reports. "More than 15,000 troops with so-called 'non-battle' injuries and diseases have been evacuated from Iraq," wrote the Department of Defense. John Pike, director of GlobalSecurity.org, told *60 Minutes* that this uncounted casualty figure "would have to be somewhere in the ballpark of over 20, maybe 30,000."

What's your problem here? The American people need to know the full casualty toll of U.S. personnel in Iraq and know it regularly and in a timely fashion. Not to do so is disrespectful, especially toward the military families, but none more so than of the soldiers themselves. As a severely wounded Chris Schneider told CBS: "Every one of us went over there with the knowledge that we could die. And then they tell you—you're wounded—or your sacrifice doesn't deserve to be recognized or we don't deserve to be on their list—it's not right. It's almost disgraceful."

Soldiers like Chris Schneider, Joel Gomez and Graham Alstrom want to know whether you are going to continue to stonewall their desire for official respect. What shall we tell them and others who seek that simple, decent official recognition? Please do not think that because you are a chronic nonresponder to critical questions, you will be able to delay this growing demand indefinitely. Your hit-and-run photo opportunities with the troops just don't cut the mustard. Stand up and face it. It is the right thing to do by them.

Sincerely,

Letters to President George W. Bush

Your Views on the Environment

Dear President Bush,

Do you generally agree that economic as well as health and ecological efficiencies, short- and long-term, accrue from more efficient utilization of natural resources (oil, gas, coal, pulp, hard rock metals, etc.), as has been demonstrated by the book *Natural Capitalism* (Hawken, Lovins, and Lovins) and companies like Interface Corporation—the largest manufacturer of commercial carpets and tiles in the United States?

What more in your Party's judgment should be done by the public and corporate sectors to defend, preserve, and nourish our depleted or polluted forests, rivers, bays, estuaries, oceans, soils and foods? In the same vein, what more would your Party do to purify the air which humans breathe from the acknowledged persistent sources of pollution (motor vehicles, industries, government activities, etc.)? Would you replace the present permissive ratification of genetically engineered crops and products by the federal government with a regulatory framework? If so, please elaborate and include whether you support labeling of genetically engineered food in the nation's markets, as the vast majority of Americans want?

Global warming. The great preponderance of non-redundant scientific analysis is that man-made greenhouse gases are increasing the overall temperature of the Earth and large portions of the Antarctic ice cap, and sections of the Andes and Alaska are evincing unusual meltdowns of glaciers and snow, including calving of glaciers in Antarctica.

We can reduce greenhouse gases by: (1) making combustion more efficient, through fuel efficiency of motor vehicles, that will save on motorists' budgets (more miles per gallon), and (2) reducing near-ground air pollution, and the resulting ailments: morbidity and mortality.

Does your Party take all three effects into account when weighing the cost-benefit of a broad policy to deal with global warming? If so, can you include written elaboration of that tripartite position? If not, please explain your disagreement.

Drinking water. Lead, other heavy metals, bacteria, viruses, toxic chemicals, and particulates have been found repeatedly in too many of the nation's drinking water systems. Underinvestment in purification technology, containment of drinking water source pollution, nonreplacement of corroded, leaching distribution pipes all combine to produce a major, but preventable long-term health hazard. What does the Party propose to do that is not being done presently—including public investment in safeguarding facilities, acquiring better technologies, improving monitoring and public notifications, and reassuring the public that bottled water is adequately tested? What is your Party's position on the corporatization of public drinking water departments and why?

For the interest of a wider, more fundamental discussion during this presidential campaign, I look forward to your response regarding these issues.

Thank you.

Sincerely,

Your Views on Corporate Taxes

Dear President Bush,

Corporate tax contributions to the overall federal budget have been declining for fifty years and now stand at 7.4 percent. Many tax analysts of differing philosophical bents believe that there should be a fundamental reappraisal of our tax laws. In that spirit, what is your position on the following approaches?

• Taxes should first apply to behavior and conditions we favor least, such as pollution, speculation, gambling, extreme luxuries, instead of taxing work, food, furniture, clothing, or books. Tiny taxes on stock, bond, and derivative transactions can produce tens of billions of dollars a year and displace some of the taxes on work and life necessities (given the large volumes of such buys and sells week after week). What is your position on the above thesis and its preferred applications? If undecided, would you like to see this subject publicly debated?

• Sol Price, founder of the Price Club (now merged into Costco), is one of several wealthy people in the past half century who have urged a tax on wealth (above an ample minimum exception). It can be very low rate, but raise significant money. Wealth is described as tangible and intangible assets. Would you support this proposal in principle? Would you like to see this publicly debated?

• Do you believe that "unearned income" (dividends, interest, capital gains) or wealth should be taxed higher than earned income, or work, inasmuch as one involves passive income, while the latter involves active effort with a higher proportion of middle- and lower-income workers relying on and working each day for these earnings?

• Simplification of the Internal Revenue Code has been

supported by almost every holder of public office yet each decade the Code has become much more complex and abstruse, and subject to both more avoidance and evasion. How would the Party delineate a policy to simplify the Code? What would be the steps taken to achieve that goal, and under what legislative strategy and timetable?

• Similarly, there has been in recent years loud bipartisan condemnation of ever more elaborate and dubious tax shelters costing the Treasury Department tens of billions of dollars a year, yet there has been no concrete action in Congress, especially with regard to the offshore tax havens. What is your Party's position and action plan—timetable and urgency—to stop this tax escapism?

• Finally, it is well known that adding one dollar to the overwhelmed Internal Revenue Service budget will return a high multiple of revenue. Yet the IRS has been deprived of these added funds. How much would you add to the IRS budget annually (cite increments over time if you are so inclined) and how would you allocate these extra funds (e.g., corporate, individual)? Estimates put the uncollected taxes from all sources at about $300 billion a year, a gap that undermines confidence in the tax system by the majority of America, including small businesses that dutifully pay their taxes.

For the interest of a wider, more fundamental discussion during this presidential campaign, I look forward to your response regarding these issues.

Thank you.

Sincerely,

Your Views on Citizen Access to Government

Dear President Bush,

I am writing you concerning your views on strengthening citizen access to all three branches of government to allow for greater participation of citizens in their government.

Executive Branch: Do you favor establishing a consumer protection agency with the right of judicial review of regulatory agencies, which passed one or another of the houses of Congress in the late seventies?

Do you favor stronger administration of the present Freedom of Information Act by reducing the delays and arbitrary denials of citizen requests?

Do you believe that citizens should have legal standing to exercise a right to a mandamus and an injunctive action against a federal agency believed to be unlawfully acting or not acting?

Do you believe that executive branch nominations requiring the Senate's advice and consent should be more open to allow the interested citizenry to testify?

Legislative Branch: Do you support democratizing the internal rules of Congress so that the minority party has opportunity to introduce amendments and engage in adequate debate?

Do you believe that members of Congress should have benefits (such as health and life insurance) that are not provided to all of the American people?

Do you believe that congressional pay should be attached to an automatic cost of living index when American workers' federal minimum wage is not?

Do you believe that each member of Congress should have his or her voting record in clear, easily retrievable fashion on his or her website?

Do you believe that the Office of Technology Assessment, closed down in 1995, should be reestablished to provide systematic technical reports and advice to Congress (its budget was then $20 million a year)?

Do you believe that congressional oversight functions need to be more extensive and demanding over executive branch departments and agencies?

Judicial Branch: Would you reduce the barriers to standing to sue the federal government for civic purposes, apart from personal or corporate damages?

Would you abolish the government contractors' defense and allow aggrieved parties (like armed forces personnel) to sue defense manufacturers that built defective weapons or other military products resulting in injuries or fatalities?

According to federal court specialists, access to these courts are being limited by tight budgets, by criminal drug cases overwhelming dockets, and by pressure on Congress to load up the federal courts with more jurisdictions (class actions, etc.) and more cases. How would you deal with such congestion, or do you believe they are not problems?

For the interest of a wider, more fundamental discussion during this presidential campaign, I look forward to your response regarding these issues.

Thank you.

Sincerely,

Your Views on Facilities for
Citizen and Consumer Action

Dear President Bush,

Inherent in the very concept of proximate self-government is due regard not just for individual rights but also for the facilities that make it easy for people to band together for common pursuits. Such a regard means that government has to respect the Bill of Rights that protects citizens from arbitrary government and also display an affirmative duty to facilitate such civic, political, and economic energies of the people (see *Here, the People Rule* by Richard Parker, Harvard University Press, 1994). The historic post office was one of the earliest examples of a very successful effort that bound the nation together, as have the objectives of the antitrust laws in the economic realm of opportunity.

In recent decades, a massive imbalance has existed between the government's programs that facilitate and fund organized corporate activity (in part known as corporate welfare) and the absence of helping American workers, consumers, small taxpayers, small investors, and residents band together. As Jean Monnet once said, nothing is possible without people, but nothing is lasting without institutions.

The following proposal can be justified in many ways. One, most practically, is reciprocity. The federal government provides advocacy (e.g., the Department of Commerce) and hundreds of billions of dollars for subsidies, free technology, R&D transfers, handouts, legal monopolies, bailouts, guarantees, natural resource giveaways along with many privileges and immunities embracing tax, appropriations, and defense laws and programs for corporate entities. Whole industries (e.g., semiconductor, aerospace, biotechnology) have arisen from government research and development programs. Massive profits have risen from government contracts and tax shelters of many kinds. Enormous business fraud is persistently eroding the integrity of Medicare procurement programs and taxpayer dollars. Along with major media outlets the General Accounting Office, congressional members, and committees of your parties and your respective administrations have documented the abuses of many of these programs which have vastly outrun any corrective or remedial actions on behalf of regular Americans. Since the people end up paying the price, it behooves the government to help the people to band together voluntarily to defend themselves and monitor their government and those who prey on it. This can be done without spending huge tax dollars, as the corporations insist be done on their behalf daily.

For consumers and investors, an insert can be placed in government mailings and transmissions and in corporate billing envelopes, statements, and other transmissions, including online. It would invite them to join nonprofit associations with all the rights to advocate, litigate, negotiate, communicate, and research that corporate entities possess. These associations would operate on voluntary memberships and voluntary dues and contributions. They would be democratically operated with any consumers or investors free to join. They could be statewide or national, independent of the government and accountable only to the laws of the land and their members. Residential utility ratepayer associations were formed in Illinois and San Diego on this model.

Such groups would redress some of the imbalance of representation and power that is now so shockingly one-sided. They would give millions of more informed Americans an organized chance to be heard and, through their full-time skilled advocates a way to participate and to prevail. "Freedom," said the Roman lawyer Cicero, "is participation in power." The government, under the influence of powerful interests, created the dangerously uneven playing field. It has the responsibility to better level that field and strengthen our democratic society. Briefly put, if the American people do not have a say, they will pay, as they have in the massive savings and loan, corporate crime, and health industry scandals.

Would you support such facilities for consumers and investors? If so, how would you go about implementing legislation toward that end? What would be your timetable? Are there any other suggestions that would indicate how serious you are about this proposal becoming a reality for millions of organized customers of bank, insurance, brokerage, mutual fund, energy, motor vehicle, mortgage, telecommunications, rental, health care, food, and other services?

For individual taxpayers, inserts can be placed in the IRS book of instructions and a prominent square space on the 1040 tax return. The message would invite taxpayers to join their own national taxpayers' organization which they would control, fund, and operate through an elected board of directors and full-time staff to watchdog the expenditures of tax funds and the equitable and efficient collection of tax revenues.

For workers, labor law reform could repeal the provisions of the Taft-Hartley Act which obstruct the ability of workers to form their own trade unions, control their own pensions, and join in solidarity with other workers to improve their standards of living. Legislation is also needed to allow workers to use card checks to form a collective bargaining unit and reduce the bureaucratic hoops presently administered by the National Labor Relations Board.

For television viewers and radio listeners, the government

would charter an audience network open to membership by any viewers or listeners and accountable democratically to its voting members who are its basic funders. The staff would operate an hour of prime time and drive time on all FCC-licensed television and radio stations that are presently using the public's airwaves without charge. Programming would reflect policies and choices of the open-door membership, the Board of Directors and the programmers, producers, editors, and reporters of the full-time staff. The network, which puts the "landlords" in charge of a little of its own property (the public airwaves), would be structured to allow diversity of views, flexible innovations and interactivity along the entire range of educational programming from the serious to the playful. (See draft statute in "Oh, Say Can You See: A Broadcast Network for the Audience," *Journal of Law and Politics*, V, no. 1 [1988].)

For individual investors, workers, television viewers, and radio listeners, would you support these facilities for voluntary associations, controlled by their members, universally accessible and member-funded under democratic procedures? If so, what would be your timetable, your level of priority and in what form would you launch your support to indicate your desired level of seriousness?

For the interest of a wider, more fundamental discussion during this presidential campaign, I look forward to your response regarding these issues.

Thank you.

Sincerely,

Will You Pledge to Not Reinstate the Draft?

Dear Senator Kerry and President Bush,

Neither of you have put forward an exit strategy for U.S. troops in Iraq or Afghanistan. This open-ended troop deployment, along with the other military commitments of the United States throughout the world, has stretched U.S. forces thin. In order to meet these commitments many soldiers have not been allowed to leave the service at the end of their enlistment (a form of a draft), thousands of troops are being shifted from South Korea to ease pressure elsewhere, the U.S. is calling up more and more reserves, and most recently the Army announced it would call back soldiers who had already left the service.

The House of Representatives voted in May to permanently add 30,000 Army soldiers over the next three years; the Senate voted in June for an additional 20,000 in fiscal 2005. But it is going to be difficult to recruit troops now that young Americans have seen what is going on in Iraq and why this country was plunged into this war of choice in the first place. Indeed, polls show more and more Americans do not support the war and want U.S. troops to come home. The Pentagon's reliance on reservists and National Guard members has grown substantially. The National Guard is being turned into an International Guard. Already, the National Guard and reserves make up about 40 percent of our troops in Iraq. Our troops are spread thin, even with the expensive outsourcing to corporations of many military functions. As Rep. Charles Rangel of New York, the lead sponsor of a bill to reinstate the draft in the U.S. House of Representatives, recently told the *New York Times*, "ultimately we will run out of bodies."

Where are the soldiers for your military policies going to come from? As a result of these factors, there is increased discussion of the return of the military draft by elected officials in Congress and commentators. I am writing to you today to urge you to publicly proclaim that you will not support a return of the draft. An unambiguous clear promise on this matter is needed to put this issue to rest.

Sincerely,

[signature]

JUNE 30, 2004

Face the True Casualty Count

Dear President Bush,

This is a request for you, as the commander in chief, to provide the American people with a full accounting of the American casualties in Iraq since the invasion—including fatalities, the injured, the sick, and the mentally afflicted (i.e., post-traumatic stress disorder).

On June 18, PBS's *NOW* reported that the Pentagon does not have a comprehensive accounting of the human toll of the war from the American side, not to mention the larger toll on the Iraqi people. If you read the transcript of that report, you will see that, according to the chief Pentagon spokesman, your administration will only report the strictly combat-related fatalities and injuries. Non-combat deaths and injuries, disease-connected sicknesses, and mental illnesses are not reported. Such a failure to fully disclose the true number of casualties—including non-combat mortality and morbidity—

to the American people and the media is unworthy of your presidency. For, consider, there would be neither trauma nor illnesses—physical or mental—were it not for the invasion. As a matter of record, any distinction between combat and non-combat casualties in Iraq is immaterial. Every last one of these casualties is inextricably tied to events in that military theater.

As of June 18, the Pentagon reports that 922 Americans have lost their lives and 5,457 have been wounded in action. United Press International investigations editor Mark Benjamin, who has traveled to American military bases to report on these casualty counts, said in a *NOW* interview: "The Pentagon has made the numbers, and when I say the numbers, I mean the casualty numbers, into such a morass of figures, that they have made it virtually impossible for reporters and the American public to figure out what's going on." *NOW*'s Michele Mitchell adds: "What's missing in the Pentagon's count of the wounded are all the other soldiers—at least 11,000 or more, injured or sickened in what the Pentagon considers non-combat circumstances." These estimates also do not account for soldiers becoming stricken with serious mental afflictions.

One condition that illuminates the gaping omissions in your administration's casualty reporting is the disease known as Leishmaniasis. Over 500 U.S. soldiers in Iraq have been infected with Leishmania parasites, which are transmitted by bloodsucking sand flies. As of February 2004, 522 soldiers had been diagnosed with the cutaneous form of the disease, which causes painful and disfiguring skin lesions. Additionally, Leishmania are capable of spreading to visceral organs; such cases can be fatal. There is no available vaccine and no safe, effective chemotherapy. Moreover, according to the Walter Reed Army Institute of Research there is potential that the parasites might enter our nation's blood supply. Not surprisingly, there is little research funding for this disease.

I call on you to report to the American people the full casualty toll paid by their sons and daughters for this war of choice—based on fabrications, deceptions, and unfounded assertions, as is now so thoroughly documented. I have been to Walter Reed Army Medical Center. I have the pictures of many of the fallen soldiers on my table. You owe their memory, their present agony, and their families the simple decency of recognizing their numbers. Will you do so?

Sincerely,

[signature]

MAY 14, 2004

Your Views on Education

Dear President Bush,

Deferred maintenance continues growing in the nation's public schools. How would you propose actually getting the job done of repairing or rebuilding the public schools?

Second, developing civic skills, experience, and motivation for our children has received the endorsement of many studies by leading educators, as is known by your Department of Education. Yet, it has not happened. If you agree, what would you propose that the federal government, working with state and local entities, do to provide this most fundamental but long-neglected pillar of elementary and high school education?

Do you believe that the "No Child Left Behind" program has been adequately funded by the federal government? If not, what would you do to correct what many teachers and administrators believe has become an unfunded mandate?

Do you think that an "overtesting syndrome" is emerging where teaching to the tests and studying for the corporate-produced standardized, multiple-choice tests that are becoming a detriment to student education, teacher-student flexibility, creative and critical thinking, and proper local control of education? If so, please elaborate and indicate what your Party plans to do about this emerging controversy.

For the interest of a wider, more fundamental discussion during this presidential campaign, I look forward to your response regarding these issues.

Sincerely,

[signature]

MAY 13, 2004

The Abuse of Prisoners

Dear President Bush,

The reported widespread abuse of prisoners by your administration adds another condition that reflects on your failure of leadership. Anticipation and prevention of such tragedies should have been routine by the top officials whom you command. How can you imagine winning the hearts and minds of the Iraqi people? You are expanding what the intelligence agencies call "blowbacks"—expanding the networking of stateless terrorists against the United States. In addition, your administration's actions put U.S. soldiers and civilians in Iraq at increased risk from the backlash to the abuse of Iraqi prisoners, most of whom the press reports were charged with no wrongdoing when imprisoned.

With the publication of photos from Abu Ghraib prison the truth is beginning to come out. In recent years, newspaper articles, human rights reports, and expressions of concern from the International Red Cross, Red Crescent, and other human services agencies have claimed that torture, degradation, and inhuman treatment had become the mode of operation under your administration in Afghanistan, Guantanamo Bay, and Iraq. This has included repeated reports in the media of deaths and suicides of people being held in U.S. military custody.

General Antonio Taguba, who wrote the Pentagon's report looking into the abuses at Abu Ghraib prison, testified on May 11 before the Senate Armed Services Committee describing systemic problems with the prison. He testified that what happened was the result of a rampant failure of leadership "from the brigade commander on down. Lack of discipline, no training whatsoever, and no supervision."

The International Committee of the Red Cross issued a report concerning prisoner abuse based on private interviews with prisoners of war and civilian internees during the 29 visits ICRC staff conducted in 14 places of detention across Iraq between March and November 2003. The report said that as far back as last May, the Red Cross reported to the military about 200 allegations of abuse, and that in July it complained about 50 allegations of abuse at a detention site called Camp Cropper— including one case of treatment that included being deprived of sleep, kicked repeatedly and injured, and having a baseball tied into the prisoner's mouth. On May 10 the Red Cross stated that "the organization's president, Jakob Kellenberger, complained about the prison abuses directly to top administration officials during a two-day visit to Washington in mid-January when he met with Secretary of State Colin L. Powell, the national security advisor Condoleezza Rice and Deputy Defense Secretary Paul Wolfowitz."

You cannot claim that you were unaware of these allegations because you are briefed daily, these allegations have been reported in the media, and human rights groups have specifically written to your administration about them. In July 2003, Amnesty International sent your administration *Iraq: Memorandum on Concerns Relating to Law and Order*. The memorandum included allegations of torture and ill-treatment of Iraqi detainees by U.S. and Coalition forces.

A May 7, 2004 letter signed by nine leading human rights organizations states: "For over a year, the undersigned organizations and others have repeatedly asked you and senior officials in your Administration to act promptly and forcefully to publicly repudiate the statements of intelligence officials and to assure that the treatment of detainees is consistent with international humanitarian law." Amnesty International also alleged torture and degradation in the treatment of prisoners and detainees resulting from the war in Afghanistan held in that country as well as Guantanamo Bay, Cuba. And, the *Washington Post* has reported that your State Department and Department of Defense had conflicts over the treatment of prisoners. As commander in chief, certainly you were or should have been aware of these assertions—often repeated in the media, by various organizations—and of the conflicts within your own administration.

Now that the photographs are beginning to make their way into the media, the public is seeing that U.S. treatment of detainees, prisoners and people held in enemy combatant status includes acts abhorred by the American people. Sadly, there will be more photos, videos, and testimonies, so more of the facts will come out.

Human rights groups wrote you on May 7 saying: "Extraordinary action on your part is now required to begin to repair this damage and, at long last, bring an end to this pattern of torture and cruel treatment."

You and your aides have a disquieting habit of not responding at all to such letters going back to the pre-invasion of Iraq early last year, when groups representing millions of Americans (e.g., religious, veterans, business, labor, retired intelligence) wrote you requesting meetings.* They did not even receive the courtesy of a reply.

In order to restore public confidence around the world, an independent international investigation is needed. The Department of Defense investigating itself, or investigation by Republican-controlled congressional committees in a presidential election year, will not be sufficient to restore the confidence of the world.

The following steps are needed:

Get the truth out through an impartial, international commission. This should include people of unquestioned integrity from within the United States and around the world. You should state that you or anyone in your administration will testify in public before this fact-finding Commission. This should include involvement of the International Humanitarian Fact-Finding Commission provided for by Article 90 of Additional Protocol I of the Geneva Conventions to look into the allegations of abuse and related U.S. investigations. The U.S. should agree to pay restitutions to all individuals whose rights were violated.

Renounce interrogation techniques that destroy basic human dignity for the purpose of eliciting valuable information. Remove those in the chain of command who in any way countenanced or ordered such activity. Direct the Department of Defense

---

* These are available at https://nader.org/iraq-letters/. There is one additional letter that was signed by myself and other consumer advocates from the Council of the European Union.

and U.S. intelligence agencies not to engage in any practices that are inconsistent with the U.S. Constitution forbidding cruel and unusual punishment, the Geneva Conventions, and the Convention against Torture and Other Cruel, Inhuman, or Degrading Treatment or Punishment. This includes banning "stress and duress" techniques, incommunicado detentions and transfer of prisoners to countries that use torture techniques. Strong and clear penalties should be announced for anyone who uses such interrogation techniques. Adequate funding should be provided to allow for investigation of allegations of abuse.

Ban the use of private civilian corporate contractors in interrogation and any direct contacts with prisoners or detainees held by the United States. These are essential governmental functions under established rules of military, domestic, and international law. You would do well to examine the corporate contracts in Iraq for waste, corruption, non-performance and favoritism—before the media gets there.

Allow access to all prisons, prisoners, detainees, and people held in noncombatant status to the Red Cross, Red Crescent, and U.N. International Humanitarian Fact-Finding Commission. This should include private interviews of prisoners as well as visits by medical personnel.

The photos showing abusive treatment are serious. They come on top of reports of U.S. military actions that took the lives of hundreds of civilians—including women and children—in Fallujah, as well as reports of over 10,000 Iraqi civilians being killed in the U.S. war and occupation of Iraq. They come at a time when it is evident that under your leadership as commander in chief there has been inadequate planning for postwar Iraq and moving that country to independence from U.S. military and corporate occupation. Further, it has now become evident that the reasons you gave for the invasion and occupation of Iraq were fabrications and deceptions. In truth, the United States and the stronger countries surrounding Iraq were never threatened by a tottering dictator with a dilapidated military having no command and control over his troops.

Richard Clarke, former White House counterterrorism advisor, has argued that the Iraq War and occupation diverted us from preventing stateless terrorism and has been counterproductive to making the United States safer. General William Odom, who served as director of the National Security Agency under President Reagan, has called for withdrawal from Iraq saying: "I don't think that the war serves U.S. interests. I think Osama bin Laden's interests and the Iranian interests are very much served by it, and it's becoming a huge drain on our resources both material and political."

The combination of these actions under your leadership as commander in chief amounts to an accumulating failure. You are clearly not able to win the hearts and minds of mainstream Iraqis. You are making the United States less safe by producing more stateless terrorist recruiting, as leading security specialists have pointed out in the media. Your attempt to restore our relations with the international community and involve them in winning the peace in Iraq is too little and too late. Polls report that the majority of Iraqis now want the U.S. to leave immediately—a sharp turnaround by desperate people who wanted Saddam Hussein out.

You need to make major adjustments by giving the Iraqi people truthful expectations, not a puppet government (see: Yochi Dreazen and Christopher Cooper, "Behind the Scenes, U.S. Tightens Grip on Iraq's Future," *Wall Street Journal*, May 13, 2004, pages 1, 8), a responsible withdrawal of both U.S. military and corporate occupations—to protect our troops by bringing them home—and internationally supervised elections with international peacekeepers from neutral countries. This withdrawal from Iraq is consistent with the recommendations of General Odom, who explained in an interview on *Nightline*: "[T]o say you can't fail at that now is to fail to realize that you've already failed. Now, when I say get out, I don't mean just pull out and walk out today. I would go through the procedures of going to the United Nations and encouraging a United Nations resolution to approve some U.N. force there. And I would be quite prepared to participate in that for a while, if we could get allies and others to come in. But then I would make it clear that I am slowly moving that responsibility to this force and withdrawing the U.S. over six months or so."

Perhaps you now see the wisdom of meeting with some of the groups representing millions of Americans—including those composed of retired military officers and intelligence officials, business, church, and labor—who asked to meet with you before you declared your unconstitutional war. They could have cautioned you about the Iraqi quagmire.

Sincerely,

MAY 11, 2004
Your Views on Energy

Dear President Bush,

Beyond what is now being done by the federal government, what quantifiable goals over what period of time would you want the share of our energy consumption to come from renewable or solar energy and to be saved by energy efficiency technologies and programs?

Please specify how you intend to achieve these goals through enabling legislation and implementation, for example: using the federal procurement dollar, mandatory engineering standards, models based on federal research and development (e.g., vehicles, lighting, heating and air conditioning, recapturing energy waste and heat, etc.), and public contests for superior technologies, such as household appliances.

For the interest of a wider, more fundamental discussion during this presidential campaign, I look forward to your response regarding these issues.

Thank you.

Sincerely,

MAY 10, 2004
Your Views on the Federal Budget

Dear President Bush,

Where do you stand on the following reallocation issues?

The military budget has been called unauditable by the GAO and other investigators and inspectors general. Congress has documented enormous, repeated waste, fraud, abuse, and duplication in the military contracting business. Think of the burgeoning federal deficit here as well. Half of the federal government's discretionary spending now goes for military budgets, post–Soviet Union. What would you do and with what strategy and timetable would you approach this continually intractable condition? Fifty-eight years after World War II, U.S. troops remain in Western Europe and East Asia, costing, directly and indirectly, tens of billions of dollars a year. Would you change this allocation and if so, how?

Weapons systems of great cost, which were designed to counter the former Soviet threat, remain in the procurement pipeline. Which ones would you drop or significantly diminish? Do you believe Pentagon outsourcing and corporatization (privatization) have gone too far (see Peter Singer's new book, *Corporate Warriors*), not far enough or should remain the same, but under tougher scrutiny? Do you believe congressional oversight of the Department of Defense, the Department of Energy's weapons program and the military contractors is adequate? If not, what would you do to improve such oversight?

• The regulatory agencies' budgets. Do you believe that the regulatory agencies (FDA, NHTSA, OSHA, EPA, FRA, FAA, CSPC, etc.)—responsible for the immense task of defending and advancing the health and safety of the American people—need more resources and enforcement to prevent or diminish hundreds of thousands of fatalities and serious injuries annually? If so, please specify.

• The corporate crime investigative and prosecutorial budgets. As reported in the mainstream business media, the corporate crime and fraud wave during the past four years has looted and drained away trillions of dollars from small investors' pension plans and workers' lost jobs. Except for the Sarbanes-Oxley Act and an overdue expansion of the SEC's budget, Congress has not yet enacted, much less proposed, a comprehensive corporate reform package, proportional to the massive corporate crime damage. Nor has Congress moved to expand the tiny corporate crime prosecution budget in the Justice Department to cope with all the corporate crimes and armies of corporate law firms representing them, nor has

Congress ever demanded the creation of a corporate crime database within the Justice Department.

Do you support the appended list of corporate reforms, in whole or in part? Please add any other reforms that you desire. Do you or your Party have a figure for the appropriate Justice Department corporate crime budget, without which the SEC referrals for prosecution cannot proceed? Do you believe the Justice Department should establish a comprehensive database on corporate crime and fraud (e.g., procurement fraud, crimes against Medicare, bribery, environmental and occupational safety crimes, corporate tax violations, looting of worker pensions, violations of regulatory standards—water pollution, pesticides, and food safety protections, etc.)? If so, specify timetable and strategy.

Uses of procurement dollars by the nation's biggest customer—Uncle Sam—offers major, efficient, proven opportunities to stimulate innovation. Would you favor a more profound direction of the procurement dollar to further statutory national missions for consumer, environmental, energy, and occupational safety by setting appropriate standards for the purchase of products like motor vehicles (Congress instructed the GSA to do this in 1964 and the GSA did it for air bags in the mid-1980s), paper, fuel, software, and other items, assuming these specifications would not undermine the original purpose of the procurement mission? If so, please elaborate the priority, timetable, and strategy to further this goal through Congress and the executive branch.

• Cost-benefit analysis on the Homeland Security budget. Last year, your OMB placed in the Federal Register an invitation to comment regarding a proposal to develop a framework for cost-benefit discipline over the way monies are appropriated and spent for a wide variety of Homeland Security expenditures. Presently, other regulatory agency budgets affecting health and safety goals are largely under this cost-benefit calculation by OMB. Do you favor extension of this framework to the large Homeland Security budget, as apparently OMB does? Would you favor a similar discipline on the vast military contract expenditures?

For the interest of a wider, more fundamental discussion during this presidential campaign, I look forward to your response regarding these issues.

Thank you.

Sincerely,

Ralph Nader

MAY 4, 2004

Your Views on Waging Peace

Dear President Bush,

Our government spends exponentially more money on preparations for war and actual wars than on waging peace, which involves rigorous attention to the prevention of conflicts and to the conditions that generate higher standards of living, justice, and cooperation. Our own country's history contains numerous successes at local, state, and national levels of "waging peace."

Given the problems afflicting the world and its immense poverty, disease, illiteracy, arms race, environmental devastation, and dictatorial-oligarchic regimes in the Third World and elsewhere, "waging peace" means in part bringing to bear the available and often inexpensive remedies (e.g., public health measures), solutions, technologies that would alleviate suffering, save many lives, unleash productive and innovative capacities in all societies, and advance security and stability within needed change.*

What are your thoughts and recommended policies and programs for these enlarged and often new directions for "waging peace"?

For the interest of a wider, more fundamental discussion during this presidential campaign, I look forward to your response regarding these issues.

Thank you.

Sincerely,

APRIL 30, 2004
Your Views on Reforming the Election Process

Dear President Bush,

Would you support full public financing of federal elections consistent with existing Supreme Court decisions? If not, would you support public financing if the funds were voluntarily contributed, as with a well-promoted check-off on the 1040 and other federal forms of up to $200 per person? Would you also support a set amount of free air time for all ballot-qualified candidates on all FCC-licensed television and radio stations? If not, would you support any constitutional amendment that would deny private contributions to candidates or political parties? If not, would you at least support a constitutional prohibition of corporations contributing or participating in elections or referenda?

---

* See wvvw.undp.orq/mainundp/propoor/ and www.Lindp.orq/mdg for more information.

What reforms would you support and fund that would diminish the number of citizens who are disenfranchised deliberately (as with citizens of the District of Columbia) or arbitrarily before election day, during Election Day, or afterward during the counting or recounting, as officially documented in Florida in the year 2000?

Which if any of the following changes would you support: a) same-day voting registration; b) instant-runoff voting; c) some kind of proportional representation to make more votes count in contrast to the winner-take-all present system; d) a national referendum to decide whether voting should become a civic duty (à la jury duty) with complete choice of candidates, write-in and binding or none-of-the-above options that allow maximum civil liberties with civil duties; e) uniform federal standards for all federal elections replacing the current hodgepodge of state rules, including draconian ballot access rules that severely restrict third party and independent candidates?

Do you believe that redistricting for congressional seats should be done more than every ten years? Should redistricting be redrawn by the state legislatures or by specially appointed nonpartisan commissions? Do you believe that redistricting should be done to pick the voters so as to provide safe seats for one party or the other? Are you concerned about how many "non-competitive" congressional districts there are in the country and, if so, what do you propose to do about it?

I look forward to your response regarding these issues. Thank you.

Sincerely,

Your Views on Corporate Power

Dear President Bush,

The large multinational corporations, with their judicially decreed status as "persons," are increasingly and pervasively replacing the sovereignty of the people. This was not the anticipation of our early state legislators two hundred years ago when they began granting state charters that to this day is the way corporations are created (investors do not create them, they finance them). Corporate charters were carefully restrained then to make sure that these artificial entities remain the servants of the people, not their masters.

Today, corporate or business interests are the main funders of elections, the main controllers of the media, the most dominant forces over our governments, the main operators of our public assets (public lands, public airwaves), the controlling managers of trillions of dollars in pension funds owned by workers, the promoters of obesity diets and obscene entertainment, the fastest commercializers of governmental functions (including military services), and the proliferators of aggressive commercial value systems that are overriding or subordinating crucial civic values that constitute a healthy, vibrant, democratic society. These corporations and their trade associations are relentlessly obtaining from governments more and more privileges and immunities which as "artificial persons" are severely tilting the balance of power and wealth against real people. The corporate ownership of patented life forms, the technological ability to change the nature of nature and alter the environment and species in dramatically damaging ways (e.g., factory fishing depleting the oceans) present in stark form the growing community debate over corporate personhood and runaway corporate power over individuals and their public representatives. A *Business Week* poll in 2000—before the latest corporate crime wave—reports that 72 percent of the American people believe corporations have too much control over their lives.

This debate has not yet reached into the political arena, which has been lagging behind the sentiments of ordinary Americans, who feel the brunt of "the Big Boys" daily and are questioning the very allegiance of these companies to our nation as they ship capital assets and work abroad and support transnational systems of governance over our own governmental institutions such as the WTO and NAFTA.* Every major religion and our greatest presidents have warned about the commercial concentrations of wealth and power. Yet, as this power has become more pronounced, the addressing of that power by the major political institutions has waned—a telling indicator indeed! The supremacy of commercial values over civic values spells trouble for any democratic society, which needs to reassert its higher calling and values of the spirit by subordinating commercial values so that they adjust to the civil society. Only when commerce is held accountable will both prosper.

In a society dedicated to "equal justice under law," does your Party believe that such imbalances between individual human beings and large corporations need to be redressed? If so, please provide details on what kinds of redress—structural changes in corporate charters, changes in corporate legal status (not a person), providing more power to the people vis-à-vis the corporations, reducing the privileges and immunities that corporations are consistently expanding, ending corporate abilities to disappear, merge, or go into temporary bankruptcy

---

* See www.citizen.org/trade for more information.

to escape serious liabilities entirely, hold top corporate executives more accountable for corporate devastations or serious crimes and misdeeds . . . to suggest a few avenues (*United States v. Park*, 421 U.S. 658 [1975]).

At the very least, would your Party support a modern equivalent to the Temporary National Economic Committee which Franklin Delano Roosevelt and the Congress established in 1938 to initiate a comprehensive inquiry into concentration and abuses of corporate power? In sending this proposal to the Congress, President Franklin Roosevelt said the following: "The liberty of a democracy is not safe if the people tolerate the growth of private power to a point where it becomes stronger than their democratic state itself. That, in its essence, is Fascism—ownership of Government by an individual, by a group, or by any controlling private power."

I look forward to your response regarding these issues. Sincerely,

APRIL 28, 2004
Your Views on Labor Issues

Dear President Bush,

The federal minimum wage has been frozen at $5.15 per hour. Had it been adjusted for inflation since 1968, it would be around $8 an hour, indicating how much today's minimum wage is below that of 1968 in real purchasing power.

What is your policy regarding raising the federal minimum wage to a living wage and to what level over the next five years would you raise it in stages? If your response is no raise, please explain how a worker facing rising prices since 1968 is expected to live on, much less support, a family on that amount of income.

The Taft-Hartley Act of 1947 is a major obstruction to the right of American workers to form their own independent trade unions. Union membership is down to 8 percent of the private workforce—the lowest in 65 years. A majority of workers are making less today than workers made in 1973, adjusted for inflation. What provisions of the Taft-Hartley Act would you repeal and what strategy and timetable would you deploy? What additional labor law reforms would you propose?

What proposals would you advance to enhance union democracy while avoiding the "freeloader" problem? What is your position on so-called "right to-work" laws in various states, from the viewpoint of federal preemption to either end them or federalize them?

I look forward to your responses to these issues.

Sincerely,

FEBRUARY 12, 2004
Misleading Americans
on Medical Malpractice

Dear President Bush,

Last week you delivered more misleading remarks on medical malpractice awards to an audience in Little Rock, Arkansas.

You similarly misled Americans in your recent State of the Union address:

"To improve our health care system, we must address one of the prime causes of higher cost: the constant threat that physicians and hospitals will be unfairly sued. Because of excessive litigation, everybody pays more for health care, and many parts of America are losing fine doctors. No one has ever been healed by a frivolous lawsuit; I urge the Congress to pass medical liability reform."

You repeat these assertions with no substantiating evidence to support this specter of "frivolous lawsuits." The Congressional Budget Office produced a report this month titled "Limiting Tort Liability for Medical Malpractice." The CBO found that "even large savings in premiums can have only a small direct impact on health care spending—private or governmental—because malpractice costs account for less than 2 percent of that spending." The report also acknowledged that medical malpractice costs have risen in part because "of reduced [insurance company] income from their investments and short-term factors in the insurance market."

You need to substantiate your claims of "frivolous lawsuits" with more than mere assertion. Judges know how to throw out of court any "frivolous lawsuits," and the truth is that jury verdicts and court payouts have decreased over the past year. So while you continually argue that a nationwide cap on medical malpractice damages would drive down health care costs, the evidence simply does not substantiate your claim.

You were a fierce defender of states' rights as the governor of Texas. But the federal preemption of states' rights that you now propose (by capping jury verdicts) rewards insurance company greed, avarice, and dishonesty by absolving them of their responsibility to injured Americans. It also protects those guilty of mismanaging insurance company investments. And, shamefully, it punishes the family and friends of the estimated 100,000 innocent victims who lose their lives from medical malpractice every year in America, and the hundreds of thousands more injured by this needless violence, according to the Harvard School of Public Health report and other studies.

Has "states' rights," as a fundamental tenet of the Republican Party platform, been tossed out of the window along with fiscal conservatism by your administration?

You must clarify these issues now. Your calls for "personal accountability" ring hollow when you continually push legislation to help absolve these negligent or incompetent doctors of responsibility for the injuries that they inflict. You also exonerate insurers from their responsibility in this situation. These are the same insurance companies who systematically avoid a focus on enormous patient suffering by failing to employ loss experience rating of neglectful, repeat offender physicians. The medical malpractice insurance sellers need to take more personal responsibility for failing to curb malpractice through loss prevention. The doctors need to take personal responsibility for failing to make state licensing board requirements more stringent to weed out the few bad apples practicing deadly medicine in every state.

As president you should not make assertions that you cannot back up. Senator Frist makes the same charge of a "flood of frivolous lawsuits" and he has refused my requests to back up what he is saying. This, President Bush, is how propaganda is defined.

Sincerely,

The Republican Party of Texas Platform

Dear President Bush,

The Republican Party of Texas was instrumental in nominating and electing you to the governorship of Texas. The state party was also working to garner the state's 32 electoral votes in the presidential election of 2000, without which you could not have been selected president under *Bush v. Gore*.

All available indications are that you generally support the Texas Republican Party's platform. Indeed, the state party expects such support and directs "the Executive Campaign Committee to strongly consider candidates' support of the Party platform when granting financial or other support." Taking no chances with any candidates pleading ignorance, each "Republican candidate for a public or Party office shall be provided a current copy of the Party platform at the time of filing. The candidate shall be asked to read and initial each page of the platform and sign a statement affirming he/she has read the entire platform. The individual accepting the signed statement shall review the initialed platform and maintain a list of those who have complied with this request. This will become effective in the 2002 election."

Since you will presumably be a Republican candidate for a public office in 2004, you will be asked by your state party to "read and initial" each page of the platform.

The "2002 Texas State Republican Party Platform" is a lengthy and specific document. It ranges over a continuum of policy recommendations that are extraordinary in the diversity of their public philosophies. While there is much there with which you probably concur, there are positions taken that make it necessary for you to clarify your concurrence or dissent before the

American people. This is the case because either your previous comments or your obligation to uphold existing laws appear to contradict some of the state Republican Party's declarations.

What follows are some of the state Republican Party's positions in the sequence that they appear in its 2002 platform:

"The Party believes terrorism is the greatest threat to international peace and to the safety of our own citizens. We also believe the current greatest threat to our individual liberties is overreaching government controls established under the guise of preventing terrorism."

"The Party opposes any attempt by the United States Census Bureau to obtain any information beyond the number of people residing in the dwelling at the time of the census and in accordance with Article 1, Section 2 of the United States Constitution."

"The Party demands the elimination of presidential authority to issue executive orders, presidential decision directives, and other administrative mandates that do not have congressional approval. Further, we demand a repeal of all previous executive orders and administrative mandates."

"The Party directs that legislation be introduced in both the United States Congress and the State of Texas to repeal existing statutory requirements to end the ever increasing, incessant, recurring, and calculated gathering, accumulation, and dissemination of finger prints, Social Security numbers, financial and personal information of law-abiding citizens by business and governments, the use of which are contrary to and destructive of our individual and collective freedom. Such legislation shall provide remedy and redress to any individual denied service for refusing to provide the above-mentioned information."

"The Party opposes any and all unauthorized access,

accumulation, and distribution of an individual's private records by a government agency or any agent working on behalf of a government agency. We oppose the creation of a federal identification card for United States citizens or the use of state driver licenses as a national identification card."

"A perpetual state of national emergency allows unrestricted growth of government. The Party charges the president to cancel the state of national emergency and charges Congress to repeal the War Powers Act and declare an end to the previously declared states of emergency."

"We support legislation enabling either party in a criminal trial to inform the jurors of their right to determine the facts and to render a verdict according to conscience."

"We call on the Legislature to allow voters the ability to recall elected officials of an irrigation district, fresh water supply district, municipal utility district, or any other special purpose district."

"The Party supports legislation to prohibit former legislators, government employees, and officials from acting as lobbyists for a foreign government and/or any business for a period of five years immediately after leaving public service."

"Our Party pledges to do everything within its power to restore the original intent of the First Amendment of the United States and dispel the myth of the separation of Church and State."

"The Party believes that all citizens have the right to be free from government surveillance of their electronic communications, including a government mandate for trap door encryption standards."

"The Party supports an orderly transition to a system of private pensions based on the concept of individual retirement accounts, and gradually phasing out the Social Security tax. We insist that Social Security benefits be non-taxable. To protect the Social Security System, its funds should not be commingled or spent with general revenues or invested in private or public corporate stock."

"The Party continues to oppose government-sponsored gambling as a means of financing state government. Government-sponsored gambling has had a devastating impact on many Texas families. Moreover, we oppose any further legalization, government facilitation, or financial guarantees relating to any type of gambling including casino, river boat, slot machine, video keno, eight-liners, and other games of chance. The Party supports the repeal of the state lottery."

"We call for the abolition of the U.S. Department of Education and the prohibition of the transfer of any of its functions to any other federal agency."

"We deplore the inordinate amount of time being forced upon teachers for state-mandated standardized test preparation to the detriment of basic academic instruction."

"The Internal Revenue Service is unacceptable to U.S. taxpayers! The Party urges that the IRS be abolished and the Sixteenth Amendment to the U.S. Constitution be repealed. We further urge that the personal income tax, inheritance (death) tax, gift tax, capital gains, corporate income tax, and payroll tax be eliminated. We recommend the implementation of a national retail sales tax, with the provision that a two-thirds majority of the U.S. House and U.S. Senate is required to raise the rate. Such reforms will encourage investment and economic growth. Lastly, such a sales tax plan must ensure that no one in America pays taxes of any kind on the necessities of life, ensuring opportunity and quality of life for low- and fixed-income Americans."

"We encourage the adoption of a National Right-To-Work

Act providing the same kind of protection from labor unions as is enjoyed by Texans under the State Right-to-Work laws."

"The Party believes the Minimum Wage Law should be repealed and that wages should be determined by the free market conditions prevalent in each individual market."

"The Party supports privatization of most government services. Public funds should not be used to fund or implement any private projects such as high-speed rail or sports stadiums."

"The Party does not support governmental subsidies, tariffs, bailouts, or other forms of corporate welfare that are used to protect and preserve businesses or industries that have failed to remain relevant, competitive, and efficient over time. The cost of such corporate welfare becomes the burden of the tax-paying public."

"We further support the abolition of federal agencies involved in activities not delegated to the federal government under the original intent of the Constitution including, but not limited to, the Bureau of Alcohol, Tobacco, and Firearms; the position of Surgeon General; the Environmental Protection Agency; the Departments of Energy, Housing and Urban Development, Health and Human Services, Education, Commerce, and Labor."

"The Party opposes all unfunded mandates by the federal and state governments. The effect of mandating services without funding is a tax increase for local government."

"The Party encourages the Congress to: . . . promote all forms of domestic energy production including ANWR, offshore California, and the East Coast, while minimizing environmental impact."

"The Party urges Congress to stop funding the IMF and any other international financing agencies, because such agencies prop up foreign tyrants and give American taxpayers' money to international bankers."

"We support business opportunity and oppose the previous Democrat administration's advocacy of intrusive government-industry partnerships based on foreign models. We urge the repeal of NAFTA, GATT, and any other international trade agreements that do not promote free trade, and withdrawal from membership in the World Trade Organization (WTO)."

"We support re-establishing United States control over the Canal in order to retain our military bases in Panama, to preserve our right to transit through the Canal, and to prevent the establishment of Chinese missile bases in Panama."

"The Party believes it is in the best interest of the citizens of the United States that we immediately rescind our membership in, as well as all financial and military contributions to, the United Nations."

Party platforms are meant by their authors and endorsers to be taken seriously. They are not mere sops thrown to one wing or another of the party in order to pacify or deceive them with verbal duplicity. In 2000, at the platform conference in Cleveland, the Democratic Party was so concerned with how the Republicans would react that the Democratic Leadership Council (DLC) controllers defeated one proposal after another by progressive Democrats that were little more than what Roosevelt's New Deal would have included as standard party philosophy, such as an updated minimum wage or a policy against poverty in the United States.

I call on you, President George W. Bush, as the leader of your Republican Party, to engage in truth-in-advertising regarding the "2002 Texas State Republican Party Platform," and let the voters of this country know where you and your fellow elected Texas Republicans stand. Did you or do you now support the Texas State Republican platform?

As you accelerate your campaigning for reelection with

Vice President Richard Cheney, it will be interesting to have your reaction to each of the above-listed Texas Republican positions. Surely, sooner or later you will be asked whether you associate or disassociate yourself from your own state party's unequivocal statements of domestic and foreign policy.

So, it will be interesting to have your reaction to each of the above-listed positions. Do you agree or do you disagree? In the interest of being suitably concise, the above are excerpts. For the full text of the Texas Republican state party platform.*

Sincerely,

SEPTEMBER 4, 2003
How Will You Use Your Tax Cuts for the Wealthy?

Dear President Bush,

It has been reported that the savings accruing to your vice president and your cabinet members from the recent legislation reducing taxes (mostly on the wealthy) are substantial. As the Citizens for Tax Justice analysis[†] demonstrates, based on the latest financial reports, the estimated tax savings from capital gains and dividends is at a minimum average of $42,158 per member to as high as $167,284 per member, per year.[‡]

Very few people are in a position to be a sine qua non for tax

---

* See http://www.yuricareport.com/Dominionism/RPTPlatform2002.pdf for more information.

† See http://www.ctj.org/ for more information.

‡ See Estimated Tax Savings of Bush Cabinet Under the New Tax Law: https://blog.nader.org/releases/2003TaxCutCabinetSavings.pdf for more information.

laws that give themselves a tax cut. You signed the legislation into law and your top associates urged its passage. Let us say that the situation calls for a special moral imperative for you, Mr. Cheney and your cabinet members to refuse publicly to take the hundreds of thousands of dollars or more in lower taxes. Such a decision would remove a clear conflict of interest and establish an honorable precedent for your successors.

There is, moreover, an additional challenge which you need to confront if you decline the aforementioned option. The moral authority to govern involves setting a good example. Over and over again you argued through the mass media that your tax cuts (2001 and 2003) would produce two consequences: first, that taxpayers would be spending more of the savings in the marketplace and thereby increase consumer demand and economic growth; and second, that taxpayers would also, in the aggregate, invest more of their money in the economy leading to expansion on the supply side of the market (the proverbial "plant and equipment and jobs" argument).

So, how are you, Mr. Cheney, and your top appointed officials planning to use your tax savings from the 2003 tax cut, given your public predictions regarding the uses of these tax cuts by the American people? Are you going to increase your spending and/or are you going to increase your investments? Notice the key word here is "increase" which is at the core of your declarations that the tax cut will increase economic growth and jobs.

You and your high administration officials have already benefitted from the 2001 tax cut. How did you and your associates increase your spending or investments, if at all?

Should you decide it is too burdensome to assemble responses from your top appointed officials (despite the deep interest by the questioning public in their responses), at the very least, place before the American taxpayers your response and that of Vice President Cheney.

Thank you.

Sincerely,

MARCH 19, 2003

Preventing Civilian Carnage

Dear President Bush,

In your March 17 address declaring your intention, assuming Saddam's unwillingness to go into exile, to take the nation to war with Iraq, you directed comments to the Iraqi people. You stated, "If we must begin a military campaign, it will be directed against the lawless men who rule your country and not against you."

The way the U.S. military, under your command, and the U.S. allies conduct the war will test the sincerity of this claim. U.S. military officials have already conceded that the war will inevitably take a substantial number of civilian lives. While there is little doubt of the brutal dictator Saddam's willingness to sacrifice his people's lives, your decisions over military tactics will be a major determinant of the extent of the civilian carnage.

Having determined to proceed with a war that violates international law on use of force and without a constitutionally required congressional declaration of war, it is now incumbent on you to conduct the war according to international humanitarian and human rights law, and to take all possible measures to avoid loss of civilian life, especially the lives of children.

Among other steps, you must renounce the use of cluster bombs and land mines in the coming conflict. These are weapons that take a devastating toll on civilians, and continue to kill and maim long after the military hostilities in which they are used have ended.

Land mines have been subjected to an international treaty, which the United States has refused to sign, that bars their use. These weapons are also arguably barred by international customary law, since those deploying them are inherently unable to discriminate in application, especially over time, between combatants and civilians. These weapons are indisputably particularly gruesome in their impact with civilians, including children, the vast majority of victims.

Cluster bombs deploy numerous bomblets, a significant number of which fail to explode. The unexploded bomblets then function as de facto antipersonnel mines, again with the greatest toll among civilians, including children. According to Human Rights Watch, "more than 1,600 Kuwaiti and Iraqi civilians have been killed, and another 2,500 injured, by the estimated 1.2 million cluster bomb duds left following the 1991 Persian Gulf War, which saw the most extensive use of cluster bombs in history."

Mr. President, given your decision in the name of the American people to embark on a discretionary war of choice against Iraq, the very least that you owe the Iraqi people is a commitment not to use weaponry that poses special dangers to civilians, during military conflict and in the period after hostilities have ceased.

Before the bombing begins, you should publicly detail the

specific commitments the United States will make to spare the loss of life in the course of the war invasion against Iraq, and the steps our nation will take to protect Iraqi populations after the war from the chaos, anarchy, and grave humanitarian crisis likely to ensue. First on the list should be a public pledge not to use land mines or cluster bombs, indiscriminate weapons that steal limbs, senses, and lives from innocents even more effectively than from combatants.

Sincerely,
Ralph Nader
Robert Weissman

MARCH 19, 2003

A Family Appeal to Stop the War

Dear President George H. W. and Mrs. Barbara Bush and Mrs. Laura Bush,

This appeal is to you as the wife and parents of George W. Bush, in the shadow of war, in part because you are the closest people of concern and in part because for months he has declined to meet with any antiwar delegations, whether composed of veterans, businesspeople, clergy, human rights advocates, labor leaders, physicians and teachers, women's leaders, intelligence and security experts, and elected officials of many city councils—all of whom represent tens of millions of Americans.* He is a president who, sadly, refuses to listen and exchange with opposing viewpoints.

This attribute is not new to you. In other contexts

---

* See https://nader.org/iraq-letters.

and in previous years, you have seen and experienced this personality trait. In his interviews with Bob Woodward and other reporters, he has often spoken of making decisions "by instinct" or "from the gut." Perhaps you have read the *New Yorker* article months ago that sensitively drew some telling contrasts between the different operational, personality, and temperamental traits between father and son. It is not a well-kept secret that the father would have approached the Iraq situation in a different manner. The overriding concern for massive civilian casualties, both from extensive military action and widespread internecine slaughters between factions inside Iraq, has not been given enough weight in the calculus of war versus tightening diplomacy—inspections, containment, deterrence, and encirclement of that country. Below is a quotation by General Douglas MacArthur in 1957 that is worthy of reflection in contemporary contexts:

"Our swollen budgets constantly have been misrepresented to the public. Our government has kept us in a perpetual state of fear—kept us in a continuous stampede of patriotic fervor—with the cry of grave national emergency. Always there has been some terrible evil at home or some monstrous foreign power that was going to gobble us up if we did not blindly rally behind it by furnishing the exorbitant funds demanded. Yet, in retrospect, these disasters seem never to have happened, seem never to have been quite real." —Address to the Annual Stockholders Sperry Rand Corporation (30 July 1957), as published in *General MacArthur Speeches and Reports 1908–1964* (2000) by Edward T. Imparato, p. 206.

Your son and husband is preparing to take the nation to war with many postwar consequences. However, each of the pillars for the foundation of his rationale for leading the nation into this discretionary war is flawed. The crucial allegations and accusations providing justification for war are unsupported, misleading, disproved or false.

The president and his administration have repeatedly justified the war against Iraq on the grounds that Iraq maintains or is on the verge of acquiring a nuclear capacity. In his March 17 address, the president stated that "in one year, or five years, the power of Iraq to inflict harm on all free nations would be multiplied many times over," a clear reference to acquisition of nuclear weapons.

There is no evidence to support these allegations. The head of the International Atomic Energy Agency (IAEA), Mohamed ElBaradei, has said there is no evidence of resumed nuclear activities in Iraq. Key evidence supporting the allegation of an Iraqi nuclear program has been exposed as a forgery. The *Washington Post* notes also that "ElBaradei also contradicted Bush and other officials who argued that Iraq had tried to purchase high-strength aluminum tubes to use in centrifuges for uranium enrichment, The IAEA determined that Iraq did not plan to use imported aluminum tubes for enriching uranium and generating nuclear weapons. ElBaradei argued that the tubes were for conventional weapons and 'it was highly unlikely' that the tubes could have been used to produce nuclear material" (Walter Pincus and Dana Milbank, "Bush Clings to Dubious Allegations About Iraq," *Washington Post*, March 18, 2003).

The president and his administration have repeatedly alleged Iraqi ties to al-Qaeda, both to date enemies of one another, and justified the pending war on the grounds of a purported Iraqi potential to share weapons of mass destruction with al-Qaeda. In his March 17 address, the president states, "It has a deep hatred of America and our friends and it has aided, trained and harbored terrorists, including operatives of

Al Qaeda." He stated, "using chemical, biological or, one day, nuclear weapons obtained with the help of Iraq," terrorists might threaten this country.

There is no evidence to support these allegations. *The New York Times* reported on February 10 that intelligence officials have "pointed out that neither the Bush administration nor the British government, which has also championed the al-Qaeda–Baghdad connection, has produced direct evidence of Iraqi involvement with the terrorist network" (Don Van Natta Jr. with David Johnston, "Threats and Responses: Terror Network," *New York Times*, February 10, 2003).

CIA Director George Tenet argued in an October letter to Congress that Saddam would not give weapons of mass destruction to terrorists unless he was facing invasion. "Baghdad for now appears to be drawing a line short of conducting terrorist attacks with conventional or [chemical and biological weapons] against the United States," the letter stated. "Should Saddam conclude that a U.S.-led attack could no longer be deterred, he probably would have become less constrained in adopting terrorist actions" (Michael Gordon, "Threats and Responses: Intelligence; U.S. Aides Split On Assessment of Iraq's Plans," the *New York Times*, October 10, 2002). Nor have the administration's intelligence agencies or foreign intelligence agencies contradicted the IAEA, because they know the Iraqi nuclear program was ended in the early- to mid-nineties by U.N. inspectors.

The president and his administration have alleged that Iraq poses a threat to its neighbors.

There is no evidence to support these allegations. Saddam has been contained since the Gulf War. A *Washington Post* story rebuts the claim that Iraqi Al Samoud missiles threaten key U.S. allies in the region: "Inspectors have found the Al Samoud-2 missiles can travel less than 200 miles—not far enough to hit the targets Bush named." It is a matter of common sense that the far stronger Israeli, Turkish, and Iranian militaries would themselves have acted to disarm and eliminate any genuine threat they perceived from the isolated, contained, encircled, and weakened Iraqi military under Saddam's brutal rule.

There are many other such examples of administration claims that are misleading or unsupported by any evidence. These include: relying on supposed British intelligence that turned out to be copied from academic papers; the reference to Iraqi defector Lt. Gen. Hussein Kamel as providing authoritative evidence of an Iraqi weapons of mass destruction program without revealing that, as *Newsweek* has reported, Hussein Kamel also told U.N. inspectors and the CIA that Iraq had destroyed its chemical and biological weapons and banned missiles (John Barry, "The Defector's Secrets," *Newsweek,* February 24, 2003); and the claim U.N. inspectors were unable to track mobile biological weapons laboratories—a claim for which Hans Blix said there is no evidence (Dan Plesch, "U.S. Claim Dismissed by Blix," *The Guardian*, February 5, 2003) and *Newsweek* reported, "Biowar experts concede that no scheme is too crazy for Saddam. Still, they say, truck-mounted labs would be all but unworkable" ("Death on Wheels," *Newsweek*, February 17, 2003).

These facts are obviously known to the administration, but the group of civilian militarists surrounding the president are less concerned with the truth than they are with whipping up a frenzy of fear that can be used to rationalize an entirely avoidable war. As you well know, there are land mines—both literal and metaphorical—embedded in this scheme, posing enormous dangers not just to the Iraqi civilian population, but boomerangs to our own national security. This latter heightened risk was pointed out by CIA Director George Tenet, as well as by many former leaders in the military, intelligence, diplomatic, and political sectors.

The clique that now has the president's ear is willing to disregard these risks to satisfy their zeal for military engagement. I can only guess what Brent Scowcroft, President George H. W. Bush's national security advisor, is now thinking about how his cluster of cautions from last year were so quickly disregarded.

Perhaps you alone now have the personal, private persuasiveness to have the president rethink this course of action, even at this late hour, and prevent the needless carnage and ongoing, multiple harms to our national interests that is sure to follow long after the military victory is proclaimed.

Sincerely,
Ralph Nader
John Richard
Robert Weissman

MARCH 10, 2003
A Man Who Has Stopped Listening

Dear President Bush,

After the completion of your long overdue full-scale news conference on March 7th, Senator Robert Byrd remarked: "He talked last night like a man who is not willing to listen any further. He has stopped listening." There are many engaged citizens who wonder whether you ever started listening or at least directly hearing views contrary to your determination to start a war, invasion, and lengthy occupation of Iraq. Indeed, it appears you have not met with a single domestic antiwar delegation, despite numerous requests from varied constituencies for a meeting.

Many commentators and reporters—having spoken with people inside your administration—have noted the isolation, the solitude, and the exclusionary characteristic of your office on this subject. Others such as Bob Woodward, who interviewed you, tell readers of your self-description as being a "black and white" type of person, of a man who makes decisions "from the gut" or from instinct. Combined with isolation from many informed contrary views, this attitude is made more disquieting by your continual invoking of God when it comes to Iraq. Viewed from abroad, this appears to millions of people as if you are embarking on a religious war. From stateside, you will forgive those Americans who instead view such allusions as indicative of a refusal to entertain empirical inputs and broader policy arguments from Americans, many of whom have been following, experiencing or studying the Iraqi situation longer than some in your very tight ideological circle of advisors.

In the past several weeks alone, a distinguished array of groups has written you about issues and has requested a personal meeting with you in the White House. Now is the time to spend a few hours listening to cogent presentations by these Americans of widely different backgrounds and insights, but mostly similar in their opposition to war/invasion/occupation. According to press reports, your travel schedule over the next two weeks has been sharply reduced to concentrate on the United Nations and other related situations which should include a decent respect for the opinions of those organizations who have asked for an audience with you.

The country is deeply and almost evenly divided according to numerous polls that ask more comprehensive questions. Meeting with representatives of these groups, which oppose your proposed policies, would afford you an opportunity for a two-way exchange. There have been too many monologues, which serve their purpose of course, but a dialogue tends to probe and clarify the issues and test the strength of opposing views.

The benefits of these meetings, were you to allow them to occur, are more than what may be described as good public relations on your part. For example, leaders of veterans' groups and former military leaders, whose letter is on its way, can convey the horrific toxic aftermath of the war/invasion to both Iraqis and U.S. troops. They know about the first Gulf War firsthand and have been closely associated with the treatment of over 200,000 soldiers who were disabled and have been receiving disability payments. Even were you to take this country to war, you would benefit from their knowledge of how under-trained and inadequately equipped U.S. soldiers are to defend themselves against what you have said is the likely prospect of chemical warfare by Iraq's brutal dictator.

From women's groups, including those back from numerous trips to Afghanistan, you'll learn about the terrible effect on the civilian population long after hostilities ended, due in part to the lack of promised follow-through assistance by the United States to the Kabul government. They can also convey the likely consequences on Iraqi families whose elderly, mothers, and children will especially suffer from lack of food, spreading disease, fires, score-settling, and fleeing refugee conditions of an awful nature.

From the perspective of working families, you will hear why this is the first time that major labor unions, with the encouragement of the AFL-CIO, have ever opposed a war by the United States, in part because it is an unprovoked war.

From the business executives, you will hear concerns about the further instability and decline of our economy with its effects on standards of living, employment and neglected domestic budgets.

From representatives of the clergy, including your own Bishop, as well as from many other Christian denominations and other major religions, you will learn the depth of their disagreement with you regarding the moral justification for this war and what they have learned from their visits to Iraq.

From leading physicians having serious experience with health conditions and capacity in Iraq, you will be informed of the scale of civilian mortality and morbidity from the looming devastation. Notwithstanding assurances to the contrary in 1991, there was severe destruction of the drinking water infrastructure leading to epidemics that most cruelly took the lives of many tens of thousands of Iraqi children.

In recent weeks, you took the time to travel to Pennsylvania and to a Washington hotel to meet with doctors complaining about their insurance premiums and malpractice lawsuits.

Surely you can meet in the White House with physicians whose compassion, insight and knowledge about the fate of millions reflect the highest obligation of the medical profession, which is prevention.

Consider how much more enriched your perspective will become after exchanging views and information with the other groups who have also asked to see you. These include: elected representatives of city councils representing tens of millions of Americans; environmental organizations knowledgeable about the environmental devastation to the region and the planet on a level even greater than 1991 that is likely from this proposed war; international intelligence specialists with past governmental experience who will tell you what many dissenters inside the Pentagon and the State Department cannot say to you about consequences and alternatives; prominent academics, historians, and civic leaders; and the next generation, from groups representing millions of college students.

More than a dozen of these letters were sent to you. Most of them have not received the courtesy of a response. None have been accorded an affirmative invitation.

The organizations requesting to meet with you represent a broad cross section of the American people. They seek a dialogue with you not out of political partisanship but because they have not been convinced that war with Iraq is necessary.

These attached requests ask for meetings of short duration but, in the retrospect of history, long significance for historians who will judge your decision-making process on the road to war-invasion-occupation.*

Sincerely,

MARCH 10, 2003
Energy Policies Hurting American Consumers

Dear President Bush,

We are writing to you as consumer organizations concerned about how your administration's energy policies are hurting American consumers, harming the economy, and increasing the number of unemployed. Your year-long push toward war in Iraq has allowed oil companies and Wall Street speculators to reap unjust rewards, as the price of oil has nearly doubled in that time.

---

* See https://nader.org/iraq-letters for the text of these letters.

We request a meeting to discuss the steps that must be taken to secure America's economic and energy security, and to ask that you initiate an investigation into the role U.S. oil company price gouging has had in contributing to high gasoline prices. We also ask that you order a cap on at-the-pump gas prices in the event of a war and inform us of your planned use of the Strategic Petroleum Reserve.

After the terrorist attacks of 9/11, the price of oil plummeted by nearly 40 percent in two months. But ever since the January 2002 State of the Union speech, where you included Iraq as an "axis of evil" country, oil prices have doubled to nearly $40/barrel—the highest level since the Gulf War.

These higher prices hit Americans in three ways. First, psychological "sticker shock" shakes consumer confidence. In February, the Conference Board's Consumer Confidence Index fell to its lowest point in nearly a decade, citing "rising oil prices" as one of the reasons.

Second, higher oil prices inflate gas prices for consumers and raise companies' cost of doing business. This particularly affects low-income communities, who are acutely affected when gas prices rise. In addition, whatever costs businesses don't absorb (through lower profits) are passed through to consumers by increasing prices for goods, which in turn increases the risk of inflation. The airline and trucking industries, along with family farms, have been hit particularly hard by the sharp increase in energy costs. High oil prices have deflated an already anemic economy and helped contribute to hundreds of thousands of additional American jobs lost this past year. At the same time, your administration has appropriated only $2 billion for low-income home energy assistance—only 0.5 percent of the $365 billion military budget.

Third, higher oil prices transfers income from Americans to

oil-exporting dictatorships like Saudi Arabia and Iraq. These two countries supply America with over 25 percent of our imports. Through the U.N.'s Oil-For-Food program, Iraq exports two million barrels of oil a day, including hundreds of thousands of barrels a day to the U.S., making Iraq the 6th largest supplier of crude oil to America. But, Iraq has been also illegally shipping oil in violation of U.N. sanctions, using foreign governments and possibly U.S. oil companies as intermediaries. Your administration has taken no action to investigate the role of U.S. corporations or of our allies in the "War on Terror" in these schemes.

U.S. oil companies are all too happy to receive the spoils of higher oil prices. A wave of mergers over the last few years has created giants—ExxonMobil, ChevronTexaco, ConocoPhillips— that dominate all sectors of the oil industry, from drilling to selling gas to consumers. As a result, the top five oil companies now control over 40 percent of all domestic production, half of the domestic oil refineries and over two-thirds of all gas stations, choking competition and allowing them to inflate gas prices on top of the global crude oil price. Indeed, the Federal Trade Commission concluded in 2001 that oil companies intentionally withheld gasoline from the Western U.S. market in order to increase prices. Because their control over the domestic market is even greater, the ability of these oil companies to manipulate prices has increased. In addition, these large oil companies continue to take advantage of the deregulated energy trading sector that allowed Enron to price gouge West Coast electricity consumers. The same lack of transparency that Enron exploited is being exploited by ExxonMobil, ChevronTexaco and other oil companies with large positions in the unregulated over-the-counter energy derivatives market.

We wish to discuss why there needs to be a $2 cap on at-the-pump gasoline prices in the event of a war. Our nation's economy is dependent upon its energy security and should not be held hostage to the interests of multinational oil companies.

To our knowledge you have never met with representatives of national consumer groups since you took office in January 2001. We hope to see you very soon.

Sincerely,

Linda Golodner, President, National Consumers League

Jaime Court, Executive Director, The Foundation for Taxpayer & Consumer Rights (FTCR)

Joan Claybrook, President, Public Citizen

Theresa Amato, Executive Director, Citizen Works

Ralph Nader

MAY 28, 2001

The Danger of Massive Tax Cuts

Dear President Bush,

Your decision to tie your economic policy to a massive tax cut places at risk the needs of local communities and millions of citizens across the nation. It is, Mr. President, as if your administration and a bipartisan majority in the Congress have declared that there are no unmet needs.

In reality, the nation has a huge backlog of needs which must be met to ensure the health and safety of citizens and the well-being of the entire economy. The tax cut will make it impossible for the necessary programs to be funded if the budget surpluses are to be absorbed by tax reductions heavily weighted for the wealthiest citizens.

Mr. President, the nation cannot continue to allow more than 15 percent of its children to grow up in poverty or to refuse to provide an adequate supply of affordable housing for inner-city neighborhoods and depressed rural areas. We are already five million units short of the need for affordable housing. There are millions of other dwellings in need of major repairs to bring them up to decent standards for human habitation. Your tax cuts will remove hopes of changing these deplorable conditions.

You have spoken often about education and the need to upgrade our schools. Where, Mr. President, will the money come from to convert your rhetoric into action? Health is of vital concern, particularly for the millions lacking health insurance and the elderly facing rising prescription costs. Will you tell them that you gave the money away in the form of tax cuts, mostly to upper-income recipients?

Safe drinking water is critically important, and problems grow as many water systems near the end of their useful life. In a detailed report of public works needs, the American Society of Civil Engineers estimates that there is a shortfall of $11 billion annually in expenditures to replace worn-out and outdated systems. There is another $12 billion shortfall in investment in wastewater systems. Some of these systems are more than 100 years old. What happens, Mr. President, when you find that these antiquated systems cannot be replaced because the money has gone out the door in the form of tax cuts?

Similarly, the civil engineers—whom I trust you do not regard as radical members of society—raise serious questions about the adequacy of our transportation system. One-third of our roads are in poor or mediocre condition, costing taxpaying drivers an estimated

$5.8 billion and contributing to 13,800 fatalities annually. Twenty-nine percent of the nation's bridges are structurally deficient or functionally obsolete. Mass transit ridership is increasing rapidly and it is estimated that capital spending needs to increase by 41 percent just to maintain these systems in their present condition, not including what is needed to keep up with the increased number of riders. Again, Mr. President, your tax cut package raises the possibility that funding will not be available to expand and maintain these transportation systems which are so vital to a growing population and particularly to working families.

A rationale put forward by your administration for the tax cut is that it will stimulate the economy. Economists differ on this point, but there is no question that investments in needed projects like transportation, water, and sewer systems and affordable housing produce new jobs and income in local communities. So, if economic stimulus is the goal, you should place high priority on these needed investments in the future of America.

Mr. President, if we do not take bold steps to deal with these unmet needs in a time of budget surpluses, when will we?

A major criticism of your tax policy is based on the fact that the benefits are heavily skewed in favor of the wealthy. For example, under the tax cut the richest 1 percent of taxpayers—citizens with annual incomes over $375,000—would receive a third of the benefits of the cuts while the bottom 60 percent of the taxpayers would get only 15 percent of the benefits.

In fact, Mr. President, you, Vice President Cheney, and members of your cabinet would be among the large beneficiaries of your proposal to repeal the estate tax. Representative Henry Waxman has estimated that your estate would save between $5 million and $11 million under the repeal of this tax (and Vice President Cheney between $10 million and $41 million) based on data from government financial disclosure forms. The estates of members of your cabinet would save an average of $5 million to $19 million each.

In contrast, Mr. President, the benefits stemming from repairs to the nation's decaying infrastructure and investments in education, health, and safety aid everyone from the poorest to the wealthiest and build a nation that we can be proud of for the future. Tax cuts are an easy political answer. We need your administration to tackle the tougher questions of meeting long-neglected needs with programs that will pay dividends for the American people for years after the tax cut has been spent and forgotten.

Sincerely,

[signature]

THE WHITE HOUSE
WASHINGTON

October 9, 2001

Dear Mr. Nader:

The President has asked me to thank you for your recent letter regarding the tax surplus and our nation's unmet needs. In light of the tragedy of September 11, I hope you will agree with me that two national priorities--two unmet needs--deserve our full attention.

First, President Bush is committed to defeating international terrorism and providing the American people with the security they want and deserve. Second, the President is committed to providing the economic leadership necessary to keep the economy thriving in the months and years ahead. As President Kennedy once remarked: "Nothing our opponents could do to encourage their own ambitions would encourage them half so much as a chronic lagging United States economy."

You and I share a desire to see that the American people are protected from harm and given every opportunity to live their lives in peace and prosperity. We may disagree on how to achieve those ends, but I am confident that we can work together on behalf of the nation.

Again, thank you for your thoughtful letter. I truly appreciate your willingness to share your concerns.

Sincerely,

Larry Lindsey

Lawrence B. Lindsey
Assistant to the President for Economic Policy

The Auto Safety Wake-up Call

Dear Vice President Gore and Governor Bush,

The fatal combination of the Firestone tire defects and the Ford rollover defect has energized the families who experienced the resulting trauma and heartbreak to seek legislation to strengthen the National Highway Traffic Safety Administration in the U.S. Department of Transportation to help prevent future cover-ups of safety defects. The legislation has been reported out of the Senate Commerce Committee and the House Commerce Subcommittee. But predictably, the auto industry lobbyists are working to stop it or reduce it to insignificance. Joining with them are the Chamber of Commerce and National Association of Manufacturers lobbyists. The families have asked members of Congress not to adjourn and seek reelection without passing strong legislation.

The key provisions concern the penalties for violating the auto safety law: Raising the maximum civil penalties from the current $925,000—chump change for multinational corporations—to $15 million (still far below what is needed) and adding criminal penalties for officers and agents who knowingly fail to recall vehicles or equipment that are defective or fail to comply with safety standards and cause death or injury. Criminal penalties were supported in testimony by Department of Transportation Secretary Rodney Slater and Ford CEO Jacques Nasser.

Also recommended by Secretary Slater and included in the Senate bill are requirements for manufacturers to provide information on a regular basis and identify trends as an early warning to the DOT. This information is already in the hands of manufacturers. It includes warranty and other claims data, lawsuits, recalls abroad or customer satisfaction campaigns that are often kept secret, accidents, injuries and deaths, vehicle components or systems failures, and other relevant information. Both bills call for updating the 30-year-old inadequate tire safety standard, but fail to require updating of other out-of-date standards such as roof crush, or issuance of a rollover prevention standard, a much-needed requirement given the propensity of SUVs to roll over. Today 25 percent of all traffic deaths involve rollover.

In the Firestone/Ford case, 101 people have been killed whom we know about and 400 injured. One fourth of these deaths (26) and even more injuries (125) have occurred in the State of Texas and another fourth in Florida (24 deaths and 106 injuries).

Criminal sanctions are common in consumer and transportation statutes. Violations by motor carriers, hazardous materials handlers, pipelines, railroads, water vessels, and airlines all are subject to criminal sanctions. Also, criminal sanctions are included in the food and drug, clean water, solid waste disposal, mine safety, occupational health and safety, consumer protection safety, and consumer product hazardous substances laws. Many economic crimes from income tax evasion to securities fraud are punishable by prison sentences. A reckless or speeding driver who negligently kills another highway user is subject to charges of criminal negligent homicide. A person rolling back an odometer can be sentenced to three years in prison, a law administered by the National Highway Traffic Safety Administration. It is past the time when these sanctions should be included in the auto safety law for knowingly failing to recall safety defective vehicles that can kill or injure or knowingly violating motor vehicle safety standards.

You have talked frequently about personal responsibility

for individuals. Surely you would agree there should not be a double standard so that corporate officials are shielded from taking responsibility for their actions, particularly those that result in death or injury.

To show your respect for the families who will forever face the pain and losses from the defective Firestone tires and Ford vehicles, I am asking you to endorse strong criminal and civil penalties for violations of the auto safety law, regular provision of relevant information to prevent deaths, and the updating of key safety standards, and to urge Congress to pass such legislation before they go home to ask citizens to reelect them to public office.

I look forward to your response. Time is of the essence if Congress is to pass this legislation before it goes home to get reelected. Postponing action until next year means more time for corporate lobbyists to delay interminably as they have since 1966 when the Automobile Manufacturers Association and its law firm, Wilmer, Cutler and Pickering, blocked the criminal penalty provisions sponsored on the floor of the House by Representative Tip O'Neill.

Sincerely,

SEPTEMBER 21, 2000
Your Views on Personal Privacy?

Dear Governor Bush,

As you should be aware, privacy is a crucially important issue in the information age. Our fundamental rights are threatened by new information technologies, and by the buying and selling of personal information. Personal information about Americans is routinely collected and abused by government agencies and by corporations for private gain.

The damage is vast. This year alone, hundreds of thousands of individuals will have their identities 'stolen' and their credit records threatened by thieves who make use of stored personal data. Workers will lose their jobs because of intrusive genetic and psychological tests. Insurance companies will deny coverage because of possible illnesses hidden in people's genes. Video cameras will track consumers and citizens throughout private and public spaces. Internet companies will secretly monitor millions of users' activities as they surf the Internet.

Meanwhile, law enforcement agencies are increasing their powers to conduct surveillance of citizens. Tens of millions in taxpayer dollars are used to pay telephone companies to make it easier to wiretap and to track the location of cellular phone users. The FBI's Carnivore system can sift through millions of e-mails.

Citizens are demanding that their personal information be protected. Polls show that individuals want legal controls and penalties for abusers. The U.S. government needs to take action, both to rein in its own agencies and to limit the abuses of private companies. Instead of action, the response has been hollow promises of "industry self-regulation."

I request that you answer the following questions about your positions on personal privacy:

Do you think the use of Social Security numbers by businesses and government agencies should be regulated?

Should patients have the right to control the collection, use and dissemination of medical information, including genetic information?

Should Internet Service Providers (ISPs) and other companies on the Internet be prohibited from misusing customer information and from selling information without their customers' permission?

What is your stance on supermarkets and other businesses that use hidden surveillance cameras to capture information from their customers? Do you think that covert surveillance technology should be regulated?

Do you support a legally guaranteed right of individuals to see all information kept about them by companies?

Should the U.S. Government create a watchdog agency to protect U.S. citizens from privacy invasions from other government offices or from corporations?

Should the U.S. support the establishment of an international convention on privacy?

Thank you.

Sincerely,

SEPTEMBER 11, 2000
Legalize Hemp!

Dear Vice President Gore and Governor Bush,

On August 24 in the early morning, 25 armed agents with the Drug Enforcement Administration (DEA), Federal Bureau of Investigation (FBI), U.S. Marshals Service, and Northern Plains Safe Trails Drug Task Force uprooted two test plots of industrial hemp planted on the Pine Ridge Indian Reservation, destroying the crop that was legally planted under the sovereignty of the Oglala Sioux tribe. The Oglala Sioux people had high hopes for this crop, believing it would allow them to achieve more economic self-sufficiency while also providing useful supplies such as building materials, as tribal leader Joe American Horse explained at a recent press conference in Washington, D.C.

Farmers in communities throughout the U.S. would benefit from the ability to grow industrial hemp, a viable crop with some of the longest and strongest natural fibers in the plant kingdom and with thousands of potential uses. In March of 1998, a coalition of individuals and organizations—including private businesses and nonprofit organizations—submitted a petition to both the Drug Enforcement Administration and the United States Department of Agriculture requesting that the agencies initiate rulemaking proceedings that would lead to the enactment of regulations permitting the domestic production of industrial hemp. Despite the prominence of many of the signers and a clearly and rationally argued case that marijuana and industrial hemp are different, there has been no response from either the DEA or the USDA to date. Sitting on this petition is an arbitrary and capricious display of administrative behavior.

In the past three years, 19 states have introduced pro–industrial hemp resolutions. Colorado, Iowa, Nebraska, New Hampshire, Oregon, Pennsylvania, Rhode Island, South Dakota and Tennessee introduced pro–industrial hemp legislation. And California, Hawaii, Idaho, Illinois, Kentucky, Maryland, Minnesota, Montana, New Mexico, North Dakota, Vermont and Virginia have passed industrial hemp legislation and resolutions. But Drug Czar Barry McCaffrey has lobbied against any moves by the states to take legislative action to address industrial hemp.

I challenge you to reveal to the American voters your position on industrial hemp and explain to them why it is illegal for farmers in the U.S. to grow a crop that has the potential to help address the global depletion of forest resources, the dependency on foreign oil, the harmful effects of petrochemicals, the excessive use of pesticides for fiber crops, and the economic depression of farming communities.

I am sure you are aware that industrial hemp is not a drug, and contains very little of the psychoactive component THC that is found in marijuana. Cumulative studies in Europe and Canada have shown that industrial hemp is not psychoactive. Therefore, smoking it will only give you a headache, not a high.

The crop, grown by George Washington and Thomas Jefferson, produces an extremely versatile fiber and oil that can be used in various applications including clothing, fuel, paper, cosmetics, animal bedding, automobile parts, food, rope, textiles, carpeting, etc.

Rather than responding to the call for industrial hemp from farmers, manufacturers, and 19 states, Bill Clinton's Drug Enforcement Administration wants to extend its bureaucratic control over products containing industrial hemp that has been legally imported from other countries. I was recently informed by Hawaii State Representative Cynthia Thielen that the DEA is preparing to propose new rules regulating industrial hemp that would, among other changes, declare any product containing any amount of THC to be a Schedule I controlled substance—the most restrictive category for controlled substances—with the exception of industrial hemp products not used or intended for human consumption, such as paper, clothing, and rope.

These actions by the United States government are ensuring that while Canadian and other farmers prosper from industrial hemp, American farmers are unlikely to see its benefits anytime soon.

While American farmers are forbidden from commercially growing this crop, American manufacturers are allowed to import industrial hemp from China and other nations and manufacture hemp products. In the current farm crisis, farmers need alternative crops, and hemp will likely be more profitable than other commodity crops. According to the Institute for Local Self-Reliance, in 1999 hemp yields grossed $308 to $410 per acre. These figures compare favorably to the $103–$137 gross made on canola and wheat crops per acre. Moreover, the market for industrial hemp has been greatly underestimated by the U.S. government. For instance, the use of natural fibers in biocomposites (such as automobile parts) is predicted to grow by 15–20 percent annually. And hemp is expected to be an important commodity for this market due to its favorable strength-to-weight ratio.

In addition to being a potentially economically viable crop, industrial hemp can also benefit the environment. It can replace wood fiber in most applications, such as building products and paper, aiding forest conservation efforts. It can minimize toxics in the environment, because when used in pulp for paper, its natural brightness avoids chlorine bleaching that produces dioxin, a powerful environmental toxin. It is also an excellent crop that needs few, if any, pesticides and herbicides, and used in rotation it chokes out weeds. Therefore, crops grown on the same field after hemp have shown increased yields. Industrial hemp also has a potential to be one of the bio-based fuels that could replace petroleum as a fuel source, thereby benefiting both national security and the environment. This benefit has attracted the support of ex–CIA Director James Woolsey, who wants industrial hemp to be grown in the U.S. Furthermore, its use in automobile biocomposites decreases energy consumption and these new components are more easily recycled than current auto parts, which are made of fiberglass.

As a result of its utility and its many benefits, industrial hemp has been experiencing a renaissance and is being grown by most industrialized countries throughout the world, with the exception of the United States. Countries such as Canada, England, Germany, and France recognize its value and grow the crop, leaving the United States at a competitive disadvantage.

I urge each of you to speak openly on this subject and to let the media, as well as working families, know where you stand.

Sincerely,

Letters to President Barack Obama

A Presidential Two-Track Plan, Revisited

Dear President Obama,

As you commence the last full two years of your presidency and on the eve of your State of the Union address to the Congress, I wish to include for your consideration the enclosed column I wrote on January 22, 1977, regarding "A Presidential Two-Track Plan." In a meeting with President Carter he indicated he had read the article.

While the attached column is self-explanatory, it is worth emphasizing that the second track is essentially an empowerment initiative that facilitates creation of many self-funded civic organizations open to all under procedures of democratic accountability.

As I wrote: "without a strong, persistent civic movement, the president can do little overall in changing the patterns of concentrated power that have bred so many first-track abuses."

This observation would be obvious were it not for the tradition of ignoring it. In a democratic society, rights and remedies, so crucial, are often not enough to achieve their substantive goals. They require "facilities" which invite organized participation at key points of citizen access and attentiveness. Harvard Law professor Richard Parker has argued in his book *Here, the People Rule* that under our Constitution, our government has an affirmative duty to facilitate the civic energies of the people.

I hope that you and/or your assistants will find a "second-track" presidency sufficiently worthy and doable to invite further details and discussions. This is not just a political/civic theory. The Citizen's Utility Board, one example of an empowering initiative, has strengthened the organized voices of residential utility consumers in your home state of Illinois.

Sincerely,

(signature)

If the lessons of recent Washington history are to be heeded, Jimmy Carter should be launching a "two-track presidency" to fulfill his campaign declarations. The first track is the familiar one. It involves treating the problems of inflation, unemployment, disease, poverty and crime on the domestic scene and the urgency of the arms race, international conflicts, and economic crises abroad. The second track involves providing citizens with the rights and remedies to assert their interests through a more democratic political and economic system. Without plowing the second track, Jimmy Carter will not have much success with the problems he wants to diminish on the first track.

Unfortunately, a president's time is programmed to place second track activities so far below the more pressing first track matters as to be nearly out of sight. But without the ideas, participation, and support of a broader-based citizenry, President Carter cannot expect to accomplish much of significance.

There were signs during the campaign that candidate Carter appreciated both the need to strengthen civic institutions outside of government and the necessity to end the isolation that grips the White House. But it will take an iron will to do this.

Consider some illustrations of the criticality that the second track holds for first track success. Carter repeatedly told Americans during the campaign that the country has gotten into trouble overseas whenever the people were left out of the decision-making process. Up to now, foreign policy has been shaped and decided by a small clique at the summit of this country's political and corporate governments. An informed and empowered civic presence in foreign policy-making is a second track challenge for Carter to facilitate.

President Carter wants to produce a genuine reform of the tax system—a first track goal. This cannot be done without displeasing powerful special interests who profit from the present inequities. It can only be done by small taxpayer participation in the reform process that builds at the community level and reaches all the way to Congress. Giving small taxpayers the legal tools of civic action is a second track mission for Carter.

The new president wants to rebuild the center cities—a prime Democratic Party platform plank. Can this be done without a second track role for neighborhood and other community organizations to both nourish and implement national policies with self reliant efforts on the receiving end?

Carter's often expressed determination to defend the human environment will conflict with defiant corporations whose executives have owned the White House for the past eight years. These companies can continue their environmental blackmail of threatening worker layoff or plant closedowns if the antipollution health laws are enforced inside and outside the factories. Without effective rights for environmental and worker safety groups to utilize the courts and the regulatory agencies—both second track objectives— Carter will be unable to resist many of these corporate pressures.

Without a strong, persistent civic movement, the president can do little overall in changing the patterns of concentrated power that have bred so many first track abuses.

During the lean and indifferent Nixon-Ford years,

the citizen movement and several Congressional committees have forged a whole series of what can be called initiatory democratic rights to make corporate and governmental power more accountable to the people they are supposed to serve. They provide the agenda for a second track presidency.

These proposals include a consumer advocacy agency, a national consumers cooperative bank, consumer and environmental class action rights, reducing the cost barriers to citizen participation in government proceedings, legal standing for citizens to sue to stop government waste and corruption, consumer and taxpayer checkoff systems to facilitate the organized representation of these constituencies.

Such proposals would be part of a second track presidency's priorities. They are not drains on the Treasury; for they are mainly self-help procedures which deconcentrate power and strengthen the fibre of grass roots initiatives.

Jimmy Carter promises to maintain an open White House and an open administration. It won't be long before Americans will learn whether the new White House operates to give them power or operates to continue instead the old practice of taking it away on behalf of an imperial corporate state. If it's the former, Carter's legacy will last for longer than his term of office.

Still Hoping for "Hope and Change"

Dear President Obama,

The end of the year and the completion of an unproductive session of Congress is an appropriate time to suggest some important matters for your close attention for next year.

Your visit to the National Institutes of Health, regarding the Ebola peril (December 2nd) and your address to some 3,000 Senior Executive Service (SES) members (December 9th) are examples of effective uses of your time to highlight the importance of the civil service sector. You helped reverse a widespread feeling among federal employees that they are the focus of what you called a "political climate where folks too often talk down government for cheap applause." Those who make such arguments against government workers are often politicians seeking or occupying public office. Stereotypical putdowns have a negative effect on morale and initiatives by the very federal employees these politicians expect to implement government policies.

While we have had our serious criticisms of government officials and staff, it is an inescapable fact that the quality of daily governance is significantly due to daily competence and diligence, not just to policy and budgets. A 2013 GAO report cites a lack of governmental employees with certain crucial skills, as well as noting that starting in 2011, about 30 percent of federal employees will be eligible for retirement by 2016.

What you can now do, free of time-consuming fundraising trips, is to schedule well-advanced presidential work days with federal departments and agencies, not just to build up morale and recognize excellence, but to delve into the depths of their missions. For example, procedural protections for conscientious whistle-blowers have improved over the past thirty years, but still have a long way to go. You recognized that point in 2008. There is a need for some hands-on presidential level management reviews and probes that shake agencies out of bad routines and bad practices that prevent improvement of such institutions.

I have spoken to many groups of civil servants and know that granular engagement by the president, which narrows the gap between promise and performance of agencies, together with follow-up by your staff, can lead to remarkable progress, savings and advancement of statutory missions. This is especially the case in the two major areas of federal regulatory enforcement and massive contract procurement. Moreover, Paul Volcker and the Partnership for Public Service have valuable proposals in the more institutionalized regions of improved governance and recruitment especially from the younger generation of Americans.

As you demonstrated, with examples in your SES remarks, the public should be informed frequently of the heroics performed daily (outside the military sphere) by civil servants in the field. I've found that it is rare for an average American to be able to name even one such heroic person in the civilian federal government.

Politically beating up on an agency like the overwhelmed Internal Revenue Service, presently run by the accomplished John Koskinen, without high-level rebuttals can also lead to self-destructive results. While it is true that the agency needs many reforms including, of course, a fairer tax code, the congressional Republicans have succeeded in cutting the budget of the IRS once again, this time to under $11 billion (to collect 90 percent of federal revenue). So tightly squeezed, the IRS simply cannot service taxpayer inquiries without inordinate waiting, cannot effectively audit giant global companies, and cannot collect more of the over $300 billion of uncollected taxes every year! So the vindictive GOP is increasing the federal deficit by its loutish behavior, as well as burdening complying taxpayers. Isn't there a role for the White House here?

Another upcoming issue—the Trans-Pacific Partnership (TPP)—requires your personal attention. Coming off your criticism of NAFTA and the WTO during your 2008 campaign, you should be responsive to the brazenly autocratic provisions overriding due process, openness and our legislative, executive and judicial branches of government, in addition to your earlier 2008 recognition of subordinating workers, environmental and consumer standards to commercial imperatives.

No doubt your advisors are informing you that any fast track shipment to Congress of this proposed trade agreement—really a treaty—will confront a formidable Left-Right alliance in the House of Representatives. The American people, increasingly informed by their local experience of hollowed-out communities and lost jobs, as well as other adversities of NAFTA and the WTO, are turning against this relentlessly ongoing silent coup d'état by U.S. global corporations and their gross lack of patriotism (you have recently described corporate inversions as unpatriotic). As your Harvard Law professors always counsel—read the full text! (See chapter entitled "Globalization" from my book *The Good Fight: Declare Your Independence and Close the Democracy Gap* [2004].)

Finally, why not have a White House Conference on the consumer/worker/retiree side of our economy. Listen to the experts on private pension looting or the sacrifices small savers are making due to a lower than one-half of one percent interest rate, compliments of the Federal Reserve, that is pressing for a 2 percent consumer index inflation rate, to the many-faceted epidemic of corporate crime—facilitated by the fine-print contract peonage (that you and Senator Elizabeth Warren have alluded to, see Faircontracts.org) to the sophisticated gouging and wrongful injuries of consumers and workers stripped of usable legal remedies and access to the courts. Special attention should be given to proposed easier facilities for consumers, in their varied roles, workers, and small taxpayers for voluntarily banding together to defend and negotiate their rightful interests. A significant shift of power from the few to the many is long overdue.

With over two years to go and no electoral restraints from the plutocracy to be concerned about, you are free to call on the "better angels" of your presidential potential for the citizenry and posterity here and around the world. There is still a chance for *some* "hope and change," is there not?

Sincerely,

OCTOBER 15, 2014

Doing More to Raise the Minimum Wage

Dear President Obama,

In the last few months, you have been making more frequent statements supporting H.R. 1010 or the federal minimum wage increase (actually a restoration to adjust to inflation) to reach $10.10 per hour over three years from the present $7.25 per hour.

With three weeks left before the November elections, the minimum wage raise needs to be "nationalized." Your supporters in Congress are firm in their belief that only you barnstorming the country, giving voice to the plight of local workers representing the low-pay occupations critical to our economy, will get the voters out behind this long overdue proposal. Both liberal and conservative workers support this lift in their living standard. Poll after poll show this convergence quite decisively.

You have left Washington for about seven days in the past five weeks to raise money for the Democratic Party from New York to Los Angeles. Surely, you can devote a similar amount of time to a campaign affecting thirty million workers and their families. You know how to make the moral and economic case for this important initiative.

As you know, the House discharge petition, filed in late February with 195 Democrats signed on, needs only 23 more legislators to bypass Speaker Boehner's ban on having a vote on the House floor. Republicans running for public office should be asked their position on getting a very popular measure to the House floor for a vote. Your staff can go to Give1010avote.org for district by district data.

Time is of the essence.

Sincerely,

[signature]

SEPTEMBER 8, 2014

Three Suggestions for the Domestic Front

Dear President Obama,

With the Democratic Party having trouble defeating the worst congressional Republican Party in modern times,* you have been searching for ways that you, as the president, can

---

* See Give1010avote.org for more information.

make change by executive action. I have three suggestions that you can initiate right after the November elections.

First schedule well-published and public half-day visits to each of 20 major departments and agencies to give visibility to what civil servants are doing for the American people. A portion of the department's or agency's time would be devoted to reviewing the areas where improvements are long overdue or could be accelerated. These working sessions would bring your management function of the executive branch to a level of detail almost always ignored by past presidents.

Such sessions would bring higher levels of urgency to such matters as the administration of the public lands, the enormous corporate frauds on Medicare by contractors and service vendors, and the seemingly intractable drain by contractors of the Pentagon budget both in what weapon systems are procured and how defense projects are mishandled. Summaries of the substance of these sessions can then be made public.

There is another compelling reason for your visits highlighting the charters of these departments and agencies. It is reflected in a recent Ipsos Public Affairs poll, commissioned by the National Treasury Employees Union long preceded by alarms issued from groups studying the federal civil service. The *Washington Post* reports that a civil service retirement wave is building, "with more than a third of career federal employees projected to be eligible for collecting their end-of-career benefits by September 2017." As president, you can highlight the unrivaled significance of civilian careers in the areas of scientific research, consumer, environmental, labor, and many other serious domestic purposes for our country. Young Americans who wish to make a difference and eschew the more lucrative, but trivial occupations that attract such media coverage, need to learn about the opportunities for government service. If there was ever an important, but noncontroversial use of the bully pulpit, this has to be one of the top contenders.

Second, just as you have attended fundraisers throughout the country for Democratic Party candidates, imagine the impact of barnstorming for a few days highlighting human faces of the 30 million American workers who make less today than workers made in 1968, inflation-adjusted. With Congress shockingly limiting its workdays post–July 2014 to about two weeks before the November elections, you can focus during the lame duck session on getting support for the House Discharge Petition, with already 195 members on board and needing 23 more to bypass House Speaker John Boehner's obstruction, to get a vote on the House floor. Representative George Miller says that H.R. 1010, the bill to raise the federal minimum wage from $7.25 to $10.10 an hour over three years, will pass if brought to a vote. Such passage will get the Senate to the 60 votes needed to overcome the threatened filibuster by the Republicans. The Republican leadership somehow thinks that blocking this overwhelmingly popular overdue measure for economic justice— one even backed by Republicans such as Mitt Romney, Rick Santorum, Tim Pawlenty and millions of conservative workers— is their political mission on Capitol Hill.

Your barnstorming can rally workers from the many occupations that produce and serve our food, take care of our ailing grandparents, do the cleaning and cleaning up of America—to name a few job categories. There are few better uses of your time before the end of the year!

Third, in previous letters I have requested your greater attention to the immense perils of viral and bacterial epidemics. You have supported a modestly larger budget for the Centers for Disease Control (which is presently funded annually at about half the cost of one aircraft carrier). But the Ebola outbreak in West Africa and the MERS virus in the Middle East illustrate the inadequate public health systems in those countries. Here is where the United States can become a humanitarian superpower and bolster its own defense as well. By both pushing to increase the budget of our government health agencies and the paltry budget of the World Health Organization (the WHO's budget, at about $2 billion a year,* is less than any one of several big city hospital revenues in the U.S.), you can advance an important humanitarian goal and strengthen our own national defense preparedness against the spread of epidemics and other health threats that so often start in East Asia and recently Africa.

Global epidemics that can spread quickly in these mobile times are a "clear and present danger" to our country. You must seriously embrace the precautionary principle through the heightened engagement of ready, able and willing public health and scientific specialists and scholars. Bring some of them together for a serious summit at the White House. If presidential leadership can put forces into motion anywhere, it is in this area of life-saving preventative action.

The use of presidential time invites many special interest pleaders. Reserve more of it to serve the vast majority of Americans who are not well organized for such pleading. They silently rely on your conscience, your awareness and your power to do the right things.

Sincerely,

---

* Alex Park reported on September 8, 2014 ("Why the World Health Organization Doesn't Have Enough Funds to Fight Ebola," *Mother Jones*) the the two-year budget for the World Health Organization is $3.97 billion.

Give $10.10 a Vote!

Dear President Obama,

After years of advocacy by citizen and labor groups, your Party has finally made raising the minimum wage for tens of millions of American workers an election issue for the coming midterms. The question remains, though: *Will raising the minimum wage simply be that—an "issue"with which to slam Republicans without any legislative effort—or will it actually be a top legislative priority this year?*

If you and other party leaders are serious about raising the federal minimum wage, you will quickly move beyond rhetoric about raising wages and focus on the concrete pending legislative path to a modest minimum wage raise to $10.10 an hour over three years: namely, *Rep. Tim Bishop's discharge petition to bring raising the minimum wage to a vote.* Rep. Bishop's petition has 195 signatures already and needs only 23 more to bypass Speaker Boehner's obstruction and force a vote on raising the minimum wage. These 23 signatures are the direct path to a long-awaited raise for millions of American workers: in the words of Rep. George Miller, who sponsored the bill, "when it comes to the floor, it will pass . . . we just need a vote." Passage in the House will ensure the 60 votes needed for Senate passage for by then the political and electoral heat will get the needed fence-sitting Senators. And yet, since the petition's introduction in late February, there has been little to no effort by Democratic leaders to pressure poverty- and labor-minded Republicans to sign. You did not even mention H.R. 1010 or its discharge petition in your Labor Day speech on the minimum wage.

With a modicum of the usual varieties of direct pressure

around the discharge petition from Democratic leaders and their circle of supporters, these 23 signatures would not be difficult to acquire. After all, 70–80 percent of Americans support raising the minimum wage, including Mitt Romney, Rick Santorum, Tim Pawlenty and Bill O'Reilly. There needs to be an intensity about this winnable effort.

To help, we have outlined 55 Republicans most likely to sign.* Among the 55: four House Democrats who have yet to sign the petition, six House Republicans who authored a letter in 2006 saying "nobody working full time should have to live in poverty"; seventeen House Republicans from districts you carried in 2012; dozens more House Republicans who have voted and spoken in favor of raising the minimum wage in the past; and many House Republicans who broke ranks to vote against food stamp cuts last fall.

It's one thing to give minimum wage workers ever-stronger speech-making; it's quite another to highlight in your remarks and push seriously for ready legislation by name. If you are truly serious about passing H.R. 1010, prioritize H.R. 1010's discharge petition during the September House session and secure the final 23 signatures so that the 30 million workers making less today—adjusted for inflation—than workers made in 1968 can get the vote they long have deserved on a much-needed raise to pay for their necessities of life. The country is ready to rise behind you on this moral and economic issue.

Sincerely,

*   See https://blog.nader.org/wp-content/uploads/2014/02/GOP-Outrageous-Votes-10-2012v3.pdf.

The "Public Sentiment"

Dear President Obama,

Abraham Lincoln once said that "With public sentiment, nothing can fail; without it, nothing can succeed." Presumably, he meant presidential action on popular issues can and should overcome influential interests.

At long last, the "public sentiment" seems to be aligning with some causes you are advancing.

First, support is increasing for restoring the federal minimum wage to account for the inflation that, since 1968, has greatly diminished its purchasing power. The federal minimum wage is presently stagnant at $7.25 per hour. You are supporting the Harkin-Miller bill (H.R. 1010 and S. 2223), which would raise it to $10.10 per hour over three years. You have already issued an executive order to require federal government contractors to pay their employees no less than $10.10 per hour, effective in 2015 (see Timeforaraise.org for more information).

Restoring the purchasing power of the minimum wage has over 70 percent public support and would lift the wages of 30 million hard-pressed American workers. Had you pushed to raise the federal minimum wage in 2010 when the Democrats controlled Congress, the House of Representatives might not have been given over to the Republican Party in those November elections. In light of this missed opportunity, you can still pressure Speaker John Boehner and House Republicans to support raising the federal minimum wage by noting that Mitt Romney, Rick Santorum and former Republican Governor of Minnesota, Tim Pawlenty, now support this effort.

Affected workers need you to step up the pressure in the remaining months of this forlorn Congress and get an existing discharge petition to the House floor for a vote.

Second, U.S.-chartered giant companies like Pfizer, Medtronic and, perhaps most foolishly, Walgreens—given its 8,000 protestable stores—are planning to move their headquarters to countries that lure them with lower tax rates, such as Ireland and Switzerland, abandon their U.S. "citizenship," and reincorporate in those jurisdictions. This is all for another tax escape to add to their existing ones, including large tax credits to Pfizer and Medtronic for research and development that corporatist lobbies have written into the U.S. tax code.

"I don't care if it's legal, it's wrong," you have indignantly exclaimed in recent speeches. You are supporting legislative efforts by Democrats in Congress (H.R.4679 and S.2360, sponsored by Representative Sander Levin (D-MI) and Senator Carl Levin (D-MI)) to prohibit such drains on corporate taxes intended for the U.S. Treasury and make the ban retroactive to May 2014.

Third, and perhaps most impressively, you are questioning the "economic patriotism" of many giant U.S. corporations who have received support (financial and otherwise) from U.S. workers, taxpayers and the public laws and benefitted from the infrastructure of our country. The mere implication that these companies are unpatriotically abandoning their native country has outraged the U.S. Chamber of Commerce (to which you paid a courtesy visit in 2011) along with the predictable *Wall Street Journal* editorial page.*

That highly vocal reaction means you touched on a vulnerability that has been on the minds of tens of millions of

---

* See http://www.wsj.com/articles/jack-lews-flee-america-plan-1405553160 for the full article.

Americans. May you continue to promote the importance of insisting on the patriotic character of corporations, since the U.S. Supreme Court (5 to 4) keeps telling us that corporations are people.

The public sentiment awaits your leadership on other positive redirections as well. Large majorities on both the Left and the Right: favor breaking up the "too big to fail" New York City banks; support cracking down on corporate crime and fraud (see the Hide No Harm Act of 2014); and, the more they know about its benefits and fairness, support a Wall Street speculation tax, a sales tax that could bring in about $300 billion a year, fund repairs of our public infrastructure, and dampen some of the reckless gambling with other people's money, such as pension and mutual funds.*

The many rallies in New York City, in front of the White House and around the country—some of which have been led by the National Nurses United†—are pressing Congress for such a transaction tax. Such activities have laid the groundwork for your exercise of the "bully pulpit."

Another easier initiative, pointed out in my new book, *Unstoppable: The Emerging Left-Right Alliance to Dismantle the Corporate State*, is to highlight, once again, the legislation that you as a Senator cosponsored with Senator Tom Coburn (R-OK) in 2006 to require that the *full text* of all federal government contracts above a minimum amount be available online.

As I've written previously,‡ putting the full text of these contracts online will: give taxpayers both savings and higher quality performances; let the media focus more incisively on this vast area of government disbursements to inform the wider public; encourage constructive comments and alarms from

---

* See http://ellison.house.gov/the-inclusive-prosperity-act for more details.

† See http://www.robinhoodtax.org/ for more information.

‡ See http://www.huffingtonpost.com/ralph-nader/government-secrecy_b_5036280.html for previous column.

the citizenry; and stimulate legal and economic research by scholars interested in structural topics related to government procurement, transfers, subsidies and giveaways.

There is already support by members of both parties in the Congress for this measure. Online disclosure would provide for greater scrutiny of some $300 billion in annual contracts by the media, taxpayer groups, competitors and academic researchers.

Yes, indeed, Mr. President, wondrous and beneficial changes can come to our country when you and Congress heed the long-standing "public sentiment," more recently called the "voices of the people," and translate that "public sentiment" into beneficial action by our government.

Sincerely,

[signature]

The Moral Authority to Govern

Dear President Obama,

The moral authority to govern is an intangible, but very real, characteristic, especially in times of harsh public events. It stems significantly from one setting an example.

You have impaired that moral authority in three areas. First, were you to tell other countries not to engage in unlawful hostilities against other people, they would respond that you have used armed force and other interventions against countries and people in ways that violate our Constitution, federal statutes, the Geneva Conventions and the U.N. Charter. Certainly that is what even your ally Israel, would cite were you to criticize and sanction their war crimes against the people of Palestine year after year, including the use of U.S.-supplied weapons for "offensive" purposes banned by federal law.

Second, from the moment in 2008 when you opted out of the federal check-off funding of post-primary presidential campaigns and raised vastly more money from donors on Wall Street, other well-to-do donors, and the Internet, your credibility regarding campaign finance reform has been diminished. This explains in part why such reform has been low on your priorities list. "Do as I say, not as I do" doesn't sound very authentic.

Third, on Thursday, July 17, 2014, two tragedies occurred. The Malaysian Boeing 777 passenger plane was shot down over southeast Ukraine, and the Israeli army, with the support of the Israeli air force, commenced a ground invasion in Palestinian Gaza. That day you were conducting two fundraisers with wealthy donors outside of Washington. Rushing to adjust back to your presidential duties didn't counter the negative imagery.

For someone who does not exactly have a Jim Farley type of personality, you certainly go to a lot of exclusive, political fundraisers all around the country. This allocation of your time is not only an unsavory distraction from your presidential responsibilities, but it comes at an opportunity cost for other types of public interest and charitable groups whose gatherings would like to hear your timely remarks. Have you or your associates ever thought of having Internet fundraisers with large numbers of people contributing smaller amounts and absorbing less of your time and that of your entourage going in and out of traffic to and from the destinations?

Unrelated to any moral authority to govern, you can, at the very least, immediately launch, with other nations, efforts to provide emergency assistance to help alleviate the humanitarian crisis presently afflicting Gazan children, women and men deprived of food, water, shelter, and medicine. They are besieged, defenseless, impoverished, and in dire circumstances.

Sincerely,

JUNE 2, 2014

Michelle: Stand Your Ground on Childhood Nutrition

Dear First Lady Michelle Obama,

One of the brightest activities to come out of the White House since January 2009 has been your visible work favoring nutritious food, nutritious gardening, and the need to reduce harmful obesity, especially among children.

As you know so well, this is an uphill struggle because of decades of the food industry saturating the taste buds of youngsters with excessive, addictive sugar, fat, and salt, leading many to a lifetime of bad food consumption.

The success of your and others' initiatives to have school lunch programs reflect nutritious and, where possible, fresh food for the children of our country, has become too much for the junk food and juice drink lobbies and their indentured, funded intermediaries. They are generating a backlash using middle-school children's rejectionist behavior as their too-facile argument.

To their above maneuvers, I have two recommendations. All nutritious food can be prepared with delicious recipes. My mother proved this point again and again, adding that fresh food has better natural flavors than the chemically doused stuff exuding from the food processing factories. Indeed, one school district, noted in the current press accounts, made this very point as evidence of their success in acceptance by the pupils.

Second, please stand your ground! For to concede waivers is to concede the regressive deterioration of what you believe to be best for the children, even those youngsters who do not

THE WHITE HOUSE

October 2, 2014

Mr. Ralph Nader
Washington, D.C.

Dear Mr. Nader:

Thank you for your support. It has been truly incredible to hear from leaders like you who are invested in ensuring our Nation moves in a healthier direction.

Since we launched *Let's Move!* in 2010, we have seen great progress in our efforts to raise a healthier generation of kids. The Healthy Hunger-Free Kids Act of 2010 is one of the achievements that makes me most proud. The passing of this bill was a big win for parents who are working hard to serve their kids balanced meals at home and don't want their efforts undermined during the day at school.

We are at a pivotal moment—new habits are beginning to take hold, and we are seeing a transformational change to a healthier new norm for children all across our country. We know change is hard, but if we keep pushing forward, we have the potential to transform the health of an entire generation of young people. I am hopeful that these changes in school lunches, snacks, and the overall school health environment will continue to strengthen, and kids across our country will grow up only ever knowing school environments that support good health and academic success.

Our strength as a Nation and our ability to responsibly shape our future depends upon tackling this issue, and I hope you continue to advocate for this important cause. Thank you again, Mr. Nader, and I wish you all the best.

Sincerely,

Michelle Obama

know what is best for them, having been turned into Pavlovian responders by cruelly clever corporate marketeers undermining parental authority.

I welcome your reaction "in the nation's service."

Sincerely,

MARCH 21, 2014
People Who Live in Glass Houses . . .

Dear President Obama,

As you ponder your potential moves regarding President Vladimir V. Putin's annexation of Crimea (a large majority of its 2 million people are ethnic Russians), it is important to remember that whatever moral leverage you may have had in the court of world opinion has been sacrificed by the precedents set by previous American presidents who did not do what you say Mr. Putin *should do*—obey international law.

The need to abide by international law is your recent recurring refrain, often used in an accusatory context toward Mr. Putin's military entry in Crimea and its subsequent annexation, following a referendum in which Crimean voters overwhelmingly endorsed rejoining Russia. True, most Ukrainians and ethnic Tatars boycotted the referendum and there were obstacles to free speech. But even the fairest of referendums, under U.N. auspices, would have produced majority support for Russia's annexation.

Every day, presidential actions by you violate international law because they infringe upon national sovereignties with deadly drones, flyovers, and secret forays by soldiers—to name the most obvious.

President Bush's criminal invasion and devastation of Iraq in 2003 violated international law and treaties initiated and signed by the United States (such as the Geneva Conventions and the U.N. Charter). What about your executive branch's war on Libya, now still in chaos, which was neither constitutionally declared, nor authorized by congressional appropriations?

"Do as I say, not as I do" is hard to sell to Russians who are interpreting your words of protest as disingenuous. This is especially the case because Crimea, long under the rule of the Ottoman Empire, became part of Russia over 200 years ago. In 1954, Soviet leader, Nikita Khrushchev gave Crimea to Ukraine, which was then part of the Soviet Union, out of sympathy for what Ukraine endured under the Nazi invasion and its atrocities. It mattered little then because both "socialist republics," Ukraine and Crimea, were part of the Soviet Union. However, it is not entirely clear whether Khrushchev fully complied with the Soviet constitution when he transferred Crimea to Ukraine.

Compare, by the way, the United States' seizure of Guantanamo from Cuba initially after the Spanish-American War, which was then retained after Cuba became independent over a century ago.

The Russians have their own troubles, of course, but they do have a legitimate complaint and fear about the United States' actions following the collapse of the Soviet Union. Led by President William Jefferson Clinton, the United States pushed for the expansion of the military alliance NATO to include the newly independent Eastern European countries. This was partly a business deal to get these countries to buy United States fighter aircrafts from Lockheed Martin and partly a needless provocation of a transformed adversary trying to get back on its feet.

As a student of Russian history and language at Princeton, I learned about the deep sensitivity of the Russian people regarding the insecurity of their Western Front. Hitler's attack on the Soviet Union took many millions of Russian lives. The prolonged Nazi siege of the city of Leningrad alone is estimated to have cost over 700,000 civilian lives, which is about twice the total number of U.S. soldiers killed in World War II.

The memories of that mass slaughter and destruction, and of other massacres and valiant resistance are etched deeply in Russian minds. The NATO provocation was only one of the West's arrogant treatments of post-Soviet Russia, pointed out in the writings of Russian specialist and NYU professor Stephen Cohen (see his pieces in *The Nation* for more information). That sense of disrespect, coupled with the toppling of the elected pro-Russian President of Ukraine in February 2014 (which was not lawful despite his poor record), is why Mr. Putin's absorption of Crimea and his history-evoking speech before the Parliament was met with massive support in Russia, even by many of those who have good reason to not like his authoritarian government.

Now, you are facing the question of how far to go with sanctions against the Russian government, its economy and its ruling class. Welcome to globalization.

Russia is tightly intertwined with the European Union, as a seller and buyer of goods, services, and assets, and to a lesser but significant degree with the United States government and its giant corporations such as oil and technology companies. Sanctions can boomerang, which would be far worse than just being completely ineffective in reversing the Russian annexation of Crimea.

As for sanctions deterring any unlikely future Russian moves westward into Ukraine, consider the following role reversal. If Russia moved for sanctions against the United States before Afghanistan, Iraq, Libya, Yemen, and other attacks, would that have deterred either you or George W. Bush from taking such actions? Of course not. Such an outcome, politically and domestically, would not be possible.

If you want continued Russian cooperation, as you do, on the critical Iranian and Syrian negotiations, ignore the belligerent baying pack of neocons who always want more U.S. wars, which they and their adult children avoid fighting themselves. Develop a coalition of economic support for Ukraine, with European nations, based on observable reforms of that troubled government. Sponsor a global conference on how to enforce international law as early as possible.

Drop the nonsense of evicting Russia from the G8—a get-together forum of leaders. Get on with having the United States comply with international law, and our Constitution on the way to ending the American Empire's interventions worldwide, as has been recommended by both liberal and conservative/libertarian lawmakers, and enjoys broad public support.

Concentrate on America, President Obama, whose long unmet necessities cry out from "sea to shining sea."

Sincerely,

[signature: Ralph Nader]

FEBRUARY 19, 2014
Convene on Climate Change!

Dear President Obama,
On February 14, 2014, you announced in California that

you will include a $1 billion fund in the proposed fiscal 2015 budget to: (1) assist communities in preparing for the impacts of climate change; and (2) fund research and technology to protect against such damage.

I am sure you do not believe this is enough. But you are dealing with a Congress that annually budgets $9 billion for a boondoggle missile defense project which has been severely criticized on technical grounds by leading authorities such as MIT professor Theodore Postol.*

Federal policies and programs to diminish and anticipate man-made climate change have largely stalled. Congress is in such a state of stasis that, other than one-minute floor statements, it seems to be in a collective state of denial, with the deniers being the aggressors in daunting active pressure by those who are alarmed but have placed their concerns on the shelf. This has been the trend since the House Democrats passed H.R. 2454, the American Clean Energy and Security Act of 2009, only to see it blocked by the minority Republicans in the Senate.

I have written a column† which suggests the need for affluent leaders of the movement to reduce greenhouse gases to step up and establish a powerful advocacy presence on Capitol Hill, member by member. Congress has been allowed to remain in a bubble, while grassroots climate change actions occur back in the districts, but without laser beam focus on the 535 legislators who are the gatekeepers for any national energy conversion program commensurate with the peril.

There is an important presidential convening function that you may wish to consider. Bring together for a day several leading scientists who have documented man-based climate change with several leading CEOs of energy companies who are deniers and/or are opposing public policies and programs

---

* See http://web.mit.edu/stgs/ for more information.

† See https://blog.nader.org/2014/02/07/climate-disasters-ending-congressional-stupor-now/ for more information.

designed to curb or replace fossil fuel contributions to climate change. Have the latter listen to the former and then engage in an exchange of responses and questions. The subject is what action is needed to reduce the future peril of tumultuous climate change on the planet, humankind, flora, and fauna. During the State of the Union Address last month, you declared "climate change is a fact."

After the conclusion of the meeting, a verbatim transcript could be released promptly for the media and the public.

The importance and uniqueness of such a gathering are obvious. It has never happened before. Only the President of the United States can make it happen. At a minimum, it will certainly broaden the public debate and the interested public audience on a major threat to the planet that receives less media attention by far than the games played by NFL teams or your favorite NBA teams.

Please consider this initiative for its many beneficial consequences.

Sincerely,

[signature]

JANUARY 16, 2014
Awaiting Three Speeches

Dear President Obama,

All the daily decisions and crises you have to confront must not preclude occasional addresses to the country that rise to the level of statesmanship, transcending the hurly-burly of politics and executive branch administration.

There are three areas where the people need the views and vision of their president.

A major address on the resources and preconditions necessary for the government to wage peace as a continual policy of statecraft and not just sporadic initiatives between waging war or engaging in other violent conflicts. Consider the enormous disparity of time, power, and money allocated to preparing for or waging military assaults with what is devoted to prevention of conflict and other fundamentals of securing the conditions for peace. The tiny U.S. budgets for nuclear, chemical, and biological arms control with the Soviet Union and other nations over the years have certainly produced positive returns of incalculable magnitude and importance.

We have military academies, but no peace academies. Vast sums are allocated for research and teaching about war and military tactics, but very little for peace studies at our schools and universities. You may wish to meet with former *Washington Post* columnist Colman McCarthy who teaches peace in the Washington, D.C.–area schools and has written pioneering books and articles that include his compelling arguments for having peace studies adopted in high schools and colleges around the country.*

In 2009 and again in 2011, I wrote to urge you to address a large gathering, in a convenient Washington venue, for the leaders of nonprofit civic organizations with tens of millions of members throughout the United States. Not receiving a reply, I sent my request to First Lady Michelle Obama, whose assistant replied saying you were too busy.

You were, however, not too busy to address many business groups and also to walk over to the oppositional U.S. Chamber of Commerce. Well, it is the second term and such a civic gathering could be scheduled at your convenience. You could use this

---

* See http://www.salsa.net/peace/conv/ for more information.

occasion to make a major speech on the importance and means of advancing the quality and quantity of civic groups and their chapters which, taken together, are major employers. Your advisors could even justify the effort as stimulating a jobs program by urging larger charitable contributions from the trillions of dollars of inert money in the hands of the upper economic classes.

Strengthening democratic processes and expanding democratic institutions and participation by the people are cardinal functions of the presidency. Indeed, Harvard Law Professor Richard Parker in his little, seminal book *Here, the People Rule* (Harvard University Press, 1994) argues that the Constitution authorizes the president "to facilitate the political and civic energies of the people."

A major address on this topic should be right up your experiential alley from both your early experience in Chicago of observing and confronting the power structure's many forms of exclusion and mistreatment of the populace and your more recent accommodation to that power structure and its influence over Congress.

As has been said, democracy is not a spectator sport. It requires a motivated citizenry, along with rights, remedies, and mechanisms that facilitate people banding together as candidates, voters, workers, taxpayers, consumers and communities. Concentration of power and wealth in the hands of the few who decide for the many is the great destroyer of any society's democratic functions. It was Justice Louis Brandeis who memorably stated that "we can either have democracy in this country or we can have great wealth concentrated in the hands of a few, but we can't have both." And another well-regarded jurist, Judge Learned Hand, declared, "If we are to keep our democracy, there must be one commandment: Thou shalt not ration justice."

As "politics" is seen by more people as a dirty word and as the people move from cynicism about political institutions to greater withdrawal from them (including public meetings, primaries, elections, and referenda), they need a president who addresses these disabling symptoms of a weakening democratic society from the local to the state to the national levels of our political economy.

Such an address will have positive reverberations beyond the general public. Depending on your scope, recommendations, and announcements, it will reach the youth of our country, our high schools, universities, workplaces, and professional schools. Why, it may even affect the moribund, technical routines of the *Harvard Law Review* (where you were resident in 1990) as well as other law schools, bar associations, and lawyers who aspire to higher estimates of their own professional significance (see my remarks "The Majesty of the Law Needs Magisterial Lawyers"* before the Connecticut Bar Association on June 17, 2013). If law means justice, as it should, then the rule of law needs presidential refurbishing to strengthen the fiber of our democracy.

I hope you will see the merit of these three suggestions. A copy of this letter is being sent to First Lady Michelle Obama, whose staff may be responsive in a different manner.

I look forward to your reaction.

Sincerely,

cc: First Lady Michelle Obama

---

* See https://blog.nader.org/2013/06/18/the-majesty-of-the-law-needs-magisterial-lawyers/ for more information.

The State of the Wages

Dear President Obama,

At last you are regularly speaking out about the need to raise the federal minimum wage, upping your 2008 proposal of $9.50 by 2011, now obsolete, and now moving to the level of $10.10 per hour to take effect over three years. That, at least, conforms your stance with that of Rep. George Miller and Senator Tom Harkin from your earlier proposal last year of $9.00 per hour over three years.

You may know that both Messrs. Miller and Harkin have publicly stated that the minimum wage should be even higher. Your determined willpower will be critical in overwhelming the likely Republican intransigence and to galvanize your steady-state congressional Democrats.

By the time $10.10 is reached, sometime in 2017 at best, it will be substantially behind the federal minimum wage of 1968, inflation-adjusted. The 1968 value, adjusted for inflation, will be $11.64 by 2017. If $10.10 is reached by 2017 and indexed to inflation, then it will be locked in at a value of $9.48 in real 2014 dollars, about $1.54 short of the 1968 real level.

In your State of the Union address before Congress, thirty million American workers, among others, want to hear you propose a higher minimum wage, reflecting the doubling of worker productivity since the nineteen-sixties along with inflation adjustments. They would respond well to your declaring that the taxpayers should not be subsidizing Walmart, Target, McDonald's, and other very profitable corporations paying their workers so little that they have to go on public assistance—food stamps, housing assistance, and Medicaid. Some corporate employers actually advise their low-wage employees on the procedures to obtain public assistance!

Outgoing CEO Mike Duke of Walmart, making $11,000 an hour, plus benefits, and CEO Gregg W. Steinhafel of Target, making $14,000 an hour, plus benefits, should be ashamed of themselves for underpaying their workers and steering them toward public assistance. You have often praised corporate executives. How about publicly challenging men like Mike Duke and Gregg Steinhafel to share some of their wealth with their deserving workers? They have earned these long-denied wage-inflation adjustments. You may compare them with CEO W. Craig Jelinek of Costco, which starts its entry-level workers at $11.50 per hour, plus benefits. Mr. Jelinek told me higher wages increase worker productivity, reduce absenteeism, reduce turnovers, and are "the right thing to do."

Let's hear it from the erstwhile "community organizer" in the well of the House of Representatives on January 28, 2014, in no uncertain terms. I'll bet it will make Gene Sperling's day.

Sincerely,

DECEMBER 20, 2013
Santa's One Wish to President Obama

The following poem was read by an activist involved in Ralph Nader's "Time for a Raise Campaign" as part of protest in front of the White House on December 18, 2013.

'Twas two weeks before Christmas: at the Senate and House,
No lawmaker was stirring, nor clicking their mouse.

Their bags are all packed for the recess with care.
We've hoped for some progress, but they've passed
   nothing there.
While congressmen nestle all snug in the beds
Of industry hacks and Fox News talking heads,
The workers who toil on minimum wage
are hurting . . . so Santa's becoming enraged!
Minimum wages have steeply declined!
From their peak at $10.70,* we've fallen behind.
You can't survive on annual $15K!
Why lose tax dough to welfare when Walmart can pay?
With Boehner! And Cantor! McConnell and Hannity . . .
Gumming up steps towards minimum wage sanity;
Ignoring workers and stirring up drama . . .
. . . Our only hope now is some help from Obama!
The president cannot pass laws in a day,
But can issue executive orders that say
That jobs which are based on contracts with the fed
Have raises in wages or those contracts are dead!
It would help set the stage up on Capitol Hill
For a too-long-awaited minimum wage bill
I know you will listen—Santa's an optimist—
To this one item on Santa's Christmas wish list
"Mr. O! if you take your executive ink
And put it to paper; 2 million on the brink
Would be helped by a much-needed, much-deserved raise
And you would have all of the North Pole's praise!"

---

*   inflation-adjusted

Justice for Nabila

Dear President Obama,

We strongly urge you to compose a letter of remorse, including an offer of compensation, to 9-year-old Nabila ur Rehman. She is a surviving grandchild of the 68-year-old Pakistani grandmother who was reduced to a grisly corpse by a drone strike you ordered last year. No claim or evidence has surfaced indicating the slain grandmother was mistaken for a jihadist or circulating among them.

The details of the apparent murder were related by the 9-year-old child recently in a congressional hearing hosted by Representative Alan Grayson (D-FL): "It was the day before Eid. My grandmother asked me to come help her outside. We were collecting okra, the vegetables. Then I saw in the sky the drone and I heard a 'dum dum' noise. Everything was dark and I couldn't see anything, but I heard a scream. I don't know if it was my grandmother, but I couldn't see her. I was very scared and all I could think of doing was just run. I kept running but I felt something in my hand. And I looked at my hand. There was blood. I tried to bandage my hand, but the blood kept coming."

Speaking as American citizens, we are ashamed of what was done to that grandmother and granddaughter and what continues to be done to innocents. Silence would make us morally complicit in the cruelty that found expression in the grandmother's killing. It would be no defense to echo the inelegant remark of a former secretary of defense: "[S]tuff happens."

Playing prosecutor, judge, jury, and executioner in secret to destroy individuals abroad on your say-so alone is fueling enmity against the United States that endangers us all—another example of blowback reminiscent of the birth of al-Qaeda from our participation in the disintegration of Afghanistan. Malala Yousafzai, a 16-year-old Pakistani heroine and Nobel Peace Prize nominee, recently informed you at the White House that "drone attacks are fueling terrorism. Innocent victims are killed in these acts, and they lead to resentment among the Pakistani people."

Your chief of staff in 2011, William M. Daley, has related his internal doubts about the effectiveness of drone killings in defeating international terrorism:

"One guy gets knocked off, and the guy's driver, who's No. 21, becomes 20? At what point are you just filling the bucket with numbers?"

We also urge you to cease all use of predator drones except during times of legal wars in areas of actual hostilities against the United States. International law, justice, and the safety of American citizens all militate in favor of such an enlightened policy.

Coupled with a contrite letter and commensurate compensation from the United States to 9-year-old Nabila and her family, these measures would be a commendable mark of simple moral decency in the presidency.

Sincerely,

Ralph Nader

Bruce Fein

Alan Grayson, Member of Congress

OCTOBER 7, 2013
Office of Non-correspondence

Dear President Obama,

In previous correspondence I have taken note of the remarkably consistent practice by the White House of neither responding (whether by you or your staff) to substantive letters on pending or proposed public policies nor even providing the courtesy of acknowledging receipt. In 2009, I had a telephone conversation with Mr. Mike Kelleher, who was in charge of handling letters to the president. He recognized that you did not have any policy about when and if you or White House staff would respond or even acknowledge the receipt of substantive letters. He said that he would get back to me were such a policy established. He never did.

This official discourtesy by the White House was not always the case. President Carter and his staff were often responsive. But as the years wore on, presidents became less and less responsive until George W. Bush and you closed the door. I know of no person sending you a policy letter, either critical or suggestive, who has received either a response or acknowledgement.

By contrast, I am enclosing two letters sent to me by A. Opalick and M. Bourque, the Executive Correspondence Officers of Canadian Prime Minister Stephen Harper. My letters raised factual concerns about the Prime Minister's urging of Verizon to enter the Canadian telecommunications market. Note both the acknowledgement and the referrals to the proper Minister. Isn't this something you can emulate— making citizens at least know that their substantive letters were received and were sent to the proper government department after possibly being read by White House staff?

I look forward to your response or that of your staff.

Sincerely,

[signature]

ENCLOSURE 1: AUGUST 26, 2013:
LETTER FROM A. OPALICK

Dear Mr. Nader,

I would like to acknowledge receipt of your correspondence of August 21 addressed to the Prime Minister regarding Verizon Telecommunications.

Please be assured that your comments have been carefully reviewed. I have taken the liberty of forwarding a copy of your letter to the Honourable James Moore, Minister of Industry. I am certain that the Minister will appreciate being made aware of your interest in this matter and will wish to give your views every consideration.

Thank you for writing to the Prime Minister.

Yours sincerely,

A. Opalick
Executive Correspondence Officer

ENCLOSURE 2: SEPTEMBER 12, 2013:
LETTER FROM M. BOURQUE

Dear Mr. Nader,

I would like to acknowledge receipt of your correspondence of September 3, addressed to the Prime Minister, regarding statements made by Verizon CEO

Lowell McAdam in response to your letter dated August 21.

You may be assured that your comments have been carefully reviewed. A copy of your correspondence has been forwarded to the Honourable James Moore, Minister of Industry, for his information.

Thank you for writing to the Prime Minister.

Yours Sincerely,

M. Bourque

Executive Correspondence Officer

SEPTEMBER 6, 2013

Barry O'Bomber and the Rush to War

Dear President Obama,

Little did your school boy chums in Hawaii know, watching you race up and down the basketball court, how prescient they were when they nicknamed you "Barry O'Bomber."

Little did your fellow *Harvard Law Review* editors, who elected you to lead that venerable journal, ever imagine that you could be a president who chronically violates the Constitution, federal statutes, international treaties and the separation of power at depths equal to or beyond the George W. Bush regime.

Nor would many of the voters who elected you in 2008 have conceived that your foreign policy would rely so much on brute military force at the expense of systemically waging peace. Certainly, voters who knew your background as a child of Third World countries, a community organizer, a scholar of constitutional law and a critic of the Bush/Cheney years, never would have expected you to favor the giant warfare state so pleasing to the military-industrial complex.

Now, as if having learned nothing from the devastating and costly aftermaths of the military invasions of Iraq, Afghanistan, and Libya, you're beating the combustible drums to attack Syria—a country that is no threat to the U.S. and is embroiled in complex civil wars under a brutal regime.

This time, however, you may have pushed for too many acts of war. Public opinion and sizable numbers of members of both parties in Congress are opposed. These lawmakers oppose bombing Syria in spite of your corralling the cowardly leaders of both parties in the Congress.

Thus far, your chief achievement on the Syrian front has been support for your position from al-Qaeda affiliates fighting in Syria, the pro-Israeli government lobby, AIPAC, your chief nemesis in Congress, House Speaker John Boehner, and Dick Cheney. This is quite a gathering and a telling commentary on your ecumenical talents. Assuming the veracity of your declarations regarding the regime's resort to chemical warfare (first introduced into the Middle East by Winston Churchill's Royal Air Force's plastering of Iraqi tribesmen in the nineteen-twenties), your motley support group is oblivious to the uncontrollable consequences that might stem from bombing Syria. One domestic consequence may be that Speaker Boehner expects to exact concessions from you on domestic issues before Congress in return for giving you such high visibility bipartisan cover.

Your argument for shelling Syria is to maintain "international credibility" in drawing that "red line" regardless, it seems, of the loss of innocent Syrian civilian life, casualties to our foreign service and armed forces in that wider region, and retaliation against the fearful Christian population in Syria (one in seven Syrians are Christian). But the more fundamental credibilities are to our Constitution, to the neglected necessities of the American people, and to the red line of observing international law and the U.N. Charter (which prohibit unilateral bombing in this situation).

There is another burgeoning cost—that of the militarization of the State Department whose original charter invests it with the responsibility of diplomacy. Instead, Mr. Obama, you have shaped the State Department into a belligerent "force projector" first under Generalissima Clinton and now under Generalissimo Kerry. The sidelined foreign service officers, who have knowledge and conflict avoidance experience, are left with reinforced fortress-like embassies as befits our empire reputation abroad.

Secretary John Kerry descended to gibberish when, under questioning this week by a House Committee member, he asserted that your proposed attack was "not war" because there would be "no boots on the ground." In Kerry's view, bombing a country with missiles and air force bombers is not an act of war.

It is instructive to note how government autocracy feeds on itself. Start with unjustified government secrecy garnished by the words "national security." That leads to secret laws, secret evidence, secret courts, secret prisons, secret prisoners, secret relationships with selected members of Congress, denial of standing for any citizen to file suit, secret drone strikes, secret incursions into other nations and all this directed by a president who alone decides when to be secret prosecutor, judge, jury, and executioner. What a republic, what a democracy, what a passive people we have become!

Voices of reason and experience have urged the proper path away from the metastasizing war that is plaguing Syria. As proposed by former President Jimmy Carter, U.N. Secretary-General Ban Ki-moon, and other seasoned diplomats and retired military, vigorous leadership by you is needed for an international peace conference with all parties at the table, including the countries supplying weapons to the various adversaries in Syria.

Mr. Obama, you may benefit from reading the writings of Colman McCarthy, a leading advocate of peace studies in our schools and universities. He gives numerous examples of how waging peace avoided war and civil strife over the past 100 years.

Crowding out attention to America's serious domestic problems by yet another military adventure (opposed by many military officials), yet another attack on another small, non-threatening Muslim country by a powerful Christian nation (as many Muslims see it) is aggression camouflaging sheer madness.

Please, before you recklessly flout Congress, absorb the wisdom of the World Peace Foundation's Alex de Waal and Bridget Conley-Zilkic. Writing in the *New York Times*, they strongly condemn the use of nerve gas in Syria, brand the perpetrators as war criminals to be tried by an international war crimes tribunal and then declare:

"But it is folly to think that airstrikes can be limited: they are ill-conceived as punishment, fail to protect civilians and, most important, hinder peacemaking . . . . Punishment, protection and peace must be joined . . . An American assault on Syria would be an act of desperation with incalculable consequences. To borrow once more from Sir William Harcourt [the British parliamentarian who argued against British intervention in our Civil War (which cost 750,000 American lives)]: 'We are asked to go we know not whither, in order to do we know not what.'"

If and when the people and Congress turn you down this month, there will be one silver lining. Only a Left-Right coalition can stop this warring. Such convergence is

strengthening monthly in the House of Representatives to stop
future war crimes and the injurious blowback against America
of the wreckages from empire.

History teaches that empires always devour themselves.
Sincerely,

AUGUST 30, 2013
The Constitutional Authority to Wage War

Dear President Obama,

Before you decide to attack Syria, yet another Arab or
Islamic country that does not threaten U.S. security, there
are certain constitutional "niceties" that you should observe.
Chronically violating the Constitution overturns the rule of law
and can produce costly blowbacks.

On August 28, you stated that bombing Syria "is not about
war, it's about accountability," obviously referring to the brutal
gassing of neighborhoods outside of Damascus. What about your
accountability to receive authorization from Congress which,
under Article 1, Section 8 has the sole and exclusive power to
declare war? Spare Americans the casuistry of your lawyers who
"legalized" your war on Libya, with no declaration, authorization
or appropriation of funds from Congress, and pushed the envelope
of the "unitary presidency" beyond the unlawful and brazen
extremes advocated by George W. Bush and his lawyers.

Nearly 200 members of both parties of Congress—now
on its August recess—demanded there be no attack on Syria
without congressional authorization. These signers have so

far included 72 Democrats. Merely secretly consulting with some lawmakers on the Intelligence Committees does not substitute for formal congressional authorization. The framers of our Constitution—whatever their other differences—were unanimous in writing Article 1, Section 8 so that no president could go to war on his own. To do so, as you have already done in the past, would be a major impeachable offense.

The media have reported that your lawyers are searching for legal justification for Tomahawk missiling Syria. They need look no more—the Constitution clearly rests the power to engage in war with Congress and Congress only. You cannot start another war! You cannot continue to be the prosecutor, judge, jury, and executioner anywhere and at any time.

You may think the foregoing overly cautious or a mere formality. But the framers held the war-making power in Congress for another reason than just thwarting a latter-day King George III tyranny. They wanted a deliberative open process to avoid reckless presidential decisions that were bad for our country and produced entanglements with warring foreign nations. Remember George Washington's farewell address on this point—truer today than in his day.

Remember what the nearly 200 members of Congress said to you—"engaging our military in Syria with no direct threat to the United States and without prior congressional authorization would violate the separation of powers that is clearly delineated in the Constitution." Congressional deliberations would ask the following questions in the open:

1. Assuming the veracity of the regime as the cause, how could a U.S. attack not make a horrible situation even more horrible, both inside Syria and in the volatile region?

2. Why are so many in the U.S. military—though they defer to civilian authority—privately opposed to such an

action? Could it be due to the lack of any strategic purpose and the violent plethora of uncontrollable consequences? See the oppositional stands, reported in the August 30th *Washington Post*, "from captains to a four-star general."

3. How are you going to avoid the kind of awful continual civilian casualties that were produced in the first Iraq war in 1991? U.S. bombings broke chemical warfare containers and led to sickness (called the Gulf War Syndrome) for tens of thousands of U.S. soldiers—many continue to suffer to this day.

4. How are you going to deal with the overwhelming majority of Muslims in the Middle East and at least 70 percent of Americans here who are opposed to you bombing Syria? Do you think that lack of domestic public support and even deeper hatred abroad are inconsequential? Your empire mentality seems to say yes.

One would think that House Speaker John Boehner (R-OH), of all people, who just sent you a detailed letter of inquiry and caution, citing congressional authority, should give you pause. Increasingly, you are coming across, even to your hardcore political supporters, as impulsively aggressive, too quick to order killing operations and too slow to contemplate waging of peace.

The Syrian civil war—riven by fighting rebel factions, sectarian revenge cycles, outside arms suppliers and provocations, and a spreading al-Qaeda force fighting the dictatorial Assad regime—can only get worse following a violent attack by your administration.

Listen to Hans Blix, the former United Nations head of the weapons inspection team in Iraq during 2002–2003 that was aborted by George W. Bush's criminal invasion that led to the continuing loss of over a million Iraqis and many more injuries, the lives of five thousand U.S. soldiers and tens of thousands of injured Americans.

Mr. Blix, former Swedish Minister for Foreign Affairs, urges an international peace conference under the U.N. Security Council's auspices attended by all governments supporting the various sides in Syria's civil war. Since all fighters in Syria are receiving their weapons from outside nations, these "supplier countries have leverage," Blix writes, to support the demand "that their clients accept a ceasefire—or risk losing further support."

Achieving this goal will require strong leadership. While it is difficult for you to move from waging war to waging peace, history documents that the latter brings better outcomes and forestalls worse slaughter and blowbacks that security experts fear could reach our country.

When your own military believes you are moving into dangerous terrain and possible points of no return, you'd better start to rethink. You'd better reread the warnings in the measured memoranda given to you by Secretary of Defense, Chuck Hagel, and the chairman of the Joint Chiefs of Staff, General Martin Dempsey.

More publicly, retired Lt. Gen. Gregory S. Newbold, who directed operations for the Joint Chiefs during the run-up to the Iraq War, told the *Washington Post*: "There's a broad naiveté in the political class about America's obligations in foreign policy issues, and scary simplicity about the effects that employing American military power can achieve." He said that many of his fellow officers share his views.

General Newbold's words seem like a rebuke not just to the Bush Neocons (pro–Vietnam War draft dodgers) who pushed the Iraq invasion, but also to you and your immediate circle of hawkish civilian advisors.

All weapons of violence—chemical, biological, nuclear, drones, conventional munitions—are used to destroy lives and habitats. The fact that using some weapons constitutes international war crimes per se is hardly consoling to the victims of other mass weapons systems.

Aggressive arms controls should be the priority of the leading superpower in the world. Why haven't you made U.S. ratification of the small arms, the land mines, and the cluster munitions treaties, adhered to by most nations, a priority?

Before you violently embroil our country in yet another Middle Eastern country's tragic turmoil, visit the government-supported U.S. Institute of Peace for intensive tutorials. Then read again Article 1, Section 8 and its originating history, which says that going to war is not your decision but the *exclusive decision of the Congress*. That may help you accept the imperative of your moral and legal accountability.

Sincerely,

JULY 9, 2013
Help 30 Million Workers Catch Up with 1968!

Dear President Obama,

Ever since your ringing announcement that you favor lifting the federal minimum wage from its frozen $7.25 per hour to $9.00 in your State of the Union Address on February 12, 2013, there has been little effort from the White House to push for this important measure. To be sure, going down to $9.00 compares unfavorably with your 2008 campaign platform which favored $9.50 by 2011. Yet, with thirty million workers in our country making less today than workers made in 1968, inflation-adjusted, it is a shameful situation. The 1968 inflation-adjusted minimum wage would now be $10.70. Is catching up to 1968 too ambitious a White House position?

You can make a $10.50 federal minimum wage, expressed by Rep. Alan Grayson's bill H.R. 1346, a front-burner national issue by Labor Day 2013, and the centerpiece of your Labor Day message to the country.

First, prominently encourage members of Congress to host a town hall meeting during their August 2013 recess exclusively focused on lifting the minimum wage.

Second, you can visit the AFL-CIO headquarters to highlight before the national media the urgency of increasing the minimum wage to help thirty million workers and their families afford the necessities of life. For far less reason and result, you walked to the nearby U.S. Chamber of Commerce headquarters and paid homage to the business barons in February 2011.

Third, you can find room in your barnstorming for business to reach out to some of those 30 million workers, who clean up after us, harvest and serve us our food, help our ailing grandparents, and much more. Excluded by the media, these striving and hard-pressed Americans need support from your bully pulpit.

According to a recently released report from Demos, the federal government indirectly employs the largest number of low-wage workers in the country, even more than Walmart and McDonald's combined. The *Washington Post* reported that a study from the National Employment Law Project (NELP) surveyed a sample of 567 federally contracted jobs. Seventy-four percent earned less than $10 per hour, 58 percent have no employment benefits, and 20 percent or more depend upon some form of public assistance.

In the absence of any serious movement in Congress to increase the minimum wage, you have the potential to exert significant influence on the wages paid to millions of low-wage workers in this country. With a simple executive order, you can fix this shameful deprivation. I urge you to sign an executive order which mandates that federal contractors be paid no less than $10.70 per hour, which would catch those workers back up with the inflation-adjusted minimum wage they would have been paid in 1968. Is this too much to ask of you?

As a former community organizer in the inner city and as a person who has risen to the highest office in the land, you should welcome these suggestions. You should have been championing this cause starting on your first day in the Oval Office. So give Gene Sperling the green light. Arouse the Democrats in Congress and give millions of Americans a reason for having voted to elect and reelect you.

Since Rick Santorum and, until last year, Mitt Romney favored an inflation-adjusted minimum wage and since the U.S. has, by far, the lowest minimum wage of the major industrial nations, how can your lack of action, after those oratorical echoes of your speech before the Congress, continue to mark your second term of office?

Hundreds of union locals, antipoverty, and nonprofit associations around the country would welcome your efforts to support the federal minimum wage catching up with 1968, inflation-adjusted, for thirty million workers.

Sincerely,

A Raise for Millions with the Stroke of a Pen

Dear President Obama,

June 25th marked the 75th anniversary of the federal minimum wage law in the United States, known as the Fair Labor Standards Act. When President Franklin Delano Roosevelt signed this legislation, his vision was to ensure a "fair day's pay for a fair day's work" and to "end starvation wages."

Seventy-five years later, there are 3.6 million Americans working for pay at or below the federal minimum wage. More extensively, *thirty million low-wage workers are making less today, adjusted for inflation, than they did 45 years ago in 1968.* They are working for a minimum wage that does not even reach the federal poverty line for a family of three and they cannot afford basic necessities like food, housing, transportation, and health care.

Had the minimum wage simply kept pace with inflation since 1968, it would stand at $10.70 per hour today instead of the current federal minimum wage of $7.25. In that time, the minimum wage has lost nearly one-third of its value while the prices of everything from food to housing to health care have been increasing—often at rates higher than inflation. Each year that the federal minimum wage is not increased, you and Congress are effectively telling low-wage workers that they are not worth as much as they were the year before and each of the dollars they earn gets stretched even further due to the effects of inflation.

Here's where you can make a decisive executive decision.

Just about a month ago, federally contracted low-wage workers walked off the job and participated in some of the largest strikes the nation's capital has seen in recent years. Despite the fact that they work indirectly for the federal government, they are still being paid poverty wages—some even explained that they were being paid *below* the federal minimum wage, which invites your administration's immediate investigation! This is disgraceful; the federal government should be providing a shining example of fair and just treatment of their contractors' workers for other employers to follow.

Your executive order to get this done would move closer to FDR's vision of ending "starvation wages." Your decision would set a good example for the rest of the business community to follow and provide the type of determined and persistent leadership that our country's political class has lacked for decades. Especially if you also limit the CEOs' and other top executives' pay for substantial federal contractors to a multiple no greater than 25 times their entry level wage. (Famed management guru Peter Drucker believed in this range as prudent corporate practice and legendary investor Warren Buffett has been critical of excessive executive compensation.)

According to a recently released report from Demos,* a public policy organization, the federal government indirectly employs the largest number of low-wage workers in the country. This is even more than Walmart and McDonald's combined. The *Washington Post* reported that a study from the National Employment Law Project (NELP) showed that 74 percent of federal contract workers surveyed make less than $10 per hour, 58 percent have no employment benefits, and 20 percent depend upon some form of public assistance.

In the absence of any serious movement in this disconnected Congress to increase the minimum wage, you have the potential to exert significant influence on the wages paid to millions of low-wage workers in this country. With a simple executive order, you can fix this shameful deprivation. I urge you to sign an executive order which mandates that federal contract workers

---

* See http://www.demos.org/sites/default/files/publications/UnderwritingBadJobs-Final-2.pdf for more information.

be paid no less than $10.70 per hour, which would catch those workers back up with the inflation-adjusted minimum wage they would have been paid in 1968. Is this too much to ask of you?

This is, of course, no substitute for a lasting federal minimum wage increase. But an executive order provides you with an option to avoid the morass in Congress and affect real positive change to millions of low-wage workers' lives and to affect that change *now*. I hope that you will recognize and seize this opportunity.

This small, but important example will make it easier for you to push Congress for a greater and bolder minimum wage increase than you did in your State of the Union address. Your proposal for a $9 minimum wage by 2015 does not go nearly far enough, remains far below what workers made, adjusted for inflation, in 1968, and doesn't even match the $9.50 by 2011 you called for five years ago during your 2008 campaign!

On the 75th anniversary of the federal minimum wage, you should sign an executive order raising the minimum wage of those working for the federal government through corporate contractors. It is the federal government's—and your—responsibility to set the example for the rest of the country to follow.

Not to mention that increasing wages could help spur on a lagging economic recovery. The *Wall Street Journal*'s story on June 24, "Slow-Motion U.S. Recovery Searches for Second Gear," discussed how the slow pace of recovery has left businesses and consumers wary. The Economic Policy Institute, in examining Senator Tom Harkin (D-IA) and Congressman George Miller's (D-CA) legislation to increase the minimum wage to $10.10 by 2016, estimated that increasing the minimum wage above $10 per hour would provide $51 billion in additional wages during the phase-in period for consumers to increase their spending for their livelihoods.

When Franklin Delano Roosevelt signed the Fair Labor

Standards Act into law, he showed courage in the face of the Great Depression, as well as considerable opposition and criticism from businesses. Is it not time, after four and a half years, for you to leave your mark, to show Americans what type of president you want to be remembered as, and to be a leader on this issue? Millions of workers throughout the country deserve a minimum wage that, at the very least, catches up with 1968.

I'm sending a copy of this letter to First Lady Michelle Obama who is said to have your ear.

Sincerely,

P.S. To find out what you can do to get involved, go to http://www.timeforaraise.org/.

Cc: First Lady Michelle Obama
Gene Sperling

Should One Man Be Prosecutor, Judge, Jury and Executioner?

Dear President Obama,

As a former lecturer in constitutional law at the University of Chicago Law School, you know that the federal government, including the Office of the President, does not enjoy limitless powers. As president, your powers are limited to those conferred either by the Constitution or federal statutes. Supreme Court

Associate Justice Hugo Black elaborated in *Reid v. Covert*, 354 U.S. 1 (1957): "The United States is entirely a creature of the Constitution. Its power and authority have no other source. It can only act in accordance with all the limitations imposed by the Constitution."

One of your illustrious predecessors, Thomas Jefferson, instructed in the Kentucky Resolution of 1798: "In questions of power, let no more be heard of confidence in man, but bind him down from mischief by the chains of the Constitution." As regards the Alien Act's empowering the president to deport any alien he unilaterally decreed was "dangerous to the peace and safety of the United States," Mr. Jefferson maintained "that transferring the power of judging any person, who is under the protection of the laws from the courts, to the President of the United States, as is undertaken by the same act concerning aliens, is against the article of the Constitution which provides that 'the judicial power of the United States shall be vested in courts, the judges of which shall hold their offices during good behavior.'"

With regard to your actions—especially those taken in the name of national security—you are obliged by your constitutional oath to explain by what authority you are acting and to answer serious criticism of your legal theories. Among other issues, you are obliged to elaborate by what authority you are empowered to: commence war without congressional authorization or appropriations; initiate war without the justification of self-defense, which is contrary to the Nuremburg precedents condemning crimes against peace; play prosecutor, judge, jury, and executioner to kill American citizens and noncitizens based on your secret assertion that the targets posed a danger—however remote and conjectural—to national security interests; imprison persons indefinitely at Guantanamo Bay without accusation or trial; intercept the e-mails and phone conversations of millions of American citizens without a judicial warrant; invoke a state secrets privilege to block judicial redress for torture or extrajudicial killings; resort to executive agreements, in lieu of treaties or federal statutes, to justify deploying the United States Armed Forces abroad; and engage in extraordinary rendition.

In light of your obligation to explain "by what authority," we were dismayed that you refused to send a witness to testify on April 23, 2013 regarding the legality of your predator drone targeted and signature killing programs before Senator Richard Durbin's Judiciary Subcommittee on the Constitution. That disdain for the rule of law and congressional oversight contrasts unfavorably with President Gerald Ford's willingness to testify personally before a House Judiciary Subcommittee on his pardon of former President Richard Nixon.

Most significant constitutional questions concerning national security escape judicial review because of technical barriers such as standing, ripeness, political question, or state secrets. That means they are decided in the court of public opinion, which must be educated about the matters by you and members of the media if the Constitution is to be adhered to and not vandalized. Public opinion repudiated the so-called "rationale" for torture concocted by the administration of President George W. Bush after you exposed the relevant legal memoranda to public scrutiny.

We urge you to explain to reporters and the American people "by what authority" you or your administration is acting regarding the aforementioned matters or comparable major actions so as to restore the rule of law as the crown jewel of the Constitution. We urge you to consider the timeless wisdom of the United States Supreme Court in *Ex parte Milligan* (1866):

"The Constitution of the United States is a law for rulers and people, equally in war and in peace, and covers with the shield of its protection all classes of men, at all times and under all circumstances. No doctrine involving more pernicious consequences was ever invented by the wit of man than that any of its provisions can be suspended during any of the great exigencies of government. Such a doctrine leads directly to anarchy or despotism, but the theory of necessity on which it is based is false, for the government, within the Constitution, has all the powers granted to it which are necessary to preserve its existence, as has been happily proved by the result of the great effort to throw off its just authority."

Sincerely,
Bruce Fein
Ralph Nader

End the Guantanamo Blot on Our National Character

Dear President Obama,

Notwithstanding Section 1028 (a)(1) of the National Defense Authorization Act of 2013, you are empowered to end Guantanamo Bay's affront to due process by releasing from imprisonment the 86 inmates whom your administration or its predecessor have found to be neither enemy combatants nor war criminals; and permitting them to arrange for travel to any foreign nation of their choosing. Section 1028 (a)(1) only limits your authority to *transfer* them into the "custody or control of the individual's country of origin, any other foreign country, or any other foreign entity . . ." But simple release, without more, is not prohibited. Of the remaining 80 prisoners, you should either charge and prosecute them for alleged war crimes or release them from Guantanamo Bay prison like the aforementioned 86.

No statute or other legal limitation blocks you from this enlightened course of action, which you have commended as who we are as a people. We are supposed to be willing to take risks that other countries shun because we find imprisoning, killing, or otherwise punishing the innocent to be morally reprehensible.

You cannot escape responsibility for the dubious legal limbo of Guantanamo Bay. You cannot simply blame Congress. President Harry S. Truman's famous Oval Office desk sign acknowledged that "The Buck Stops Here." Your oath of office compels you to honor the Constitution, not to evade it.

You must terminate forthwith Guantanamo Bay's blot on the character of this nation that gratuitously provokes retaliation and enmity.

Sincerely,
Bruce Fein
Ralph Nader

MARCH 18, 2013
Widening the Entitlement Debate

Dear President Obama,

An axiom of politics is to avoid using the words of your opponents. The Republicans in Congress are pressing to have you concede a reduction in what they call "entitlements," mostly meaning Social Security, Medicare, and Medicaid.

The Democrats also use the word "entitlements" in resisting the madness of the cruel, oligarchic proposals of Paul Ryan, John Boehner, and Eric Cantor. But neither they, nor you, include under entitlements the vast giveaway of corporate welfare—subsidies, inflated contracts, handouts, loan guarantees, bailouts, tax expenditures, and others too numerous to mention. These are real and significant entitlements. Corporate recipients do not pay for these giveaways. They use these freebies to cloak corporate mismanagement, increase retained corporate profits, and boost staggering executive compensation.

Peoples' entitlements, by contrast, are paid in significant degree by the taxes of the people who receive them, when they retire or are in need of health care. Quite a difference!

Don't fall for the cornering maneuver by the Republicans to get you to agree to reductions in *benefits* from Social Security, Medicare, and Medicaid. You know this tactic, but you need to be more vocal. Insist that *huge savings can come from the vendors* who unlawfully or deceptively take profits from Medicaid and Medicare. The long article in *Time* magazine by Steve Brill titled "Bitter Pill: Why Medical Bills Are Killing Us" (March 4, 2013) documents some of the rampant price gouging by the health care industry.

There is also the outright billing fraud on Medicare and Medicaid which both the GAO and the leading specialist, Professor Malcolm Sparrow of Harvard University (author of the book *License to Steal*), have declared to be at least 10 percent of health care revenue. That overall would exceed $270 *billion* last year and the large part ripped off from Medicare and Medicaid is in the tens of billions yearly. Please note this is just *billing fraud and abuse* which your Department of Health and Human Services can document. I am sure Professor Sparrow would be glad to help.

Add a serious enforcement program to reduce both unnecessary health services, as documented by the Dartmouth Medical School team, as well as costly medical malpractice and medical errors and you have a long range plan for major efficiencies. And taking away the remaining subsidy of Medicare Advantage received by the health insurance companies would further facilitate preserving benefits for those who paid for and relied on these social compacts.

As for Social Security, propose an increase in the amount of those with higher incomes having to pay Social Security taxes. This single move would relieve the pressure years from now on reducing benefits for the needy elderly.

Many citizens would look forward to such clarifications of language and action that embrace equities and remedies scarcely discussed in this deliberately narrowed debate on "entitlements."

Sincerely,

JANUARY 15, 2013
Pardon John Kiriakou

Dear President Obama,

We the undersigned are writing to urge that you pardon former CIA officer John Kiriakou. Motivated as a father devoted to his children, Mr. Kiriakou recently pleaded guilty to one count of violating the Intelligence Identities Protection Act of 1981 to avoid the government's threat of long-term devastation of his cherished family.

He pleaded guilty to the crime of providing the name of a former colleague to an author who was writing a book and searching for former CIA officers to interview, an act which seems much less censorable than Deputy Secretary of State Richard Armitage's disclosure of the CIA's Valerie Plame to reporter Robert Novak with impunity. Mr. Kiriakou's disclosure never was made publicly available and occasioned no harm to the United States. Indeed, it assisted in ending waterboarding, the crime of torture as you and your attorney general have acknowledged. In contrast, Mr. Armitage's disclosure was shared to the world by Mr. Novak, and reportedly placed in danger persons who had associated with Ms. Plame. The reporter of Mr. Kiriakou's information unilaterally shared the name with the American Civil Liberties Union.

We believe that commutation is appropriate in this case for a number of reasons:

First, Mr. Kiriakou is a highly decorated, fourteen-year CIA counterterrorism veteran who has spent his entire adult life in public service, including two years as a senior aide to Senator John Kerry. He was the leader of the team that captured an al-Qaeda leader Abu Zubaydah in Faisalabad, Pakistan, in 2002. He is the recipient of twelve CIA Exceptional Performance Awards, the Sustained Superior Performance Award, the Meritorious Honor Award with Medal, and the Counterterrorism Service Medal.

Second, Mr. Kiriakou is an antitorture whistle-blower who spoke out against torture because he believed it violated his oath to the Constitution. He never tortured anyone, yet he is the only individual to be prosecuted in relation to the torture program of the past decade. The interrogators who tortured prisoners, the officials who gave the orders, the attorneys who authored the torture memos, and the CIA officers who destroyed the interrogation tapes have not been held professionally accountable, much less charged with crimes.

Third, there is precedent for leniency. In 2007, I. Lewis "Scooter" Libby was granted a commutation after being found guilty of four felony counts—obstruction of justice, making a false statement, and two counts of perjury—related to the Valerie Plame affair. Mr. Libby did not spend one day in prison. Similarly, in 2001 President Clinton pardoned Samuel L. Morison, the only person ever convicted of espionage for leaking classified information to the press.

Mr. President, do not allow your legacy to be one where only the accurate whistle-blower goes to prison.

We urge you to take action in this matter. Please do not let this injustice stand. Commute John Kiriakou's sentence.

Sincerely,
Bruce Fein
Ralph Nader
Joan Claybrook

Nominate Hagel and Fight the
Bloated Pentagon Budget

Dear President Obama,

Now that you have won your last election, there is no longer any conflict of interest between your electoral aspirations and what needs to be done for our country and its people—present and future generations.

It is customary for citizens to expect more from their president's second term for just that reason. However, such expectations have rarely been met. Character and personality tend to combine with other factors to make second terms even less productive than first terms.

Thus far, since Election Day, your decisions have not reflected these higher expectations whether domestically or in foreign/military affairs. Certainly in your handling of the Republicans or in your presumed solidarity with the Democrats in Congress, the past continues into the present. Character and personality in leaders are quite decisive traits in shaping a president's legacy. The next four years will require you to start addressing long overdue demands for our country.

Since November 6, Election Day, there has been one departure from your practice of selecting nominees unlikely to be opposed by interest groups allied with or influential over the Democratic Party or the Republican Party. That is the reported selection of former Senator Chuck Hagel as secretary of defense.

The reasons for your reported choice of Mr. Hagel are seen as laudatory, given the bloated, redundant, deficit-ridden, unauditable Pentagon budget that consumes half of the entire discretionary federal budget post–demise of the Soviet Union.

Should you back down on your reported decision in the face of widely criticized "vicious attacks" on Mr. Hagel, to use the phrase by four former U.S. national security advisors from both parties, you will, as they note, "discourage future prospective nominees from public service when our country badly needs quality leadership in government."

The place to "cut and run" is on your basketball court, not in the Oval Office.

Sincerely,

AUGUST 23, 2012
Take Labor Day Seriously

Dear President Obama,

Labor Day 2012 is approaching. Besides your usual Labor Day message, you should consider making this a major event dedicated to America's workers.

The meaning of Labor Day has been overtaken by the commercialists who see it as a day for shopping and sales. With your bully pulpit there are strong leadership messages regarding long overdue attention to the plight of tens of millions of workers, without unions, laboring for wages below the inflation-adjusted minimum wage of 1968! Thirty million workers are receiving wages between the present, eroded federal minimum wage of $7.25 and the 1968-adjusted minimum wage which would be $10.35.

Support of an inflation-adjusted minimum wage polls at 70 percent. This support includes Rick Santorum and Mitt

Romney, until the latter waffled earlier this year. The moral and economic arguments are overwhelming. Workers have been shortchanged for years while the top fifty largest corporations, which employ two-thirds of low-wage workers in the U.S., had their CEOs averaging about $9.5 million in compensation (or about $1 million every six weeks).

I'll leave the political pluses for you and your advisors inherent in standing for "catching up with 1968" (see H.R. 5901 sponsored by Jesse Jackson Jr. and other House members). Releasing tens of billions of dollars in consumer spending by these hard-pressed Americans is good for a recessionary economy.

You have on your White House staff two of the most knowledgeable people on the need for a minimum wage upgrade. Professor Alan Krueger, U.S. chairman of your Council of Economic Advisors, is a leading scholar in this field to rebut the propagandists from the Chamber of Commerce, where you visited earlier this year. Gene Sperling was involved in the last adjustment of the minimum wage in 2007 and would be an excellent advocate on this topic.

Many organizations are on the record favoring a living wage including labor, religious, social service, antipoverty, women's associations, and others with millions of members around the country that await your call. (They should be on the ramparts themselves without waiting, preferably.) Recall your 2008 pledge of $9.50 by 2011 and your words on this point in your July 2007 address in Anacostia and other speeches. No one can call you an oratorical newcomer on the minimum wage. Bring all together for a briefing and news conference, including the AFL-CIO's chief, Richard Trumka, followed by an event or two on Labor Day.

How many times have the monetized minds of the business

lobbies called on the government to weaken safeguards "to keep up with the global competition?" Well, since the U.S. had the lowest minimum wage by far among major Western industrial nations, you'll help American workers keep up with the wages (but not the social safety net) of laborers in Western Europe and Canada.

There have been 17 tax cuts for small businesses under your administration. They have already gotten their consideration. It is time for you to address the perceived and desperate needs of thirty million American workers who have waited too long for their government to act in an era of Wall Street bailouts and tax cuts for the wealthy.

If there is anyone arguing the opposite case for the status quo in the White House, I would like their names so that I can hear their assertions.

Sincerely,

JUNE 7, 2012
Attend the Take Back the American Dream Conference

Dear President Obama,

Can you imagine President George W. Bush and Vice President Dick Cheney refusing, year after year, to go a few blocks from the White House and address the largest congregation of supporters, Republicans, conservatives, corporatists—call them what you will—and getting away with it?

Well, that is what you and Vice President Joe Biden have

been doing to the largest annual gathering of liberal politicos and activists in Washington, D.C., overseen by your faithful supporter, Robert Borosage.

The "Borosage Convention" brings together several thousand people over the course of its three days with its workshops, plenary sessions, and other events. Why do you not only decline to appear—while choosing to attend business conventions and media extravaganzas at the same or nearby hotels—but you so signal your refusal that Mr. Borosage et al.'s "Take Back the American Dream Conference," June 18 to 20, does not even tender a public invitation for fear of having an embarrassment being interpreted by observers and reporters as a rebuke.

You traveled to India a while back to promote Boeing products and Harley-Davidson motorcycles. How about this: Will you address the Conference if its organizers display three shiny Harley-Davidson motorcycles and a large model of the Boeing Dreamliner with salespeople from both companies standing by with pamphlets and promotional DVDs? Will that be enough to induce your presidential presence before a large ballroom full of your probable supporters who have come to Washington, D.C., from most of the fifty states?

Please ponder the pathos of these people yearning to give you a standing ovation, but not wanting to be publicly rejected and therefore dejected. Can you spare some time for people who you know have nowhere to go? If they aren't important enough, as a result, to be addressed as collaborative citizens, perhaps your sense of pity could serve to activate Limousine One to take you and your staff to their gathering at the Washington Hilton Hotel.

Remember voters are sometimes fueled by enthusiasm. Please ponder.

Sincerely,

Your Choice on Wisconsin:
Be a Leader or Be a Calculator

Dear President Obama,

On June 5, 2012, hundreds of thousands of your supporters, including firefighters, police, nurses, and teachers will go the polls to recall Governor Scott Walker, the arch-reactionary, the opponent of the basic right of collective bargaining, and many other decent, established policies.

Political observers are saying that if the Republicans defeat your Democratic Party on Tuesday, it will have wide ramifications throughout the country and will probably cost you Wisconsin this November. Last year, I noticed how quiet you were about the large and resourceful demonstrations in Madison that were so inspiring to many of your supporters around the country. You did not go to speak to these good Democrats. Your political operatives in the White House even turned thumbs down on the request by the Wisconsin state federation of labor that Vice President Joe Biden—a self-styled "union man"—address one hundred thousand working people and students before the state capitol in Madison.

So, the main public organizations and demonstrations against the draconian Republican assault on your constituents and on long-standing Democratic Party policies—their rights and their livelihoods—were not supported by either you or an otherwise eager Joe Biden at any of those Madison turnouts.

Are you a leader? Or are you a calculator? Either way your status as "missing in action" in Wisconsin, as writer Paul Hogarth put it yesterday, is not smart, expedient politics. It is one thing not to champion the priorities of your labor supporters—such as pressing to raise the minimum wage to

$9.50 an hour by 2011, which you promised in 2008. It is quite another to betray these working and unemployed people to the cruelties of a massively funded Walker campaign which, if it wins, promises to turn Wisconsin into WisKochsin.

Perhaps you have private polls that support your absenteeism from the state. Perhaps you have other calculations not shared by the legendary calculator in chief Bill Clinton who is going to Wisconsin tomorrow to support the workers.

Whatever your hidden motivations are for inaction in situ, people will be asking over and over again whenever you go to fat-cat fundraisers, to foreign countries promoting Harley-Davidson motorcycles, to ESPN knowledgeably picking the winners for each level of the March Madness basketball tournaments, to business gatherings on Wall Street and elsewhere, this question:

Barack Obama did not have the time nor the interest to come and help us during the last days of our historic struggle against the cruelest, most craven, most corporatist–indentured Republican Party in history. Where was he?

Unless you fly to Wisconsin before Tuesday, you'd better HOPE that the polls CHANGE and the good people of Wisconsin turn out Governor Walker. Otherwise, you'll be up against the memories of your abandonment all the way to November that will not be restricted to the boundaries of the Badger State.

Sincerely,

MAY 4, 2012
Michelle: Why Won't Barack Speak to Civic Groups?

Dear First Lady Michelle Obama,

At the suggestion of some knowledgeable people I am writing you to convey a message to President Obama that was sent to him thrice in the past three years without response.

I urged him to address a convocation of the leaders of 1,000 national civil groups—antipoverty, consumer, environmental, worker, good government, et al.—at a ballroom in a downtown Washington Hotel. In 1976, President-elect Jimmy Carter attended such an occasion and recognized the critical importance of such organizations, with their millions of members back home, to a functioning democratic society.

Since my first letter to him on this subject, President Obama has gone to foreign countries to promote U.S. corporate products (e.g., high-priced Harley-Davidson motorcycles in India) and visited factories hundreds of miles from Washington for the same purpose. Recently, he reiterated that he would go anywhere in the world to promote U.S. exports.

Certainly as a matter of convenience and recognition, speaking to a thousand civic/labor organizations a few blocks from the White House about justice, democracy, and civic empowerment is a comparatively easier case to make.

So as a Princetonian "in the nation's service," would you please inform him of the above request and forward his response to me? Scores of letters to the president from many civic groups, including ours, have gone unanswered by anyone in the White House. So we are appealing to the East Wing.

Thank you. Your work for fresh, nutritious food and exercise to reduce obesity and elevate health is very admirable.

Sincerely,

Dear President Obama,

There is an old saying in southern politics that "you dance with the ones who brung ya." While I have read about your many meetings and dinners with Republican politicians, corporate executives, right-wing columnists and commentators, and assorted other people and groups representing agendas and ideologies opposed to both your candidacy and presidency, missing has been any major outreach to the liberal and progressive civic constituency in our nation's capital. These are the many groups, supported by millions of dues-paying members around the country, who have held down the fort, so to speak, in the most difficult days of Nixon, Reagan, the two Bushes and Clinton.

These organizations are well known to you. They cover the important advocacy areas of peace, civil liberties and civil rights, antipoverty and health, consumer protection, environment, labor safety, protection and reform of labor laws, plus many traditional charities that minister to the needy. While these associations are mostly nonprofit and do not engage in electoral activities, there is little doubt that you received a majority of the votes from their memberships. They would add that their policies resonated more closely with your views than with those of your major opponent, Senator John McCain.

I wish to make a strong suggestion that you meet soon with the leaders of these groups in a major auditorium or ballroom in Washington, D.C. Just after his election in 1976, Jimmy Carter accepted an invitation to do just that at a hotel near the White House. The ballroom was full and the event was considered by all to be a great success with much substance exchanged formally and in the informal interactions and subsequent contacts with the president and his associates.

The national civic community should play a significant role in shaping your agenda. Many took note of your comment that you wanted to escape being "in a bubble" while president in the White House. You kept your Blackberry to stay in touch with the outside world, especially Chicago. Well, here is a grand opportunity to secure another way to avoid the bubble.

Sincerely,

THE WHITE HOUSE
WASHINGTON

July 17, 2012

Dear Mr. Nader:

Thank you for writing to the First Lady to invite President Obama to speak to group of leaders of civic and labor organizations in Washington, D.C.

President Obama values each and every invitation he receives. However, the constraints of his schedule and the volume of requests are such that the majority must be declined. It is with sincere regret that the President will be unable to participate in the gathering of national civic leaders.

Thank you for your interest in including President Obama in your event. We appreciate your understanding and extend our best wishes to you in planning the gathering.

Sincerely,

Michael S. McSwain
Associate Director for Scheduling Correspondence
Office of Scheduling and Advance

Vetoing the Corporate Crime Facilitation Bill

Dear President Obama,

As you know, this country has recently faced one of the worst financial crises in our history. In the aftermath, millions were left unemployed, without a home, saddled with enormous college loans, and struggling to get by. The economy continues to lag to this day, and many millions of Americans remain out of work and looking for a job. For that reason, voters have been desperate for their national elected officials—you and Congress—to take decisive action to create more jobs. The so-called JOBS (Jumpstart Our Business Startups) Act is not a true job creation bill—it is a ravenous beast in sheep's clothing.

The misnamed "JOBS" Act is riddled with cuts in investor-protection regulation, glaring giveaways, and monster-truck-sized loopholes. Republicans claim that the "JOBS" Act will create jobs by lowering the cost of capital for "small" start-ups to raise money by offering IPOs. But what do the bill's authors consider a "small" start-up (referred to in the bill as "emerging growth companies")? According to Title I of the bill, any company that makes up to *$1 billion* in revenues! Companies that reach revenues of this size are not *small* businesses. Kathleen Smith, the chairwoman of Renaissance Capital (a firm based in Greenwich, CT that deals with IPOs), recently stated at a Senate Banking Committee hearing that this would apply to *more than 90 percent* of companies that go public! At the same hearing, Lynn Turner, former SEC chief accountant and accounting consultant at LitiNomics, stated that by this standard, 98 percent of IPOs since 1970 would have been considered "emerging growth companies."

Furthermore, by raising the ceiling for these exemptions to such sky-high altitudes, you know many companies considering

IPOs will come up with—and use—accounting gimmicks to keep their revenues below the benchmark. Richard Eskow of the Campaign for America's Future even suggests that some companies may split in two to remain below the $1 billion threshold. Contrary to claims from the proponents of the "JOBS" Act that small businesses and start-ups are strangled by regulation, Bloomberg News reported that the SEC has "long exempted companies with less than $75 million in sales from some of the law's [Sarbanes-Oxley] most onerous provisions." Raising the ceiling to such an astronomical level will open the door to a variety of financial shenanigans.

As a president who was left to pick up the pieces in the devastating aftermath of the policies of your predecessors that deregulated and failed to properly oversee Wall Street, one expects you would act prudently and veto this fraud-centric legislation. Start-ups can be some of the riskiest investments since they haven't had the opportunity to establish themselves, may require large initial quantities of capital, and often see large losses in the time it takes them to become profitable (or in many cases, bankrupt). The "JOBS" Act would allow these risky companies to launch without proper regulatory safeguarding. It would eliminate much of the personnel and financial disclosure for these start-ups that is typically in place to protect investors and consumers.

More disturbing, this bill might not just create loopholes for these newly defined $1 billion "emerging growth companies"—but for larger corporations as well. Title V of the bill loosens requirements for companies to register with the SEC. It increases the number of "shareholders of record" that require a company to register with the SEC from 500 to 2,000. The *New York Times* has quoted John C. Coffee Jr., a prominent securities law professor at Columbia, explaining that many "individual stockholders are not shareholders of record but beneficial owners whose shares are held by a brokerage firm, which is the owner of record." Consequently, larger corporations worth many billions of dollars (and which may have thousands of *beneficial owners* instead of shareholders of record) would be able to avoid registering with the SEC and the transparency that comes along with it.

Did we learn nothing from the "dot com" bust, the Enron scandal, or the home mortgage financing debacle? In light of the fact that some of the major causes for the recent financial crises were the lack of openness in certain financial markets and products, and the failure to understand these complex financial products, their risk, or the risks involved in these markets, it is shocking that both indentured Democrats and Republicans have allowed the so-called "JOBS" Act to get so far. It tears down regulations put in place after these recent financial disasters that lost millions of Americans their jobs and trillions of dollars of their savings and pensions. And by removing crucial transparency, it throws a shroud of uncertainty over the operations of these "emerging growth companies."

The list of individuals and organizations that are opposed or have voiced their concern about this legislation is long. It includes: former SEC Commissioner Arthur Levitt and former SEC Chief Accountant Lynn Turner; academics like Columbia Law School Professor John Coffee, Harvard Professor of Business and Law John Coates, and University of Florida Finance Professor Jay Ritter; consumer and investor advocates like the AARP, Americans for Financial Reform, the Consumer Federation of America, the Council of Institutional Investors, and Public Citizen, among others; unions, including the AFL-CIO, AFSCME, and the NEA; and even members of the business community who have warned of the consequences of this bill, including Bloomberg News, the Main Street Alliance, Motley Fool Mutual Fund Manager Bill Mann, and Renaissance Capital's K. On top of all of that, the current chairwoman of the SEC, the ever-cautious Mary Schapiro, has warned about the potential for this legislation to actually undermine investor confidence and make it harder for start-ups to raise capital—presumably something that would harm job creation.

I urge you to look past the title of the bill—the "JOBS" Act—and consider the serious consequences of signing such legislation into law. Slapping the acronym "JOBS" on the bill does not mask the damage this legislation will produce. If you bow to political pressure of the worst kind and sign this bill into law, the beacon of hope that many Americans have been waiting for in the past three years will be further dimmed. So will your legacy in this area. The "JOBS" Act presents you with an opportunity: you can stand with the American people and protect consumers and investors, or you can yet again defer to the monied interests of avaricious corporations and enable more of their corporate crime wave.

I urge you to defend the American people from certain future fraud and abuse in this congressional attack and destruction of existing law and safeguards of many years standing by vetoing the "JOBS" Act.

Repeat—Veto this congressional enabler of corporate crime, fraud, and deception.

Sincerely,

State of the Union 2012

Dear President Obama,

As you prepare your State of the Union address, please be advised that those who support you are very cognizant of what you do not mention in such annual presentations to the nation. For example, last year, environmentalists were shocked that climate change received no attention. Nor did raising the minimum wage, as you promised in 2008, to $9.50 by 2011.

My recent column titled "Congress Needs to Get to Work"* reminds and recommends what you and the congressional Democrats should be advancing this year. They are not only needed legislative actions, but are also both significant and popular.

Try to avoid being drawn into corrosive conflicts with the congressional Republicans on matters you could have avoided by learning how to bargain for more when you give up much. An example is your concessions on the Bush tax cuts in late 2010, for which you should have demanded concurrence for raising the debt limit. Think of the time that struggle absorbed in 2011!

To call a reduction of the employee side of the payroll tax a "tax cut" for 160 million Americans is beyond disingenuous. You know who pays for this maneuver once this can is kicked down the road.

The many organizations in this country striving to stem the rising poverty in this country have wondered why you never mention "the poor" in your speeches. They are aware of the Clintonesque code that only referred to "the middle class" and never to "the poor" or "to low-income people" who now

---

* See https://blog.nader.org/2012/01/18/congress-needs-to-get-to-work/ for more information.

number nearly 100 million Americans. They did not expect that Barack Obama also would have employed this language of avoidance.

You do not want them to feel they are being taken for granted.

Sincerely,

[signature]

SEPTEMBER 2, 2011

Wanted: Labor Day Enthusiasm

Dear President Obama,

Happy Labor Day! This is your third opportunity as president to go beyond your past tepid Labor Day proclamations.

You could convey to 150 million workers that you stand with them by honoring your campaign pledge to raise the minimum wage to $9.50 over three years. You can add that a $9.50 minimum is still less than what workers made under the minimum wage in 1968, adjusted for inflation, when worker productivity was half of what it is today. Besides, businesses like Walmart have received windfalls year after year due to the minimum wage lagging behind inflation for decades.

Your second promise in 2008 was pushing for card check legislation—a top priority for the AFL-CIO, whose member unions helped elect you. "Give me the card check," Rich Trumka, now AFL-CIO president, told me in 2004, "and millions of workers will organize into unions."

I may have missed something but when was the last

time you championed card check after you took your oath of office? Did you bring labor together, the way you brought big business together for their demands, and launch a public drive to overcome many of the obstructions workers now have to confront under the present corporate-driven union-busting climate?

I met with Mr. Trumka recently. It seemed he's given up on you for the card check or minimum wage. With such low expectations, you probably can make organized labor a little more enthusiastic for you if you simply mentioned these two measures in your next State of the Union address. You could even break an old taboo and say that the notoriously anti-worker Taft-Hartley Act of 1947 needs to be changed. Just talking about those issues will "keep hope alive" for "change you can believe in."

Even better, mention these with a paragraph on the spreading poverty—yes, finally use that word "poverty" which is decidedly not "middle-class." Last January, your State of the Union address ignored poverty—accelerating child poverty, hunger, homelessness, mass unemployment and underemployment, do add up to that phenomenon. If not deeds or action, at least just give them some words.

As big business abandons American workers and takes jobs and industries to communist and fascist regimes abroad—regimes that know how to keep workers in their place at 50 or 80 cents an hour—reactionary Republican governors are stripping public employees of their collective bargaining rights. These Republicans are laying off their teachers and other workers so they do not have to repeal the corporate welfare drains on their state treasuries. Dozens of corporate welfare tax abatements, subsidies, giveaways, bailouts, and other freebies are embedded in their state laws.

When the Wisconsin workers protested and filled the square in Madison, Wisconsin, they were expressing your "fierce urgency of now." But you would not go and address just one of their rallies to support their jobs and rights.

Just before the last big rally of some 100,000 people from all over Wisconsin, the state federation of labor invited the vice president to speak to them in Madison. The White House said no. Isn't Joe Biden known for saying "I'm a union guy?"

By comparison: *Can you imagine a national Republican presidential candidate refusing an invitation to speak to 100,000 Tea Partiers?*

But then these Democratic workers, you may believe, have nowhere to go in November 2012. That's right, they don't have to go anywhere; they can stay right at home along with their volunteer hours and Get-Out-The-Vote calls. Political withdrawal is real easy to do. Remember 2010. Remember the sharp drop in the youth vote. You may be met with less enthusiasm than congressional Democrats encountered in 2010.

Sincerely,

JUNE 29, 2011
Don't Abandon Elizabeth Warren!

Dear President Obama,

Yesterday's *Washington Post* published a page-one article headlined "President Waging A Charm Offensive. Obama Woos Big Donors to Help Fund Early Campaign Expansion."

Later in the article appears this unseemly behavior by a public servant paid for by public funds:

"A key player in the closed-door donor recruitment is White House Chief of Staff William M. Daley, a former banking executive who has huddled in recent weeks over breakfasts and dinners with business leaders and Wall Street financiers in Chicago, New York and Washington—seeking to ease tensions over new financial regulations and other administration policies."

How rancid is the behavior described in the article compared to your no-more-business-as-usual rhetoric during your "hope and change you can believe in" 2008 campaign! What assurances are being given by your staff in order to ensure that donations do not become what NBC's David Brinkley once called "legalized bribery"?

Yesterday's *New York Times* has a column by Andrew Ross Sorkin about the campaign fundraising activities involving big-time financiers. He writes: "While Wall Street executives still complain about the president's name-calling and pressure for a regulatory overhaul, many say privately that his bark has been worse than his bite."

It could be that your political advisors, viewing the unimpressive field of Republican wannabes for 2012, have neglected to crank in your stay-at-home voters who would exceed their number in 2010 by a substantial measure.

Not giving Elizabeth Warren a recess appointment (and using your presidential authority to assure a recess)—to head the Consumer Financial Protection Bureau that she is now building at her post in the Treasury Department will produce many stay-at-home voters. These are the Americans for whom over three years of dashed hopes in many fields view abandoning the authentically admired Professor Warren as the last straw!

Given the crimes and derelictions that looted or drained trillions of savers' and workers' money in 2008–2009 and that collapsed the economy with its resultant unemployment and bailouts, they want law and order for Wall Street.

This letter is being sent to your political advisor David Plouffe and to Vice President Biden.

Sincerely,

P.S. By the way, have you met with Professor Warren in the last year, as you do with Wall Street CEOs?

JUNE 3, 2011

Letter from E.coli O104:H4

Dear President Obama,

My name is E.coli O104:H4. I am being detained in a German Laboratory in Bavaria, charged with being "a highly virulent strain of bacteria." Together with many others like me, the police have accused us of causing about 20 deaths and nearly five hundred cases of kidney failure—so far. Massive publicity and panic all around. You can't see me, but your scientists can. They are examining me and I know my days are numbered. I hear them calling me a "biological terrorist," an unusual combination of two different E.coli bacteria cells. One even referred to me as a "conspiracy of mutants."

It is not my fault, I want you to know. I cannot help but

harm innocent humans, and I am very sad about this. I want to redeem myself, so I am sending this life-saving message straight from my petri dish to you.

This outbreak in Germany has been traced to food—location unknown. What is known to you is that invisible terrorism from bacterium and viruses takes massively greater lives than the terrorism you are spending billions of dollars and armaments to stop in Iraq, Afghanistan, and Pakistan.

Malaria, caused by infection with one of four species of Plasmodium, is a parasite transmitted by Anopheles mosquitoes that destroys a million lives a year. Many of the victims are children and pregnant women. Mycobacterium tuberculosis takes over one million lives each year. The human immunodeficiency virus (HIV) causes over a million deaths each year. Many other microorganisms in the water, soil, air, and food are daily weapons of mass destruction. Very little in your defense budget goes for operational armed forces against this kind of violence. Your agencies, such as the Centers for Disease Control, conduct some research but again nothing compared to the research for your missiles, drones, aircraft, and satellites.

Your associates are obsessed with possible bacteriological warfare by your human enemies. Yet you are hardly doing anything on the ongoing silent violence of my indiscriminate brethren.

You and your predecessor George W. Bush made many speeches about fighting terrorism by humans. Have you made a major speech about us?

You speak regularly about crushing the resistance of your enemies. But you splash around so many antibiotics (obviously I don't like this word and consider it genocidal) in cows, bulls, chickens, pigs, and fish that your species is creating massive *antibiotic* resistance, provoking our mutations, so that we can breed even stronger progeny. You are regarded as the smartest beings on Earth, yet you seem to have too many neurons backfiring.

In the past two days of detention, scientists have subjected me to "enhanced interrogation," as if I have any will to give up my secrets. It doesn't work. What they will find out will be from their insights about me under their microscopes. I am lethal, I guess, but I'm not very complicated.

The United States, together with other countries, needs more laboratories where scientists can detain samples of us and subject us to extraordinary rendition to infectious disease research centers. Many infectious disease scientists need to be trained, especially in the southern hemispheres to staff these labs.

You are hung up on certain kinds of preventable violence without any risk/benefit analysis. This, you should agree, is utterly irrational. You should not care where the preventable violence comes from except to focus on its range of devastation and its susceptibility to prevention or cure!

Well, here they come to my petri dish for some more waterboarding. One last item: You may wonder *how* tiny bacterial me, probably not even harboring a virus, can send you such a letter. My oozing sense is that I'm just a carrier, being used by oodles of scientists taking advantage of a high-profile infectious outbreak in Europe to catch your attention.

Whatever the *how* does it really matter to the need to act *now*?

E-cologically yours,
E.coli O104:H4 (for the time being)

Professor Warren: Our Working Class Hero!

Dear President Obama,

An interesting contrast is playing out at the White House these days—between your expressed praise of General Electric CEO Jeffrey R. Immelt and the silence regarding the widely desired nomination of Elizabeth Warren to head the new Consumer Financial Regulatory Bureau within the Federal Reserve. On one hand, you promptly appointed Mr. Immelt to be the chairman of the President's Council on Jobs and Competitiveness, while letting him keep his full-time lucrative position as CEO of General Electric (the corporate state expands). At the announcement, you said that Mr. Immelt "understands what it takes for America to compete in the global economy."

Did you mean that he understands how to avoid all federal income taxes for his company's $14.2 billion in profits last year, while corralling a $3.2 billion benefit? Or did you mean that he understands how to get a federal bailout for GE Capital and its reckless exposure to risky debt? Or could you have meant that GE knows how to block unionization of its far-flung workers here and abroad? Perhaps Mr. Immelt can share with you GE's historical experience with lucrative campaign contributions, price-fixing, pollution and those nuclear reactors that are giving people fits in Japan and worrying millions of Americans here living or working near similar reactors.

Compare, if you will, the record of Elizabeth Warren and her acutely informed knowledge about delivering justice to those innocents harmed by injustice in the financial services industry. A stand-up law professor at your alma mater, author of highly regarded articles and books connecting knowledge to action, the probing chair of the Congressional Oversight

Panel (COP) and now in the Treasury Department working intensively to get the CFRB underway by the statutory deadline this July with competent, people-oriented staff.

There were many good reasons why Senate Majority Leader Harry Reid (D-NV) called Professor Warren and asked her to be his choice for chair of COP. Hailing from an Oklahoman blue-collar family, Professor Warren is just the "working class hero" needed to make the new Bureau a sober, law and order enforcer, deterrer and empowerer of consumers vis-à-vis the companies whose enormous greed, recklessness, and crimes tanked our economy into a deep recession. The consequences produced 8 million unemployed workers and shattered trillions of dollars in pensions and other savings along with the dreams which they embodied for American workers.

Much more than you perhaps realize, millions of people, who have heard and seen Elizabeth Warren, rejoice in her brainy, heartfelt knowledge and concern over their plight. They see her as just the kind of regulator (federal cop on the beat) for their legitimate interests in a more competitive marketplace who you should be overjoyed in nominating.

Yet there are corporate forces from Wall Street to Washington determined to derail her nomination—forces with their avaricious hooks into the Republicans on Capitol Hill and the corporatists in the Treasury and White House.

You have obliged these forces again and again over the last two years, most recently with the appointment of William M. Daley, recently of Wall Street, as your chief of staff.

How about one nomination for the people? The accolades on hearing the news of Elizabeth Warren's nomination may actually exceed the enduring indignation were she not to be nominated. Just feed the Senate Republicans to the mass media that would cover the nomination hearings, and note all that calm, solid, wisdom and humanity that she communicates without peer. See who prevails.

Selecting Elizabeth Warren and backing her fully through the nomination process will always be remembered by Americans across the land. Not doing so will not be forgotten by those same persons. This is another way of saying she has the enthusiastic constituency of "hope and change"—that is "change you can believe in!"

I look forward with many others to your response.

Sincerely,

P.S. If you doubt this observation and would like to see one million Americans on a petition favoring her selection, ask us and see how long that would take.

MARCH 28, 2011
Promoting Auto and Motor Safety Coach Legislation

Dear President Obama,

A few days ago, Transportation Secretary Ray LaHood told some long-time auto safety advocates in his office that the Department wants to see the two bills—the auto safety and the motor coach safety legislation—enacted this session. Last December, all was set for these two bills to be passed—a clear majority in the House (led by Rep. Waxman) and 99 Senators

signed off on unanimous consent (led by Sen. Rockefeller).
One Senator, Dr. Tom Coburn, refused to release his hold.
We conversed with him several times and tried to respond
to his procedural and substantive complaints within his own
framework of thinking and not knowing, but to no avail.

Last year, I was not aware that as a Senator you and your
wife befriended Senator Coburn and his wife and became
social friends, notwithstanding the differences in your views
and outlook. Had I known this, I would have urged Secretary
LaHood to request your direct involvement, though this should
have been done by his and your own initiative for the life-saving
results of these two thoroughly deliberated safety bills.

Can you still urge Senator Coburn to concur this session and
declare to your Democratic allies in Congress that you are going to
speak out and push for this legislation? Most families extended or
not, including yours, have been tragically affected by road crashes.

By the way, the *Hill* newspaper had a picture of you in a
vehicle not wearing your seat belt. Are you now belted? You do set
an example for others in what you do.

Sincerely,

FEBRUARY 1, 2011
Give D.C. the Vote!

Dear President Obama,

Secretary of State Hillary Clinton reflected your sentiments
when she commented on the Egyptian uprising with the words
"We want to see free and fair elections."

But in the District of Columbia, where you and Secretary Clinton reside, there are no "free and fair elections" for electing representatives with full voting rights to Congress. There is only the continual disenfranchisement—unique to all other national capital cities in purported democracies—for the hundreds of thousands of voting age citizens in the District of Columbia.

You stated that the United States "will continue to stand up for the rights of the Egyptian people." Presumably that includes the right to have members of Parliament, with full voting rights, elected by the Egyptian voters.

Although you declared in the 2008 election that you supported voting rights for the District—at the very least one voting member of the House of Representatives if not two voting Senators—you used little if any of your political capital or the bully pulpit and muscle to get even the most modest measure through Congress.

Will you now stand up for the voting rights in Congress for District voters, especially since the Republicans in the House have just taken away what committee-level voting rights Delegate Eleanor Holmes Norton has had?

Here is a suggestion to get started and one that will enhance a spirit of solidarity. Why not invite 100 of the exuberant, bilingual, peaceful Egyptian demonstrators to come to Washington, D.C., and help rally District residents in a massive gathering for their democratic rights in front of the White House at Lafayette Park? Before you address them, you can look out the window of the White House and see the colonials' signs and banners and hear their chants.

They might even announce a staggered general strike whereby at the beginning of each month they come to work 30 minutes later in the morning so that in six months, they go to work at noon. Some employers, especially nonprofits and commercial concerns with a sense of self-respect and human rights, may actually encourage such commitment and join with them.

During this elevating protest, people can discuss what it means to the District of Columbia when Congress can over-rule the City Council's decisions, vanquish referenda results, distort its budget, and decline to adequately reimburse the District government for incurring many federal governmental expenses, as precisely outlined recently by Colbert King in the January 29th *Washington Post*. Conversely, they can ponder with you what is not even contemplated by District residents because of their thralldom to the congressional veto.

So, come home with your rhetoric, Mr. President; come home to liberate your District of Columbia. What is your response?

Sincerely,

(Anyone interested in helping voting rights for Congress in D.C. can call the White House switchboard number at 202-456-1414 and express your opinion.)

JANUARY 10, 2011
The Roots of the Midterm Malaise

Dear President Obama,

The sentiments expressed in this letter may have more meaning for you now that the results of the midterm elections are clear. You have seen what can happen when a number of your supporters lose their enthusiasm and stay home or do not actively participate as volunteers.

In your first two years, you developed a wide asymmetry between your association with big business executives and the leaders of national civic and labor groups whose members are in the tens of millions. You have met repeatedly at the White House and other locales with corporate officials, spoken to their gatherings, and even traveled abroad with them to promote their exports.

Recently on your trip to India with a covey of business leaders, you vigorously touted their products, some by brand name (Boeing and Harley-Davidson's expensive motorcycles). Your traveling companions could not have been more gratified as you legitimized their view that WTO trade rules were a net plus for employment in the United States as well as India. Imagine—the president as business agent.

Contrast this close relationship with profit-making firms, many subsidized by the taxpayers in various ways, and probed for health, safety, or economic violations by regulatory agencies, with your refusal to openly and regularly address the large nonprofit civic groups. Before your inauguration, I wrote requesting that you do what Jimmy Carter did just after his election when he addressed and interacted with nearly one thousand civic leaders at a Washington hotel. They addressed a broad array of issues: environment, food, labor, energy, consumer, equality for women, civil rights, civil liberties, and other endeavors for a better society. It was a grand and productive occasion.

You know that the civic groups—often called the Independent Sector—employ many thousands of people around the country often on shoestring budgets with no profits in mind. They work for health, safety, economic and environmental well-being, for living wages and access to justice, for peace and the rule of law in domestic and foreign policy. Yet you, as president, do not adequately attach your cachet in their favor and give them the visibility that you give commercial businesses. Strange! For profits and jobs, yes I'm coming says the president. For justice and jobs, no I'm not coming says the president.

It is time to associate yourself with civil society, name some with approbation as you have done with companies, express your support for the expansion of their budgets and activities—in short, identify with them.

Please note that when you invite the CEOs of Aetna and Pfizer numerous times to the White House and cut deals not exactly in the patients' best interest, while you decline to invite old friends and mentors on these health insurance and health care subjects like Dr. Quentin Young in Chicago, people are perplexed and communicate their displeasure via their networks.

Last Friday, the *Wall Street Journal* reported that on February 7 you "will cross Lafayette Park from the White House to the headquarters of the U.S. Chamber of Commerce, [your] longtime political nemesis." What about walking next door and visiting your political friends at the headquarters of the AFL-CIO, whose member unions represent millions of working Americans?

You can discuss with Richard Trumka, a former coal miner and the new president of the AFL-CIO, your campaign promises in 2008. Repeatedly you said to the American people that you supported the "card check" and a "federal minimum wage of $9.50 in 2011." The 1968 minimum wage, adjusted for inflation, would be about $10 today. (The federal minimum wage is currently $7.25.)

Raising the minimum wage to nearly what it was back in 1968, in purchasing power, would increase consumer demand by over $200 billion a year. Isn't that what this economy needs right now, not to mention the boon it would be to long-deprived, underpaid workers and their families? After all, businesses of all sizes have received a variety of substantial tax breaks during this windfall period of a stagnant federal minimum wage. Isn't it time for some equity for the people?

On a related note, over a year ago Mr. Mike Kelleher, the man in charge of letters written to you, said he would get back to me about your policy on replying to letters that deal with substantive matters, whether under your signature or the signature of your assistants and department heads. I have not heard from Mr. Kelleher.

Let me give you an example. Months ago, I wrote to inform you that several prominent environmental and energy groups, such as Friends of the Earth, Greenpeace, and the Union of Concerned Scientists, were at their wit's end trying to arrange a joint meeting with Secretary Steven Chu. He repeatedly declined to meet, though he has often met with nuclear energy business executives and has gone so far as to tout nuclear energy's desirability in an op-ed. The environmental groups wanted a serious exchange with him on your administration's energy policies, including your request to Congress for very large loan guarantees by taxpayers for utilities that want to build more nuclear plants.

My letter asked you to intercede and urge Secretary Chu that it is only fair and constructive to hear what these groups have to say. There never was an answer from the White House or the Department of Energy. You know that for years many citizen advocates have worked hard to improve the federal government and they have rarely experienced such discourtesies of no replies.

Perhaps you do not care. But you should know that there are people who do. What is your response?

Sincerely,

The Office of Juvenile
Justice Deserves a Leader

Dear President Obama,

For two years, your administration has failed to appoint
a chief administrator for the federal government's juvenile
justice agency, the Office of Juvenile Justice and Delinquency
Prevention (OJJDP).

As an Illinois State Senator, you were in the forefront of the
drive to change the states laws, which automatically permitted
the transfer of youth to the adult criminal justice system. You
said then that "it's not the kind of state I want to live in where
we are afraid of our children and we are continually building
more prisons, as opposed to building more schools."

Is it not time for you to find a leader for the Office of
Juvenile Justice and Delinquency Prevention? Although some
candidates have been interviewed, there are few signs of the
political will to reach a decision with the urgency it deserves.
The administration needs to nominate an administrator who
has the experience, vision and energy to guide federal support
for youth justice in a way that simultaneously addresses the
harms caused by youth violence as well as the damage caused
by their incarceration.

Sincerely,

DECEMBER 6, 2010
On Extending the Bush Tax Cuts

Dear President Obama,

Increasingly credible press reports say that you are going to join with the Republican minority in the Congress and support the two-year extension of the Bush tax cut for the rich, along with cuts for those who make under $200,000 (individual) and $250,000 (couples) that the Democrats were favoring. It has become a widely noticed habit of yours to concede or to adopt both the Republican terms of policymaking and Republican policies and programs. Enclosed is a recent column where I wrote an imaginary private letter from former President George W. Bush to you, by way of providing examples of this recurrent practice.

You may or may not know what extending the tax cuts for the rich, worsening the deficit and burdening the next generation with the fiscal obligations, not to mention further restricting your options for public works programs and employment, will do to your electoral base. For many of your 2008 voters, this will indeed be the last straw for any active support they might have considered providing you.

It may be that you believe that trading off $120 billion in retained income for the rich is worth persuading the Republicans to support $18 billion for an extension of unemployment benefits to people out of work. With your Party controlling both the White House and the Congress until January 1, 2011, that is a remarkable definition of political, moral, and strategic weakness that will signal even greater capitulations to the Republicans during the next two years.

Remember MacGregor Burns's distinction between a transformational leader and a transactional leader.

Sincerely,

After nearly two years out, I can imagine George W. Bush writing his successor the following letter:

Dear President Obama,

As you know I've been peddling my book *Decision Points* and while doing interviews, people ask me what I think of the job you're doing. My answer is the same: he deserves to make decisions without criticism from me. It's a tough enough job as it is.

But their inquiries did prompt me to write to you to privately express my continual admiration for the job you are doing. Amazing! I say "privately" because making my sentiments public would not do either of us any good, if you know what I mean.

First, I can scarcely believe my good fortune as to how your foreign and military policies—"continuity" was the word used recently by my good friend, Joe Lieberman— has protected my legacy. More than protected, you've proven yourself just as able—and I may say sometimes even more so—to "kick ass," as my Daddy used to say.

My pleasant surprise is darn near limitless. Your Justice Department has not pursued any actions against my people—not to mention Dick Cheney or me—that the civil liberties and human rights crowd keep baying for you to do.

Overseas, all I see are five stars. You are roaring in Afghanistan, dispatching our great special forces into Yemen, saying, like me, that you'll go anywhere in the world to kill those terrorists. When you said you would assassinate American citizens abroad suspected of "terrorism"—that news came over the radio during breakfast when I was eating my shredded wheat and I almost choked with amazement. You got cajones, buddy.

I was hesitant about crossing the border into Pakistan—but you, man, are blasting away. Even Dick, who would never say it publicly, told me he is impressed.

The Leftists are always trying to have your policies show me up negatively. Hah—they're having one hell of a tough time, aren't they?

Me state secrets, you state secrets. Me executive privilege, you executive privilege. Me stop the release of torture videos, you backed me up. Me indefinite detention, you indefinite detention. Me extraordinary rendition, you extraordinary rendition. Me sending drones, you sending tons more, flying 24/7. Me just had to look the other way on collateral damage, you doing the same and protecting our boys doing it. Me approving nighttime assassination raids, you're upping the ante especially since General Petraeus took over. Me beefing up Defense, you not skipping a beat. Me letting the CIA loose, you told them to operate at large. Me demanding no pictures of our fallen troops, you doing the same, but allowing the families to go to Dover which I should have done.

There is one big difference. I never cracked a law book. You are a top Harvard lawyer and teacher of constitutional law. So when you do what I did, man, it's—what's the word—legitimization!

Domestically, sure you rag Wall Street, but you continued the big bail out of the bankers and their supporting cast. Sure, you're tougher with your words, but they deserve it—remember I said that the Wall Streeters "got drunk" and "got a hangover."

What I get such a kick out of is how you handled the unions and libs who backed you with dreams of "hope and change." How smoothly you let them learn they got nowhere to go, just as we used to tell our conservative wing the same thing (though now they've been reborn as growling Tea Partiers). So, card check, single payer, rolling back my Party's passage of legislation in Congress—you made them forget it!

You have been such a great president—backing me on so many things—keeping most tax cuts and shelters, support for my oil and gas buddies (my base), big loan guarantees for nukes, keeping Uncle Sam from bargaining down pharma, expanding free trade, not going tough on China (my Daddy especially liked this one), avoiding class struggle rhetoric, and so on.

You want to know how confident I am about you? Even though you called waterboarding "torture," I proudly admitted approving its use to protect our country and its freedoms. Isn't that really what the presidency is all about, along with honoring our troops and the entire national defense efforts? Semper fi.

Sincerely,

George W. Bush

P.S. My mother Barbara is a big fan. She calls your term so far *Obamabush*. Cute, aye, for someone who was never a wordsmith.

NOVEMBER 11, 2010

The Public Interest and GM's IPO

Dear President Obama,

The U.S. government bailout of, and acquisition of a majority share in, General Motors was an exceptional action, taken in response to exceptional circumstances. The U.S. stake in GM obviously poses novel managerial challenges to the government. The appropriate response to those challenges, however, is not to run from the responsibility through passive ownership and premature sale at a loss to taxpayers. We write as GM prepares to undertake an Initial Public Offering (IPO) of stock that will reduce the government stake in the company to 43 percent. We urge that the government, as primary owner, arrange for the suspension of the IPO and then begin exercising the responsibilities attendant to ownership. We would like to highlight some of the numerous reasons for, and applications of, these recommendations.

1. Ensuring the best return to taxpayers

The government obviously has a serious fiduciary duty to taxpayers to obtain the best possible return on our investment in GM. This should not be the government's only consideration in managing its GM stake, but it should be a priority.

News reports indicate the planned IPO will cause taxpayers to realize a $4.9 billion loss. Certainly no one can predict the future of GM or the markets with any certainty, but many analysts have offered the view that GM's financial prospects are very positive. Simply recognizing how severely the Great Recession has crimped auto sales in the United States gives credence to this view; annual sales remain down by more than 25 percent from a few years ago. Many analysts believe that the IPO is being driven by a government desire to exit from GM ownership as soon as possible, even at the expense of better recoupment of the taxpayer investment.

Investor prudence thus counsels for maintaining the government's current share, and delaying a sell-off so that the government can capture likely improved returns in the future.

2. Protecting jobs and investment in the United States

We believe the government emergency investment in GM was necessary and proper, though we were and remain critical that the government imposed conditions on its investment to lower GM costs, but not to advance broader public interest objectives.

The primary rationale of investing in GM had to be to preserve jobs and prop an economy in a severe downward spiral. As we pointed out at the time of the government investment, it was incumbent on the government to ensure that GM maintained production in the United States. There may be a rationale for GM to produce overseas for overseas markets, but it should not be opening new facilities abroad to ship back to the United States; and choices about facilities closings should favor keeping U.S. plants open, especially for vehicles produced for the U.S. market. There is a broader concern: the U.S. government has an interest in ensuring that the locus of GM's research and product development remains in the United States.

As majority shareholder in GM, the United States has the ability to direct or influence the company's investment decisions. As the U.S. reduces its share, so its capacity to influence such decisions diminishes. Had the government invested in GM for pecuniary reasons, the legitimacy of affecting such decisions would be lessened. But the government did not invest in GM for pecuniary reasons. It invested precisely to preserve U.S. jobs and manufacturing capacity. It is now incumbent on the government to manage its investment to advance these objectives.

Underscoring the importance of suspending the IPO to ensure protection of the U.S. national interests in GM, are reports that various foreign auto manufacturers—including China's SAIC—and sovereign wealth funds are considering purchasing large blocks of shares in GM.

3. Addressing climate change, safety and environmental challenges
Looming over all the other great challenges facing the

country and the world is the threat of catastrophic climate change. Addressing climate change is going to require massive, across-the-board changes in the way we generate, distribute, and consume energy. No area will be more important than transportation.

Your administration has taken some positive steps toward increasing vehicle fuel economy standards, but we need even more to achieve transformational change.

Holding a majority stake in one of the world's largest auto makers, even if due to a historic anomaly, positions the U.S. government to directly advance the transformational changes we need. In addition to prodding the automakers to do better, through always-contentious and often-undermined regulatory processes, the government can and should direct GM to dramatically increase its investments in electric cars and other transformational technologies, and to make sure safety is not compromised with such new technologies.

The ability to direct such investments will decline as the U.S. share in GM declines.

Such direction makes even more sense given the second gift from TARP to GM in the bailout—a provision allowing GM to keep a $45 billion tax loss carryforward that normally is erased in restructuring. GM can avoid that amount in future tax liability on its profits.

4. Preserving our democracy from influence from unaccountable corporate entities

Whether by government directive or some very modest sense of propriety, GM suspended its lobbying and campaign contributions while undergoing the government rescue.

But now, outrageously, with the government still a majority shareholder, the company has resumed lobbying. To peruse GM's lobby disclosure forms is to see a corporate entity working to shape policy on a broad range of issues, including: auto and truck safety,

Wall Street reform, taxes, appropriations, climate change, fuel efficiency, trade (including trade agreements with Korea, Peru, and Colombia, and negotiations at the World Trade Organization), and currency valuation.

Why in the world is a majority government-owned—that is, publicly-owned—entity permitted to lobby the U.S. Congress and executive agencies, often against your own administration's legislative and policy positions, such as the Motor Vehicle Safety Act of 2010 legislation to correct statutory deficiencies resulting in the Toyota debacle, presently pending in the House and Senate? With the ballot boxes barely counted, the Alliance of Automobile Manufacturers (of which GM is a prominent member) is already reneging on fuel economy rules it agreed to with your administration less than two years ago.

The government, as majority shareholder, should not permit this to occur; and it should not permit its shareholding stake to be reduced in such a way that GM gains greater latitude to affect policymaking.

As the government was preparing its rescue of GM, we highlighted each of the concerns mentioned here, and urged that they be addressed as part of the rescue process. Those recommendations were, unfortunately, ignored. But it is not too late for the government to exercise its control of GM responsibly and to advance vital public interest objectives. We urge you to act to suspend the IPO.

Sincerely,
Ralph Nader
Joan Claybrook
Clarence Ditlow
Robert Weissman

AUGUST 2, 2010
In the Wake of Talmadge Creek, Revive the Office of Pipeline Safety

Dear President Obama,

The spill of nearly one million gallons of oil from Enbridge Energy Partners' pipeline into Talmadge Creek in Michigan on July 26 further demonstrates the necessity for you and Secretary LaHood to pay immediate attention to the hapless, industry-indentured Office of Pipeline Safety (OPS), which has been, like the Minerals Management Service, in a long fraternal relationship with its industry.

Following a pipeline explosion in 1965 at Natchitoches, Louisiana, which took 17 lives, engineer Fred Lang and I pressed Congress to pass the Natural Gas Pipeline Safety Act of 1968. Almost immediately, the pipeline industry—both gas and oil—moved to capture it and its advisory committee. The history of OPS has been largely one of self-regulation with standards essentially written by the industry below the needs of safety and the availability of practical technological capabilities.

Today, there are two million miles of pipelines under the jurisdiction of OPS, including many miles offshore. It has never had enough inspectors.

On January 21, 2010, OPS wrote to Mr. Terry McGill, president of Enbridge Energy, that "you have committed a probable violation of Pipeline Safety Regulations, Title 49, Code of Federal Regulations." This tentative charge related to one of the worst nightmares of pipeline safety engineers—internal corrosion. Nonetheless, OPS decided, after reviewing "the circumstances," "not to conduct additional enforcement action or penalty proceedings at this time." The agency advised Enbridge "to correct the item identified in this letter."

Had OPS issued a corrective action order at any time during the first half of 2010, the environmental water contamination calamity would not have occurred. The creeks and streams would be fishable and a source for drinking water for the nearby communities. The fear of further water contamination to Lake Michigan would not have been expressed by Michigan's governor.

OPS seems not to value "corrective action orders" that are preventive. Instead, they "usually" reserve corrective orders for the period after the "accident, spill, or other significant immediate or imminent safety or environmental concern." These words signify OPS's relaxed response to law enforcement or to policing in ways that deter and preclude.

There are those so-called regulatory agencies, with low general media visibility, that have responsibilities to head off major environmental disasters. Earlier, I advised you to pay closer attention to those agencies that are known to be heavily industry influenced inside and out, including the Federal Railroad Administration and the Nuclear Regulatory Commission. I hope that you do. You and the country do not need another BP gusher situation that proper regulation could have prevented.

Sincerely,

The White House's Canned Response
on the Auto Industry

Dear Friend,

Thank you for contacting me regarding the American automobile industry.

Since its inception, this industry has been like no other. It has been an emblem of the American entrepreneurial spirit and a symbol of America's success. It helped build the middle class and sustain it throughout the 20th century. American automobiles have been a source of pride for generations of workers who have produced some of the finest cars the world has ever known. Millions of jobs depend on this industry, and it can play an important role in our Nation's future economic growth.

Unfortunately, year after year, leaders in Detroit and Washington have papered over problems and kicked tough choices down the road. Now is the time to confront these problems and do what is necessary to solve them.

As president, my job is to ensure that if tax dollars are being put on the line, they are being invested in a real fix that will make the auto industry more competitive. Ultimately, though, the survival of this industry cannot be dependent on an unending flow of taxpayer dollars. Our Government's direct involvement in the auto industry should end as soon as responsibly possible.

We will continue to pursue the goal of a re-tooled, re-imagined auto industry that can create jobs here at home and help usher in a new era of economic prosperity. To learn more about this and other issues, please visit: WhiteHouse.gov.

Again, thank you for writing.

Sincerely,

Barack Obama

Warren for Consumer Financial Protection Bureau Director!

Dear President Obama,

It is time for you to give taxpayers, consumers, and investors a reason to believe that you are truly interested in consumer protection by nominating Professor Elizabeth Warren to be the Director of the much-anticipated Consumer Financial Protection Bureau (CFPB).

Professor Warren combines rigorous scholarship, a superb sense of needed change and clear ways to communicate those needs to families and individuals around the country. Consumer leaders know that Professor Warren has been a strong and talented chair of the Congressional Oversight Panel (COP), which has been reviewing the current state of financial markets and the regulatory system.

In addition, Professor Warren had the vision and good sense to propose and advocate for the creation of an entity much like the Consumer Financial Protection Bureau.

It is troubling that Shahien Nasiripour, *Huffington Post* business reporter, wrote in a July 15, 2010, article: "Treasury Secretary Timothy Geithner has expressed opposition to the possible nomination of Elizabeth Warren to head the Consumer Financial Protection Bureau, according to a source with knowledge of Geithner's views."

It is equally troubling that on NPR's *The Diane Rehm Show*, Senator Christopher Dodd, chairman of the Banking, Housing and Urban Affairs Committee attempted to further undermine Professor Warren. Today's *National Journal Online* reports that when asked about Warren, "Dodd said that 'no idea is terribly creative if it can't sell' and he asked rhetorically about Warren, 'Is she confirmable?'"

With Senator Dodd showing a lack of leadership or willingness to fight for Professor Warren, and with Treasury Secretary Geithner seemingly preferring someone who is more willing to fight for Wall Street speculators with other people's money than consumers and investors on Main Street, it is imperative that you issue a strong and clear statement of support for Professor Warren now.

Wall Street's "picks" for high positions in your administration have met with your concurrence again and again. Now it is time for the overwhelming choice of Professor Warren by consumer groups in Washington and all the country to be respected.

If you wish to make this an adverse political issue for November, you can. Or you can be a responsive leader and secure Senate confirmation for the people's choice.

Sincerely,

JULY 7, 2010
Labor Day 2010

Dear President Obama,

Presidents issue a statement on every Labor Day. This year's September commemoration for American workers offers a special opportunity for your words to resonate with a brighter reality for millions of low-income laborers, many of whom have no health insurance, nor any paid sick leave.

I am referring to a solemn campaign pledge you made to American workers in 2008, to further raise the minimum wage to $9.50 an hour by 2011, index it to inflation and increase the Earned Income Tax Credit to make sure that full-time workers can earn a living wage that allows them to raise their families and pay for basic needs such as food, transportation, and housing.

The federal minimum wage was raised to $7.25 on July 24, 2009, and remains at that level. Were the federal minimum wage in 1968 just indexed to inflation, apart from any recognition of major worker productivity gains, it would be at least $10.00 by now. (In addition, the real costs of getting to and from work are greater than they were in 1968.)

Politifact.com from the *St. Petersburg Times*, which keeps meticulously fair records of how many campaign promises you have kept, stated: "We have reviewed his public statements since taking office and couldn't find any mention of his plans to raise it to $9.50. We also searched statements made by Obama to see if, since taking office, he has provided a plan, or at least a broad outline, of how he plans to implement this proposal. We didn't find one."

The labor movement is not expecting you to press for the repeal of the pernicious, antiworker portions of the Taft-Hartley Act of 1947. Organized labor is upset, however, at your lack of any mention or urging of Congress to enact the Employee Free Choice Act which you repeatedly supported as a presidential candidate. At the very least, provide the unorganized, voiceless workers of Walmart, McDonald's, and other low-wage businesses, paying their CEOs thousands of dollars *per hour*, with a minimum wage of $9.50 that is still less than what it was in 1968 in real purchasing power.

Begin the process of fulfilling this campaign pledge by declaring on Labor Day 2010 your recommendation to Congress that it enact a $9.50 federal minimum wage and put some White House muscle behind that demand. It would be good to include at long last farmworkers under that legislation as well. After all, these workers do not push paper all day; they grow and harvest our food!

I look forward to your response to the people in this regard.

Sincerely,

[signature]

Where Is Secretary Chu?

Dear President Obama,

For over a year, we have been requesting a meeting with Secretary of Energy Steven Chu to discuss various aspects of energy policies that have been neglected. At first, his office responded that it would be best to wait until Secretary Chu had filled key tall positions. Then his office recommended an appointment with a subordinate, notwithstanding that the request was for a meeting with leading civic groups.

We know that he has met many times with corporate officials from industry and commerce. We know that he has published at least one article exclusively promoting atomic energy. We know, from our meeting with other secretaries (labor, education, and agriculture), that they found meeting with civic leaders a beneficial experience.

It is sad and self-limiting that he has not seen fit to meet with these groups, which have been proven right so often. They have many years of experience, knowledge, and accurate analyses of wrongheaded energy choices, subsidies, deregulation, no regulation, and the absence of concrete plans for worst-case scenarios to further distinguish the better from the least good choices of energy sources. They know the weaknesses of the various energy regulatory agencies under your administration, including the Minerals Management Service.

On behalf of the organizations listed below, I urge you to encourage Secretary Chu to meet personally with us. A convenient date for all can be arranged sometime this summer.

Sincerely,

List of groups:
Beyond Nuclear
Friends of the Earth
Greenpeace
Nuclear Information Resource Service
Physicians for Social Responsibility
Public Citizen's Energy Project
Union of Concerned Scientists

MAY 28, 2010

Security from Transportation Security

Dear President Obama,

It is important for citizens to give their president cautionary alerts about serious potential risks to the public's health.

Enclosed is a letter from members of the University of California San Francisco (UCSF) science faculty (including a member of the National Academy of Sciences and an internationally known and respected cancer expert) sent to your science advisor, Dr. John Holdren, on April 6, 2010.* These scientists express their deep concerns about the rapid deployment of the full-body backscatter X-ray scanner in U.S. airports without sufficient safety review by an impartial panel of experts. A call to Dr. Holdren's office reveals that he is studying the letter and has not yet responded to the UCSF scientists.

Another highly respected radiation expert, Dr. David Brenner of Columbia University's Center for Radiological Research, has also raised serious concerns about exposing millions of airline passengers to radiation without an independent scientific review.

Security experts have also questioned the effectiveness of these scanning devices, concluding that the devices can be easily defeated by concealing explosives in body cavities.

It was wasteful enough for the Transportation Safety Administration (TSA) to install the "puffer" security devices at U.S. airports and then withdraw them because they were found to be "unreliable" at a cost of $30 million to taxpayers. Now, a far larger amount of taxpayer money is being spent on these scanning devices by the Department of Homeland Security (DHS), which claims it is not obligated to observe the Administrative Procedures Act.

I suggest that you give your attention to this emerging risk. Preventing cancer should be a presidential priority.

Sincerely,

*See http://www.npr.org/assets/news/2010/05/17/concern.pdf for the full text of this letter.

Establish a Financial Consumers' Association

Dear President Obama, Senator Dodd, Senator Schumer and Senator Shelby,

On the eve of the portentous Senate debate over the extent to which the financial industry is to be held accountable so as to avert future megacollapses on the backs of taxpayers, workers, and consumers, a great gap has been left unattended.

That gap pertains to the continued powerlessness of the investors and consumers—the people who bear the ultimate brunt of Wall Street's recklessness, avarice and crimes and who have the greatest interest in strong regulatory enforcement.

Among all the amendments filed for the upcoming Senate debate, only amendment number 29, introduced by Senator Schumer, provides a facility to establish an independent non-governmental nonprofit Financial Consumers' Association (FCA).

Amendment 29 includes the following for funding this unique institution:

"—the financial industry has enjoyed virtually unlimited access to represent its interest before Congress, the courts, and State and Federal regulators, while financial services consumers have had limited representation before Congress and financial regulatory entities"; and

"—the Federal Government has a substantial interest in the creation of a public purpose, democratically controlled, self-funded, nationwide membership association of financial services consumers to enhance their representation and to effectively combat unsound financial practices."

Anyone modestly familiar with the history of regulatory failures knows that the gross disparity of power and organized advocacy between big business and consumers outside of government leads to an absence of fair standards and law enforcement.

It also leads, as everyone knows, to massive taxpayer bailouts, subsidies, and guarantees when these giant banks and other financial firms immolate themselves, after enriching their bosses, while engulfing tens of millions of innocent people in the subsequent economic conflagration.

Given all the privileges and costly rescues for culpable corporations that flow regularly from Washington, D.C., adopting ever so mildly the principle of reciprocity makes a powerful case for facilitating a nationwide Financial Consumers' Association—one that would be composed of voluntary memberships by consumers who, through their annual dues, will sustain the FCA for an expert place at the table.

Senator Schumer, when he was a congressman during the savings and loan bailout in the nineteen-eighties, introduced such a proposal. But the bankers took the $150 billion bailout and blocked this reciprocal respect for depositors in the House Banking Committee.

Then, Representative Schumer and his supporting colleagues on that committee understood that without the supposed beneficiaries of regulatory authority being organized to make regulation and deterrence work, the savings and loan collapse could happen again. And so they became prophetic beyond their wildest nightmares.

Before he died in a plane crash in 2002, Senator Paul Wellstone recognized the need for such a facility, when he introduced the Consumer and Shareholder Protection Association Act.

A key enhancing feature in Amendment 29 is a requirement that invitations to membership in the FCA be included in the billing envelopes or electronic communications of financial institutions with their customers. At no expense to these vendors, these notices would ensure that the maximum number of consumers are invited to join and fund such a democratically run, educational, and advocacy organization.

In early 2009, I met with Chairman Christopher Dodd and explained the nature and importance of the FCA and Senator Schumer's earlier role in advancing this civic innovation. He seemed receptive to the idea and urged us to have his colleague Senator Schumer take the lead, which he has done with Amendment 29 just a few weeks ago. Senator Shelby and I have also discussed the FCA proposal.

The major valiant, but overwhelmed consumer groups, who experience daily this enormous imbalance of power between corporations and consumers, presently stacked by unprecedented amounts of federal funds and bailout facilities for the misbehaving companies, support the creation of a self-funded FCA.

The federal government has long paid for facilities in the U.S. Department of Agriculture for agricultural businesses to band together and assess themselves to promote beef, corn, cotton, and other commodities to increase their profits. By contrast, the FCA, once launched, would be composed of consumers paying their own way to preserve their hard-earned savings from predatory financial speculators.

Allow one prediction. Even if the ultimate legislation comes out stronger than expected on such matters as derivatives, rating agencies, too big to fail, using depositor funds for speculation, and the consumer financial regulatory bureau, unless the consumer-investor is afforded modest facilities to band together with their experts and advocates, the laws will hardly be enforced with sufficient budgets, personnel, and regulatory will power.

Give the consumer a modest round in this prolonged deliberation following the destructive events of 2008.

Sincerely,

[signature]

NOVEMBER 24, 2009

Stand Up and Appoint!

Dear President Obama,

Every year, over 40,000 people die on the highways in our country. About 58,000 workers perish due to workplace-related diseases and trauma. The National Highway Traffic Safety Administration (NHTSA) and the Occupational Safety and Health Administration (OSHA) are charged with preventing these casualties, along with injuries and illnesses of an even greater number.

Having worked at the founding of these two regulatory law enforcement agencies in the sixties and early seventies, I have been sorely disappointed at their lassitude and obeisance in recent decades as the so-called regulated companies learned to game them, co-opt them, stifle them and delay them. For instance, OSHA did not initiate and issue a single chemical control regulation during the Clinton and Bush administrations!

Upon your election, some of us entertained the thought that you would command a reversal, even if modest, of these passive agencies. As of today, these agencies remain headless. No one has been nominated to head NHTSA, after the first candidate changed his mind months ago, and your OSHA nominee David Michaels has been held up in the Senate.

As of today, fully 45 percent of your positions, confirmable by the Senate, are still not filled, ten months after your inauguration.

Isn't it time for you to make a public statement backed by a compelling demand on the Republicans in the Senate to let you staff our government at the highest levels or at least bring these nominees to a vote on the Senate floor? The voiceless deserve no less.

Speak out, Mr. President, forcefully and visibly.

Sincerely,

AUGUST 5, 2009
GM and Chrysler's Victims

Dear President Obama,

We are writing again to urge you to restore the obliterated rights of victims of defective GM and Chrysler cars. Our earlier letter of July 14 has received no reply.

The bankruptcy process for GM and Chrysler that your Wall Street task force directed left those persons who allege injuries as a result of defective vehicles sold by these companies, and with pending or not-yet-filed claims, without redress. Their legal claims against the companies for compensation for their injuries, or family members' claims for lost loved ones, were extinguished by the dictatorial bankruptcy process. In the case of Chrysler, future victims of defective products on the road will be without opportunity for redress; GM belatedly agreed to accept liability for future victims.

When we wrote you last month on this topic, there appeared some possibility for a legislative or administrative remedy for these double victims—first, by corporate wrongdoing; second, by an unjust bankruptcy process—in connection with efforts to address concerns of closed-down dealers. The likelihood of such an arrangement now appears diminished.

Thus it is imperative that you and your administration assure these persons a modicum of justice. As the dominant shareholder in GM and an overseer at Chrysler, the government could instruct the companies to accept liability. You could require they purchase insurance policies to cover claims against them for defective products. Or, the worst option (but far better than inaction), the government itself could provide a compensation fund for these victims.

In addition to the identifiable suffering of those already victimized by Chrysler and GM's defective products (you can acquaint yourself with the anguishing stories of some of the victims*), there is the matter of future victims of defective Chrysler products. Hundreds or thousands of people will foreseeably be victimized by dangerous products sold by old Chrysler. All of them will be disbelieving when they discover that not only do they have to come to grips with their injuries, or loss of family members, but that they have no legal claim against Chrysler. The obvious remedy to prevent this problem is to require Chrysler to accept liability for future injuries. If your administration declines to take this step, however, then it must lend support to a petition now pending at the Federal Trade Commission, calling for the roughly 30 million old Chrysler cars now on the road to be accompanied at resale by prominent disclosure statements regarding Chrysler's immunity from civil liability for defective cars.

---

* See https://nader.org//files/8014/1021/0074/BankCaseStoriesPhotoF.pdf for stories of the victims.

Mr. President, there is no doubt that managing the GM and Chrysler transition process required hard choices and tradeoffs. But whether to victimize again the victims of these companies' unsafe cars was not among those hard choices. We urge you to reverse course on this matter, and ensure that past and future victims are provided with the opportunity to seek compensation in courts of law.

A few weeks ago, we spoke to the gentleman at the White House in charge of letters to determine what your response policy is, other than to continue George W. Bush's policy of not responding, nor even acknowledging receipt. We await his answer and hope to hear from you about the above-noted travesty of justice.

Sincerely,
Ralph Nader
Robert Weissman

MAY 29, 2009

Holding GM Accountable, Follow-up*

Dear President Obama and Mr. Henderson,

We are writing to follow-up on our letter of May 26. We wish to reiterate our overriding message: Before any irreversible moves are made—including, especially, entrance into voluntary bankruptcy—the GM/task force reorganization plan should be submitted to Congress for deliberative review and decision. We also wish to highlight several major concerns with a precipitous bankruptcy declaration that have emerged over the last several days.

---

* See page 273 for original letter from May 26, 2009.

First, the previously understood rationale for bankruptcy no longer applies. We noted in our prior letter that there were creative negotiating strategies to address the problem of reaching an accommodation with the bondholders. Recent developments indicate that claim to be true, as GM and the auto task force have revised the proposed allocation of equity in a restructured GM, and reached agreement with at least the most prominent bondholders. Although a June 1st bond payment is due, it certainly seems that that payment could easily be wrapped into the new bondholder offer, as effectively will be the case if GM enters bankruptcy.

With the bondholder problem moving toward resolution, or at least now clearly resolvable, there is no evident rationale for bankruptcy other than an unstoppable momentum of some hidden agendas. Given the high stakes, including the many concerns we raised in our previous letter (among them, the effects on consumer confidence in the GM brand and the socioeconomic impacts of potentially excessive downsizing), inertia is no reason at all.

Second, the matter of how GM's holdings in China will be treated in bankruptcy, an issue we highlighted in the previous letter, continues to demand attention before a filing. Kevin Wale, president and managing director of GM China, told CNN that "Our business is run as separate joint-ventures here in China in partnership with SAIC . . . so we're profitable, we fund our own investment and we would be largely independent of any action that took place in the U.S." Yet the GM assets and profits in China must be included in any bankruptcy proceeding, and available to creditors, claimants, and litigants who could, conceivably, petition to take the company into Chapter 7 liquidation. Has GM clearly presented to the government its valuable holdings, large profits, and contractual obligations in

China? The task force has indicated some uncertainty about these questions.

Third, proceedings in the Chrysler bankruptcy have highlighted the manifold injustice being perpetrated on victims of defective Chrysler products—and likely to be perpetrated on victims of GM products. In the Chrysler proceeding, top Chrysler officials have acknowledged that they were ready and able to do a deal with Fiat that established successor liability for the emergent Fiat/"good Chrysler" company. In the course of bankruptcy or in preparing for bankruptcy, however, they reversed course, apparently just because they could. Now, hundreds of Chrysler victims are on track to have their claims extinguished, unless the bankruptcy judge or other court overrules this element of the bankruptcy plan.

There are many differences between the bankruptcy of the private company, Chrysler, and the pending GM bankruptcy, but the GM restructuring plan is similar to Chrysler in the anticipated creation of a bad/old GM and a new/good GM that emerges without liabilities. Do you plan to follow the Chrysler approach? Have you given consideration to the suffering of real adults and children that will follow from such a move? (Not to mention the political backlash.)

One such real person is Amanda Dinnigan, a 10-year-old girl from Long Island, New York. Amanda was injured by an allegedly faulty seatbelt in a GMC Envoy that snapped her neck in a crash. Her father, an ironworker, estimates her health care costs at $500,000 a year. Her decline in quality of life will obviously be tragic. Will a discretionary decision not to establish successorship liability in a discretionary (voluntary) bankruptcy leave Amanda and her family—and thousands of others like them—with no access to justice? If you intend to proceed with maneuvers effectively to extinguish their claims, you should at least talk to some of them first, and confront the human consequences of such actions.

The GM/task force bankruptcy plans appear geared to saving the General Motors entity—but at a harsh and often avoidable cost to workers, communities, suppliers, consumers, dealers, and the nation's manufacturing capacity.

At this late stage we again urge you to reconsider the bankruptcy filing plans, and to enable deliberative and meaningful congressional review—as many members of Congress are seeking—of the restructuring plans before irreversible steps are taken. After all, Congress is more than a potted plant. The first branch legislated, after public hearings, the 1979 Chrysler bailout and the complex Conrail restructuring a few years later.

Sincerely,
Ralph Nader
Robert Weissman
Charlie Cray

MAY 26, 2009
Holding GM Accountable

Dear President Obama and Mr. Henderson,

There is no question that the reorganization of General Motors, after decades of managerial failure and amidst the most severe economic downturn of the last 70 years, is a matter of enormous complexity. But the publicly available information about GM and the auto task force's plans raise many disturbing questions. Given both the significant public investment in the reorganization, and the extraordinary public interest in seeing the reorganization succeed in achieving public objectives, it would be a mistake to proceed with reorganization plans crafted behind closed doors and not publicly vetted. Before any irreversible moves are made—including, especially, entrance into voluntary bankruptcy—the GM/task force reorganization plan should be submitted to Congress for deliberative review and decision.

To the outside world, the priority of GM and the task force seems to be to preserve GM as a going concern. Less apparent is: to whose benefit?

Would it make sense for the government to invest tens of billions of taxpayer dollars in GM to enable it to shift much more of its production for the U.S. market outside of the United States? The answer is, plainly, "no," highlighting the larger principle: From the public's standpoint, the reorganization makes sense only if it serves the public interest.

There are numerous features of the GM/task force plan that, on their face, appear to contravene this public interest. Perhaps there are legitimate rationales for the choices made; if so, they should be presented and debated in the Congress, as was the 1979 Chrysler bailout and the Conrail restructuring. Among the many unanswered questions and concerns expressed by Members of Congress and the public about the GM/task force plan:

• Has the task force evaluated the social ripple effects on suppliers, innovation, dealers, newspapers, banks, and others that hold company stock and/or are company creditors, and other unique harms that might stem from bankruptcy? Has it conducted any kind of formal or informal cost-benefit analysis on the costs of a GM bankruptcy and excessive closures, including the social effects of lost jobs (including more than

100,000 dealership jobs alone), more housing foreclosures, the government expense of providing unemployment and social relief, lost tax revenues, supplier companies that will be forced to close and impacts on GM industrial creditors?

• Does GM really need to close as many dealerships as have been announced? Is the logic of closing dealers to enable the remaining dealers to charge higher prices? (See, for example, Peter Whoriskey and Kendra Marr, "Chrysler Pulls Out of Hundreds of Franchises," *Washington Post*, May 15, 2009.) And if so, why is the government facilitating such a move, since dealers do not cost GM, given its "adhesion-like" contracts?

• Has the task force maintained the Bush administration-imposed obligation for unionized auto workers at GM and Chrysler to accept wages comparable to those in non-unionized Japanese company plants in the United States? This requirement is especially troubling given the low contribution of auto manufacturer wages to the cost of a car (10 percent), and that it may set off a downward spiral of wages, with the nonunion plants no longer needing to compete with union wages, and union wages following those in nonunion plants.

• Why isn't the task force obtaining guarantees that, after restructuring with U.S. taxpayer financing, GM cars sold in the United States will be made in the United States? What is the conceivable rationale for permitting GM, sustained by taxpayer dollars, to increase manufacturing overseas, especially in dictatorships, for export back into the United States?

• How will bankruptcy affect GM's overseas subsidiaries, with special reference to China and GM's corporate entanglements with Chinese partners? Are these GM assets and their profits being exempted from conditions being imposed on domestic operations? If there is such a disparity, is it reasonable and unavoidable?

• How will bankruptcy affect GM's obligations to parties engaged in pending or future litigation in the courts with GM regarding serious injuries suffered because of design or product defects in vehicles sold prior to the bankruptcy? There are suffering human beings who are wondering about monetized minds ending their day in court.

• How will bankruptcy affect GM's obligations to parties engaged in lemon litigation—suits to get auto design or manufacturing defects fixed or cars replaced?

• Is the task force insisting on too many plants closing and the elimination of too many brands?

• What guarantees are the task force, supposedly representing the taxpayers' investment, obtaining to ensure that the GM of the future invests in safer and more fuel-efficient vehicles, and what investments will the new company make in ecologically sustainable technologies? How will a potential bankruptcy filing affect, ignore or preclude any such future investments and commitments?

There are also the acute business judgment questions:

• Will a bankruptcy filing go as smoothly and quickly as GM and the task force believe? Doesn't the complexity of the GM corporate entity, contrasted with Chrysler, highlight the limitations of relying on the Chrysler precedent, which is in any case not yet established?

• What will be the effect of bankruptcy on consumer confidence in the GM brand? What has changed to dispel the conventional wisdom of six months ago, which held that bankruptcy would be disastrous for consumer purchasing confidence?

There are difficult questions, as well, about whose interest GM, the corporate entity, is advancing. It is plainly not advancing interests of its powerless owner-shareholders, who will see their equity dissolve to near worthlessness. GM's bondholders and creditors are unhappy with the proposed reorganization plan. More public stakeholders—workers, consumers, victims of defective products, and communities— are also ill served by important features of the plan, as we suggest above. Exactly what principles are guiding GM's handling of the reorganization?

Moreover, do both of you realize the difficulties of full disclosure of properly valued assets and creditors worldwide that even lenient bankruptcy courts require to meet the fiduciary obligations of top GM executives? On this point, Mr. Henderson's imagination is more fertile than the outsider president.

An expected June 1st bankruptcy declaration looms over any meaningful consideration of these and many other questions by Congress and the public. The task force declares June 1st as its deadline because of a scheduled bond payment. But there must be creative negotiating strategies to avoid that purported obstacle. In any case, the $1 billion due in bond payments pales in comparison to the extraordinary sums poured into AIG ($180 billion plus), Citigroup ($330 billion in loans and guarantees) and other financial-speculative firms. (The question of the legality of any government funds for GM and Chrysler is for another day.)

This is a moment that calls for leadership, including the steadfastness to defend the importance of our deliberative democratic institutions. There's too much at stake, with too many social, economic, and political consequences for a bankruptcy declaration and the reorganization plan to proceed without congressional action.

Sincerely,
Ralph Nader
Robert Weissman
Charlie Cray

Consumer Protection in the Obama Era

Dear President Obama,

Underneath many of our country's economic problems is the thirty-year collapse of consumer protection—both of the regulatory kind and of the self-help kind known as proper access to justice.

Last month, major consumer groups sent you a letter proposing action to rein in exploitation of consumers as debtors, as buyers of oil, gas, and electricity, as patients needing health insurance and as eaters wanting safe goods.

Under the Bush regime, the words "consumer protection" were rarely uttered and the Bush administration almost never initiated any proconsumer efforts, even with massive evidence before it, such as predatory lending and credit card abuses.

You need to recognize and elevate the GDP significance of fair consumer policies, along with their moral and just attributes at a time of worsening recession.

I suggest you focus on the state of the poorest consumers in the urban and rural ghettos. As you know from your days with the New York Public Interest Group (NYPIRG) and as a community organizer in Chicago, the consumers in these areas are the most gouged and least protected. That the "poor pay more" has been extensively documented by civic, official, and academic studies, and numerous local newspaper and television news reports.

Unfortunately, neither Congress nor the executive branch have paid adequate attention to the tens of millions of people who lose at least 25 percent of their consumer dollars to multiple frauds and shoddy merchandise. You should establish special task forces in the Justice Department and the Federal

Trade Commission on their plight and on the many proven, but unused remedies to assure a fair marketplace with effective enforcement and grievance procedures.

Working with and galvanizing local and state agencies to enlarge their capacity and staff—with stimulus monies—can produce a triple-header, making the federal effort more effective, providing valuable jobs and freeing up billions of consumer dollars from the financial sinkhole of commercial crimes.

It requires the visibility and eloquence of your personal leadership to launch this long overdue defense of poor people.

A second area of action is simply to update major areas of regulatory health and safety that have been frozen for thirty years. These include modernizing standards for auto and tire safety, food safety, aviation and railroad safety, and occupational health and trauma protection.

New knowledge, new marketing forays, and new technologies have accumulated during this period without application. It is the obsolescence of so many safety standards hailing from the fifties, sixties, and seventies that permits the tricky, corporate advertising claims that products "exceed federal safety standards."

Note for example that the SEC has never come close to regulating the recent explosion of myriad collateralized debt obligations (CDOs). The massive speculation in this area is destabilizing the national and world economies.

Third, you need to articulate and provide a high profile to what Western Europeans have long called "social consumerism." Citizens are consumers of government services for which they pay as taxpayers. In return they are entitled to prompt, accurate, and courteous responses to their inquiries and to their perceived needs as embraced by the authorizing statutes.

To begin with, Americans need to be able to get through to

their government agencies and departments. Being put on hold interminably with automated messages to nowhere, not receiving replies of any kind to their letters, and generally getting the brush-off even with the deadlines explicated in the Freedom of Information Act have been a bipartisan failure.

However, under the Bush regime, not answering serious letters from dedicated individuals and groups on time-sensitive matters of policy and action—as with the Iraq War and occupation—became standard operating procedure, starting with President Bush himself.

This stonewalling has turned people off so much that they do not even bother to "ask their government" for assistance, and that includes an astonishingly unresponsive Congress (other than for ministerial requests such as locating lost VA or Social Security checks).

As you shape the Obama White House, bear in mind that the "change you can believe in" is one of kind, not just degree.

Sincerely,

JANUARY 9, 2009
Advice for the President-elect

Dear President-elect Obama,

You have been receiving a great deal of advice since November 4, 2008 from people and groups who either want you to advance policies not covered in your campaign or who want you to be more specific about initiatives you emphasized.

There are two suggestions which may not be among your

stacks of recommendations that need to be considered before you take office on January 20, 2009.

First, the public would benefit from a concise recounting of the State of the Union and where the Bush administration has left our country. As is your style, you can render such a bright line of serious problems inside and outside the government in a matter-of-fact manner. Otherwise, a blurring of who was responsible for what can taint your presidency.

Second, you need to make a clean break from the Bush regime's law of rule to our declared commitment to the rule of law as in the firm adherence to constitutional requirements and statutory and treaty compliance. There is a Bush-Cheney stream of criminal and unconstitutional actions which are on autopilot day after day. You have pointed out some of these abominations, such as a policy and practice of torture and violations of due process and probable cause. The task before you is to break these daily patterns just as soon as you ascend to the presidency or be held increasingly responsible for them. This can be significantly accomplished by executive orders, agency or departmental directives, whistle-blower protections, enforcement actions, and explicit legislative proposals.

With Americans wishing you well in this most portentous of times, the last thing they want to see is you tarnished by the preceding rogue regime and its ruthless monarchical forays. To avoid this contagion of power over law and its contiguous accountabilities at a time when you are striving for a "clean slate" administration, you must be decisive and eschew any excessive harmony ideology which has seemed to be your nature vis-à-vis those who are powerful but are opposed to your views.

One possible impediment to your making a comprehensive clean break for restoring the rule of law is that you have too easy an act to follow. There are a long list of violated civil liberties that need to be restored (the American Civil Liberties Union has compiled a list of immediate actions for you to take), and resolute commitments must be made so that it is clear the United States, for example, will not engage in, or countenance, torture. Only a few restorations, however, would produce a sense of relief and flurry of accolades—but they are hardly sufficient.

There are also regulations and interpretations of statutes that scholars believe to have been erroneous as a matter of law. As one guide for your new era of overdue regulation or re-regulation—given the corporate wrongdoing these days—you may wish to refer to the Center for Progressive Reform's report, *By the Stroke of the Pen.*

The Bush lawlessness and state terrorism are like a contagious disease. If you do not remove their sprawling incidence, you will become their carrier. This means you must move fast to eject the mantle of war criminality and repeated unconstitutional outrages committed in the name of the American people here and abroad.

Sincerely,

NOVEMBER 11, 2008
An Inclusive Inauguration

Dear President-elect Obama,

The day of a new president's inauguration—your day is January 20, 2009—is a highly symbolic occasion, as well as a legal one. From your early postelection remarks and photographed advisors and associates, you are making clear that you are interested in a wide nonpartisan embrace of Democrats, Republicans, business executives, and some labor and minorities who will be represented at the ceremonies. Included, no doubt, will be your principal opponents—John McCain and Sarah Palin.

May I suggest that you include the independent and third party presidential and vice-presidential candidates who were on enough state ballots to win an Electoral College majority, theoretically? There were only four—Chuck Baldwin, Robert Barr, Cynthia McKinney and the undersigned.

I have not spoken to any of them about this recommendation. To avoid any semblance of self-interest, I will delete my name from this list and watch the event on C-SPAN.

No recent president-elect, to my knowledge, has ever invited his smaller competitors to the inauguration. Who can forget the pioneering difference such candidates have made throughout American history—starting with the antislavery Liberty Party in 1840 and continuing through the women's suffrage, labor, farmer, and social justice agendas in the 19th century?

Into the 20th century, these candidates presaged Social Security, Medicare, unemployment compensation and, of course, the great civil rights and worker demands of Eugene Debs, Robert LaFollette, Norman Thomas, and the prophetic environmentalist Barry Commoner. Given such historically significant roles, it would be functionally gracious for you to start this invitational tradition in the spirit of a more competitive democracy.

Thank you for your consideration.

Sincerely,

Index

costly aftermath of, 193
draft and, 95–96
Hussein in, 11, 13, 76, 104, 126, 131–32
mosques destroyed in, 80–83
mothers and grandparents against, 73–77
refugees from, 12, 16
Rice and, 13, 101
terrorism in, 11, 13, 41–42, 45, 81, 131
"Iraq: Poor Families Sacrifice, War Corporations Profit" letter, 68–72
IRS. *See* Internal Revenue Service
Israel
    Bush, George W., and, 17, 24–27, 44–51
    Lebanon attacked by, 3, 17, 25–26, 44–51
    Obama, Barack, and, 173–74
    Palestine and, 3, 17, 24–27, 50, 173–74
    Suez Canal and, 24, 49

Jefferson, Thomas, 1, 150, 207
Jelinek, W. Craig, 186
JOBS (Jumpstart Our Business Startups)
    Act, 225–28
judicial branch, citizen access to, 90
Jumpstart Our Business Startups Act. *See*
    JOBS Act
"Justice for Nabila" letter, 188–89

Kamel, Hussein, 132
Kay, David, 78
Kelleher, Mike, 190, 245
Kellenberger, Jakob, 100–101
Kerry, John, 83, 95–96, 213
Khrushchev, Nikita, 177
King, Colbert, 242
Kiriakou, John, 212–14
Koskinen, John, 160
Krueger, Alan, 217

Labor Day, 216–18, 230–32, 259–61
"Labor Day 2010" letter, 259–61
labor issues, 114–15, 231–32, 260. *See also*
    unions
labor law reform, 93
LaFollette, Robert, 283
LaHood, Ray, 239–40, 255
land mines, 127, 132
Lang, Fred, 255
Laski, Harold, 1
"Leave No Child Behind" program, 98–99
Leavitt, Michael, 63
Lebanon, 3, 17, 25–26, 44–51
"Lebanon, Part 1" letter, 47–51
"Lebanon: A Nation Under Attack" letter,
    44–47
"Legalize Hemp!" letter, 148–52

legislative branch, citizen access to, 89–90
Leishmaniasis, 97
"Letter from E.coli O104:H4," 234–36
    benefits of, 1–2
    collectively signed, 5
    e-mails and, 4
    form, 4–5
    ink-and-paper, 1
    media coverage of, 1, 5, 7–8
    online, 8
    to presidents, 1–8
    responses to, 2–8, 14, 52, 83, 143, 175,
        190–92, 224, 257, 270
    robo-signed, 5
Levitt, Arthur, 227
Levy, Gideon, 25, 50–51
Libby, I. Lewis "Scooter," 214
Libya, 177, 179, 193
"Limiting Tort Liability for Medical Mal-
    practice" (CBO), 116
Lincoln, Abraham, 1, 23, 169
Lindsey, Lawrence B., 143

MacArthur, Douglas, 129
Madison, James, 22
Malaysian Boeing 777, 173
Mann, Bill, 228
"'A Man Who Has Stopped Listening'" letter,
    133–37
marijuana, 149–50
Mason, George, 22
Mayfield, Max, 58
McAdam, Lowell, 191
McCaffrey, Barry, 149
McCain, John, 223, 283
McCarthy, Colman, 182, 195
McGill, Terry, 255
McKinney, Cynthia, 283
McSwain, Michael S., 224
McWane, Inc., 34
media, letters and, 1, 5, 7–8
Medicaid, 185, 210–11
Medical Innovation Prize Fund, 65
medical malpractice, 115–17
Medicare, 92, 108, 164, 210–12, 283
Memorandum on Concerns Relating to Law
    and Order in Iraq, 101
Michaels, David, 267
"Michelle: Stand Your Ground on Childhood
    Nutrition" letter, 174–76
"Michelle: Why Won't Barack Speak to Civic
    Groups?" letter, 222–24
midterm elections, 242–45
Miers, Harriet, 21, 62, 67–68
military